Conflict
Dialogue

*This book is dedicated to my Mum and Dad,
and to my brothers Paul, David, and Timothy.*

Conflict Dialogue

Working With Layers of Meaning for Productive Relationships

Peter M. Kellett

The University of North Carolina at Greensboro

SAGE Publications
Thousand Oaks ▪ London ▪ New Delhi

For information:

Sage Publications, Inc.
2455 Teller Road
Thousand Oaks, California 91320
E-mail: order@sagepub.com

Sage Publications Ltd.
1 Oliver's Yard
55 City Road
London EC1Y 1SP
United Kingdom

Sage Publications India Pvt. Ltd.
B-42, Panchsheel Enclave
Post Box 4109
New Delhi 110 017 India

Printed in the United States of America.

Library of Congress Cataloging-in-Publication Data

Kellett, Peter M.
Conflict dialogue: working with layers of meaning for productive relationships / Peter M. Kellett.
    p. cm.
Includes bibliographical references and index.
ISBN 1-4129-0930-9 (cloth) — ISBN 1-4129-0931-7 (pbk.)
  1. Interpersonal conflict. 2. Interpersonal communication.
3. Conflict management. 4. Negotiation. I. Title.

HM1121.K45 2007
303.6—dc22   2006001788

This book is printed on acid-free paper.

06 07 08 09 10 10 9 8 7 6 5 4 3 2 1

Senior Acquisitions Editor:	Todd R. Armstrong
Editorial Assistant:	Camille Herrera
Project Editor:	Tracy Alpern
Copy Editor:	Marilyn Power Scott
Typesetter:	C&M Digitals (P) Ltd.
Proofreader:	Theresa Kay
Indexer:	Rick Hurd
Cover Designer:	Michelle Kenny

Contents

Acknowledgments

My special thanks must go to all of the people who have shared their personal conflict stories with me, both in and out of the classroom. In particular, I thank those who have given me permission to include their stories in this book. Their generosity and openness make this work both possible and worthwhile for me.

I am also grateful to the following reviewers: Pat Arneson, Duquesne University; Angela Laird Brenton, University of Arkansas at Little Rock; Roberta A. Davilla, University of Northern Iowa; Larry A. Erbert, University of Texas at El Paso; Claudia L. Hale, Ohio University; and Christopher O. Lynch, Kean University.

Introduction

The following is a true story that, in some ways, reads like the start of many roommate conflict stories—in fact it almost sounds like a roommate story archetype: Things started out so well . . . now we all hate each other and communicate by nasty sticky notes! In between these two states is a conflict over something that seems quite trivial as we are looking back on it. We are all probably familiar with such typical story lines. As you will see, this conflict is about a specific dispute—who gets what room—although intimately tied to the specific decision is the obvious deeper meaning of who has more prestige and privilege in the house and who becomes marginalized into the small space. A deeper read reveals additional layers of meaning attached to the subsequent tangible actions of the roommates as they live out their conflict together.

Three young, Native American women—Carmen, Beth, and Kathryn—are starting college and decide to move in together to share an apartment; Carmen and Beth are cousins. The three are excited about their new place and the adventures they would share living together. However, the three bedrooms are unequal in size, and the master bedroom has its own bathroom. Besides the large master bedroom, there is a medium-sized one and a small one. The young women are faced with the difficult task of deciding who gets which room. They draw straws, and Carmen gets the master bedroom, Kathryn the medium-sized room, and Beth the small one. Then the real conflicts begin. . . .

Beth was furious that she got the small room; she expected at least to get the medium-sized room. She tried to "guilt trip" Carmen into giving up the master room, but Carmen stood her ground and, as she says in her story, "However I acted in this situation would set the precedent for me in the future. It did . . ." Sarcastic comments and put-downs from Beth began to characterize their roommate communication. Apparently, for example, Beth's mother told Beth to be understanding of Carmen's desire for the room since her room at home was so small—clearly a put-down on the relative financial status of Carmen's family. Put-downs evolved into revenge and sabotage. Beth would be rude, put Carmen down in front of others, and purposely forget important information. Revenge evolved into betrayal. Carmen had begun dating a much older man, something that her parents would not approve of, and something that would become fast-traveling gossip in their tightly knit Native American community in eastern North Carolina. Carmen entrusted Beth with the private information and later found out she had let the news out, and the whole community was buzzing with the gossip. Carmen also found out that Beth had been saying behind her back that she was trying to act "white"—a slap in the face and a slur for her as a Native American. Carmen put all her feelings into a letter and left it for Beth. She seemed to ignore it, so Carmen taped it to Beth's computer. Beth continued to ignore it although it turns out she had read it the first day it was left for her. Apparently she ignored Carmen's letter to get back at her. All the relationships deteriorated, and soon Beth and Kathryn were not speaking. Carmen and Kathryn are worriedly expecting a grand finale as Beth moves out. What will she do as her final act of revenge and payback?

You probably have several questions that you would like to ask to dig deeper into this story, and that's probably a sign of a good story: Good stories generate good questions. Perhaps the two main questions are, first, why was the room ineffectively negotiated? Second, why was the deeper relational conflict not effectively managed? Besides these, there are lots of questions that pop to my mind to get at the meaning and conflict dynamics of the story. These include, Why would Beth be so resentful? What did the room symbolize beyond merely prestige and status within the home? Is there some deeper power struggle or competitiveness between the cousins that is being displaced from their family relationships or community status and brought to life in this context? Is Beth projecting her own dark desires and motives for power and status in the house onto Carmen? How can a seemingly fair and agreed-upon way of making a decision lead to betrayal? How is the letter an important element in the story? How are the betrayal and the "white" slur connected to Beth's assumption that Carmen had betrayed her by taking the big room? What do we not know that might make this make sense? What would you love to know that would help you understand their conflict? These are some of the questions that came to mind for me. This process of digging by using smart questions is at the heart of the interpretive technique you will learn in this book.

We often never know the full story, but smart interpretive guesswork can often lead to some keen insights into the various layers and dimensions of a given conflict. In understanding these layers and their interrelationships lies the wisdom to know why the conflict takes the form that it does and possibly insight into how to manage it more effectively based on that wisdom. I hope that you find this approach to conflict as fascinating and as rewarding as I do as you learn to go from smart questions to making recommendations for changing conflict behavior.

As part of my ongoing fascination with how people manage and negotiate their relationships with others, I have listened to probably thousands of conflict stories over the years, many just like the one involving Carmen, Beth, and Kathryn. One of the lessons or morals in the vast majority of stories is that people would negotiate resolutions to their conflicts much more effectively if they understood the meaning of the conflict for each other and negotiated through the conflict based on that meaning. This lesson suggests that we (1) ought to examine our stories for opportunities to negotiate more effectively; (2) ought to, where possible, approach negotiations dialogically, that is, as opportunities to search for mutually beneficial solutions; (3) ought to become more aware of how to use narrative or story dynamics to enhance our negotiation and dialogue techniques; and (4) ought to examine our conflicts with a focus on how to understand the meaning of the conflict in terms of why it exists, why it takes the form that it does in our relationships, why it has the outcomes that it does, and what prevents the participants from choosing more dialogic negotiation. Imagine how these "oughts" might have made a difference to the conflict of Carmen and her friends if they could go back to a productive point in the conflict before it became divisive.

These core concepts form the basis of the chapters of this book, and each chapter is an invitation from me to you, to engage these core concepts as ways of understanding conflict. In this book you will be invited to interpret conflict stories as a way to imagine more creative ways to engage in conflict effectively. You will be asked to apply concepts and techniques from the field of conflict management to the experiences of yourself and others in your real worlds. You will learn to critically question how we approach conflict and to hopefully learn valuable lessons from the process of engagement between concept, other people's stories, and your own experiences.

Carmen may have lost the friendship with Beth forever, and the conflict dynamics and result may have been inevitable given the deeper dynamics of their relationships and the symbolic meaning of the conflict. But if she and her roommates were to carefully consider the concepts and techniques that we will be exploring, the result may have been quite different. If not, she could at least understand why the conflict took the form that it did, learn how to not repeat the same conflict again, and perhaps know how to create the conflict experiences that are more productive for all involved. This book comes out of the simple observation that we can improve our conflict communication and that such improvements will, in many cases, result in more productive and peaceful relationships.

The invitation to engagement with these concepts in this book is done through the use of *personal narratives* that I have express and written permission to use. (Note: The collector of each story is indicated in parentheses beside its title, and story characters' names have been changed for the usual reasons.) You will engage with the conflicts of others through the stories that they have told me. I could only include a small fraction of the stories I have been told, and I could only include a few main concepts in each of the parts of the book, but hopefully both the stories and the concepts covered will be representative enough and engaging enough to pull you into the complex and fascinating world of how people engage in, and how they might rethink, their conflicts. You will also learn to use these stories shared by other people as a way in to examining and questioning your own conflict practices and the stories you tell about your conflicts. Along with learning how to collect good stories, you will learn to ask *good theoretically grounded questions*—lots of questions, in fact. These questions will help you to engage with the stories and learn as much as possible from them about how we all do conflict. Ultimately, the concepts, stories, and questions will hopefully inform the *technique* of how you analyze and manage conflict effectively.

Part I

Conflict Stories, Dialogue, and Negotiation

Concepts and Techniques

1

Stories and the Meaning of Conflicts

❖ ❖ ❖

Do what you can in your conflicts to bring peace to your relationships . . . Take what you can from your conflicts to build the life narrative that brings peace to you.

—Kellett and Dalton (2001, p. 183)

The stories we tell . . . guide and direct the way we feel, think, and act.

—Pearce and Pearce (2004, p. 47)

In the many hundreds of conflict stories I have listened to and collected, there is, in almost every case, room for improvement as well as important lessons about what was done well that can be taken from them. As the first foregoing quote suggests, one of the main goals that I have, in taking you through the research process of collecting conflict stories and analyzing and learning from them, is for you to discover opportunities to improve your skills in engaging in conflict where necessary and where possible. My assumption is that this improvement in how you and I manage conflict will in turn enable us to live more peaceful and productive relationships. The first main challenge in achieving these goals of improving our conflict communication is figuring out how to collect enough of the details of how we do conflict to enable us to reflect on them, critique them, see what we do effectively, and look for those opportunities for improvement. Direct observation of conflict behavior as it unfolds in naturalistic settings is certainly one approach to data collection.

As the second quote suggests, I believe that one of the best ways to study conflict is to collect conflict stories that are detailed enough to help reveal the meaning of the conflict for the people involved. This is one step removed from direct observation of behavior, but perhaps it also contains additional rich data that direct observation does not have in terms of how people make sense of their conflicts and how they construct the meaning of the conflict as they look back on it through their stories. A good conflict story, like a really good fossil specimen for the paleontologist, contains enough information that a researcher of communication can figure out why the conflict occurred, why it occurred as it did for the people in question in their specific (cultural) environment and historical moment, and what some possible alternatives for doing conflict more effectively might be.

This chapter equips you with the interpretive tools and background in narrative theory and methodology to collect and analyze a story for the meaning of the conflict. I believe that to explicate the meaning of the conflict for the people involved is the key to both understanding the conflict and developing ways of approaching the conflict more productively. The next chapter focuses on the principles of dialogue and negotiation as a framework for how you can approach all of the case studies in this book and your own stories. For now, let's explore the techniques and principles of a narrative approach to studying conflicts.

As an interpretive researcher concerned with *understanding* communication, you will need the key skill of sensitivity to the multilayered and often multifaceted nature of meaning as you examine stories; developing this skill is the prime function of this chapter. Careful and thorough examination of a particular conflict from as many angles and perspectives as possible is important. Conflicts between people who have ongoing intimate, personal, familial, neighboring, or working relationships can sometimes be simple disputes over specific tangible things. More commonly, however, conflicts are about both specific disputes and also deeper relational themes or issues that are played out through the conflicts. Good management of a conflict will depend on your ability to read the conflict broadly and deeply and work at managing it on several levels at once. Resolution of a conflict is of course the most desirable outcome, but that is often difficult to achieve—hence the use of the term *management*. Let's begin with a simple example to illustrate the opportunities and challenges of a narrative approach to interpreting the meaning of conflict stories.

The other day, a former student from my conflict management class—Mike—stopped by to discuss his life since graduating. As he talked about his life as a recent graduate and as a newlywed, he related a family conflict to me that perfectly illustrates these challenges and opportunities. Specifically, he had a long-term goal of going into the ministry as a pastor. Since graduating, he had been working in several capacities in his church to build up his experience before applying to seminary. He was, however, unpaid in these roles. This left his new wife as the breadwinner and him as the "house husband and volunteer," as he put it. Although this caused some role and identity tensions for him, it did not cause conflict within the marriage so much as it did with his wife's parents—his in-laws. They could not understand why he would not get a full-time job and be the so-called man of the house. They became vocal in their disagreement with the young couple's choices, and this caused some minor but frustrating tensions and conflicts that spread into other topics.

As you might imagine, it is a delicate conflict with long-term family implications, so Mike wants to handle it effectively and not make a potentially damaging communication mistake. This conflict is about the specifics of getting a full-time job, providing for the family materially, putting ministry second after these tasks, and so on. Clearly, there are also more symbolically meaningful dimensions to the conflict as the couple tries to figure out the long-term purpose of their lives and follow their dreams and what it means to be a man of the house and a man of God. At the same time, another layer to the conflict has to do with the in-laws wondering what these choices mean for their daughter's life, what these things say about who she married and why she married him, possibly even what all of this says about them as parents, and even why the young couple is not following their advice. So the conflict symbolizes tensions between images of husband roles, goals, family involvement, and how much say these people have in each other's lives. The conflict *means* these and perhaps many more things as you might discover if you continued to unearth the layers of connected themes in the conflict.

If you were studying Mike's conflict, what would be a good story—a relatively complete piece of data—that you could put on the table and analyze? How would you collect such a story? What besides his story would you want to collect, and what questions might you have for all involved that you think would give you necessary details and the big picture of the conflict so that you could begin developing ideas for how they might effectively manage it? These are the key questions you will be able to answer through this chapter.

Understanding that the specific behavior under dispute is connected to these more symbolic layers of meanings, I advised him to understand the differences in meaning for him and for his in-laws and then use that understanding as he manages his conflict with his in-laws. This is also what you will learn to do through this chapter and as you progress through the book.

This chapter provides a theoretical and practical framework for helping you to collect conflict stories and understand the meaning of conflicts through narrative research techniques common to the communication field. We have access to the meaning of conflicts through the stories people tell. In the next chapter, you will learn a specific technique for analyzing and managing conflicts based on the meanings you uncover. This chapter builds the necessary foundation by illustrating how stories in the form of personal narratives—accounts of conflicts that capture as fully as possible the experience of a conflict from the first-person perspective—can be used to access the meanings of the conflict.

Main topics and learning goals in this chapter:

- What makes a good conflict story?
- Why stories are good starting points for interpretive research
- The challenges and opportunities of meaning for the narrative researcher
- How to collect a good story as research data
- Lessons from the field of practice

❖ WHAT MAKES A GOOD CONFLICT STORY?

Folger, Poole, and Stutman (2005) define conflict as "the interaction of interdependent people who perceive incompatibility and the possibility of interference from others as a result of this incompatibility" (p. 4). If we accept this basic definition of conflict, then a good piece of data in the form of a conflict story will do the following: First, a good conflict story will represent the interaction, the communication, between the people concerned. The story should show how the people interacted and that the interaction was conflicted in nature. Second, the story should also show how the interaction is connected to the deeper issues associated with both sides' sense of interdependence, their being in a relationship, and their difference or opposition on the issues in dispute. Third, the story should contain clues in the characterization of self versus the other and their relative motives to their perceived senses of interference. In most conflict stories, there will be good guys, bad guys, and a story plot that supports the rhetorical goal of the storytellers in showing their experience of interference. We can expand the definition of Folger et al. (2005) slightly to include the sense that conflict interaction typically occurs in patterns and cycles of expression. These patterns can occur and recur in short bursts or over many years, even many generations, and they are often related to characteristics of psychology as well as the cultural context of the conflict. Note that in Mike's conflict, the perceptions of his in-laws were connected to cultural values and assumptions about gender roles and expectations. Fourth, then, a good conflict story should show how the conflict is an expression of broader and deeper patterns and give some sense of why it got expressed as it did. (Are there patterns of avoidance that affect the expression of the conflict, for example?) If we also add to our definition that conflicts are often not simply about a specific incompatibility but that they are often connected, often tangentially or symbolically, to other relational issues or themes, then this gives us a fifth dimension of a good conflict story. Fifth, conflict stories should, where possible, give the researcher insight into the deeper meaning of the more specific dispute or incompatibility that is evident in the conflict. The story should at least hint at the connection between the specific conflict being related in story form and the broader connection to, and meaning in, the relationship. The story should show if the conflict serves a creative purpose in effectively ending a relationship, for example, or enabling people to move closer to each other.

These definitional criteria of conflict and story data quality give us a good start at developing research questions and observational criteria for collecting or creating a good story. These criteria also give us the following key words that you can keep in mind as you examine stories: *conflicted interaction*, *relational dispute*, *characterization*, *patterns*, and *deeper meaning*. As you do a first read through of the story of Antoine and Torise, consider these five key definitional characteristics of a conflict. You should see quickly that, yes, they definitely have a conflict. Then we will work through some criteria from narrative theory and research that help us understand why it is also a good piece of data for us to examine.

An Example of a Good Story

"From Cloud Nine to Bikini Bottom" (Antoine)

As we were on our way back from Wal-Mart one day, I turned the music down and said,

"Hey Torise, I was talking to a friend of mine, and he was talking about how he and his girlfriend love watching *The Simpsons* together. I told him I love *The Simpsons,* but Torise doesn't really get down like that. He thought it was real messed up and asked me if there was anything that we liked watching together besides movies. I was like ummm . . . *American Idol* and *Real World.* He thought that the lack of a common interest, even in something small like TV, might be a problem. What do you think?"

Torise looked away and said, "Well, I never thought we had much in common anyway, we just complement each other."

I was shocked by this, as I always assumed we had a lot in common, and that's what I thought I loved about the relationship. But my friend's comments did make me question that. I remember trying to come up with something to lighten the mood, but I don't remember it coming out. By the time I soaked all this in, we were pulling up to my apartment.

"Is something wrong?" I asked. "I mean it's like . . . something just doesn't feel right between us, like something just isn't there. Like the love is lost or missing."

In tears, she replied, "I know what you mean. I just don't have the same feeling that I expected. I mean things just don't feel right."

"I know," I replied with my head down, trying not to acknowledge the tears. "But I don't know what to do. I got to go."

I got up to get out of the car and go home and I saw that she was still crying, so I got back in the car to console her.

Violently sobbing, she said, "I just don't think there is anything we can do. I don't know if there is any way that things could change back to how they used to be. My feelings just aren't as strong as they used to be, and I don't know if we can work this out."

We both sat in her burgundy Accord, tense after she revealed something that I had long assumed but had not come to terms with. I remember sitting there with thoughts burning a trail in my psyche. I thought, "What the hell is going on, and what am I supposed to do in this situation? Did I just hear what I think I heard? Does she mean what I think she meant?" As I sat nervous and dumbfounded as passersby gave me cutting eyes and evil looks as if to say, "What did you do to this girl to make her cry?" Little did they know, I thought, as I sat in the seat slumped in shock. I never felt the urge to cry—honestly, I felt like a huge weight was off my back.

In retrospect I don't remember my response, I just remember feeling empty but also relieved. I was still shocked even though I had known for a while. I wanted to believe that her feelings had not changed, but they had and who knows for how long. It was at this point that I knew we would never be together. However, while she pondered the decision and questioned if the relationship could be repaired, I soon after made the decision to end the relationship.

(How It All Began)

Me and Torise had been friends since I was 13 years old, through a mutual friend, her cousin Patrick. We had always been cool, we even went to the prom together, which was the time where my crush for her developed. It wasn't until we got to college that we became very close friends.

My sophomore year we were both either involved with, or interested in someone else. My feelings for her hadn't changed, and I felt one day she will realize that we would make a great couple. It wasn't until things did not materialize with a guy she had a crush on that I think she realized that we might would have something. Then one day, we both decided to go to the circus. I thought, "Man, this might be my chance," because she was going to have to spend the night in my dorm room (which was a single room!). So I anxiously drove down to Chapel Hill and went to the circus. I remember being nervous the whole night, trying not to mess up. Later that night, we went to a party that my friend was throwing at his apartment. We danced, laughed, and joked and just had a great time together. That night in my bedroom, we were both so nervous that we barely slept. I remember thinking, "If I fall asleep, I am liable just to jump on her, and if I say how I feel, it might ruin a great night." So we both stayed up just talking and joking the whole night.

We got back to her dorm room, and I remember just not wanting to leave. She got up off the bed and had tears in her eyes. I asked her what was wrong, and she just couldn't say. I said, well, write it down and I said, there's something I want to tell you, too. So we sat on her bed filled with pillows, teddy bears, and silence. I remember me holding a green pen and a scrap of paper, and I just explained how I felt about her. Luckily she did the same, and once we exchanged our notes, we just embraced. To end the day, we slow danced, and I asked her to be my valentine. From that day on, we were inseparable.

(The Buildup to the Conflict)

The first 8 months of the relationship were great; we were just on cloud nine. We rarely argued. I was happy, and everything was cool. We had a lot of conversations about how we felt our relationship was so much better than other relationships our friends were involved in, and we were just happy with life. However, by the time of my fall semester, we began to grow apart. I was very busy and started to have some commitment anxiety. I found it hard to talk to her about a lot of topics that were important to me. The majority of our conversations were initiated by me, and it began to drain me.

We would not talk for a few days, and she would ask me if I had a decision yet, or what she could do about the situation. I felt almost suppressed by the pressure to make it work. A few weeks later, we hung out around our hometown, and it was a very passionate and fun weekend. The following week, she was going to the Bahamas with some friends. Before she left, she asked me if we were getting back together. I told her that I wasn't sure but that this was a good place to start. We could just see how it goes. Who knew this comment would change things forever.

(Action Scene)

I still remember how nervous she was about the conversation we had soon after she returned from the Bahamas. I remember joking about her meeting a hot guy down there. Then she told me, "'Toine, I met somebody in the Bahamas, we met. . . . " My mind went blank. I knew what was coming up before she said it. "We kissed and had a great night together, and we exchanged information. I'm sorry, but I just didn't know where you and me were going!" I remember just responding with "Wow" and feeling surprised.

From this point, I tried to get over it and make things work with her. Things were going OK until one argument where she said she was still going to keep in touch with him. We broke everything off, and that was that. A month or so later— on Valentine's Day, ironically—I drove down there unexpectedly to tell her that I truly loved her and that I wanted her back and was sorry for pushing her away. She said she wasn't sure. For months we were back involved physically, but she was still involved with Mr. Bahamas. They seemed to be working on a relationship. I remember sitting at her parents' small kitchen table and, once again crying, she told me she wanted to see how things worked out with the other guy. If it didn't work out with him, she said there may be a chance for us. I was heartbroken, but a few months later, for some reason, I took her back.

(Aftermath)

I never could get over the Bahamas incident. It just ate at me. I began to realize that everything that seemed so good about our relationship may not have been true. A lot of the problems that existed before the Bahamas trip were unresolved conflicts. When I tried to bring it up, we just ended up in an emotional display from her and me trying to keep the peace. I was frustrated and unhappy with the relationship, but I knew that so much had been invested in it that I just couldn't give up. And I did love her.

By the fall, our conversations consisted of arguments or awkward silences. She had begun a new full-time job and had moved back to our hometown. This made it harder as we were 2 1/2 hours away. Our lives were different, too, with me in school and her working full time. I didn't feel that the relationship was benefiting me any more. I approached her by saying that I did not feel in love any more and that I thought she felt the same way. She was in denial about it up until the conversation in the car at Thanksgiving where it all came out.

"Mr. Bahamas—The Other Side of the Story"

What follows is the other side of the story, which was collected and shared by Antoine. As you get Torise's side of the story, it will probably reshape and deepen your understanding of their relational conflicts. It will also broaden your understanding of the multifaceted nature of meaning, in the sense that examining the meanings of the various participants in the story will help you to piece together the often complex differences and similarities between them. The exercise will also help you understand the politics of narrative representation in the sense that seeing various versions of a conflict can help you question the choices that any one participant makes in how the story is told *and* not told as this expresses his or her standpoint in the conflict. Examine the story closely and jot down your thoughts and questions. Then consider the discussion questions that follow the story.

(Torise's Story)

Looking back on the situation, I think there were some minor signs that I should have paid attention to that led to our breakup. I can remember times when Antoine would ask me why were my eyes so big and that he liked girls with small, seductive eyes. Or why my butt didn't poke out at the top, or why I snored or had big feet, or why I didn't pay more attention to the world and current events, or why I cried when we had an argument, or why I wasn't what he considered *strong*. Thinking back, there were a lot of little things like that, which leads me to believe that no matter how good I was to him or how much I tried to improve myself, I could never be what he wanted me to be. I think that Antoine saw a lot of good in me, but when he saw someone who had the qualities that I don't have, then he was intrigued by her and began to think that maybe I am not what he needed. This is an underlying reason for all of the conflict we had.

There were other issues. I messed up when I went on a trip to the Bahamas. Things started getting better just before my trip, so I asked Antoine if this was a sign that we were getting back together. He was unsure. So I went to the Bahamas feeling somewhat single. I met a guy there and kissed him. I felt guilty, but I did like him. I told Antoine when I got back, and he was hurt but said he was OK with it. I don't think he really told me his true feelings because he would bring it up in conversations even after he said it was cool. Things weren't going well with the Bahamian guy, and I started to like Antoine again. So we gave it another try.

In addition to the Bahamas thing, I think that Antoine and I were too close as friends to make it as a couple. I mean, I think he treated me more as a friend than a girlfriend, although there was plenty of passion and romance. For instance, we went to a concert in DC. I was expecting to have a romantic weekend with him. I had never been away with a boyfriend before. He didn't hold my hand or show me any affection at the concert. We went sightseeing, and he still treated me that way. There were a few times when this sort of thing happened.

But the biggest thing that I felt led to the breakup was the lack of time—and distance. When I moved back to Kinston, it was hard to deal with the distance, although we made a huge effort. But our phone conversations were starting to get brief. I would automatically ask him, "Are you busy?" when I called as he always seemed to be busy, and I couldn't talk through the things he wanted me to talk about when he called.

All of this took a toll on the relationship because in October, Antoine told me he was not in love with me any more. He wanted me to evaluate the relationship for myself. I started thinking about past guys and how good they were and started wondering if Antoine would make a good husband. I overanalyzed it and scared myself into thinking I wasn't in love with him.

I think Antoine held onto the relationship as long as he could, partly to see if it could work and partly to spare my feelings. I held on because I loved him and because I wanted a future together. He bluntly decided that we should break up, and I didn't feel that I had much say in it. I think that because he found another girl to talk to, the decision was made quicker than I expected. He complained sometimes that he would sit home while his friends were out looking for girls. I think he missed that and wanted someone closer. I ultimately think that what my cousin Patrick said was right—Antoine has too short an attention span to stick with one girl. I also think our long distance was important. Plus, I think he has a long list of requirements for a girlfriend, and if a girl doesn't meet them all, then he's not satisfied and will start thinking about other options.

Discussion Questions for Exploring
Why This Is a Good Conflict Story

• How well does the story, told from both sides, show the conflicted communication and interaction between Antoine and Torise? Are there conversations that you wish we had access to that we do not?

• In what ways does the story show their struggle between being interdependent as a couple and being different or even oppositional? What specific differences are they struggling with, and how does the story of their struggle seem real to us as the audience? Look closely at their expectations for relationships, boundaries, rules, definitions of *commitment*, fidelity, love, and assumptions about power.

• How does the story bring to life their senses of interference of the other or opposition (or incompatibility) with the other on key issues just outlined? How do they each portray themselves and the other and their relative motives in ways that further hint at their opposition on these issues?

• How does the story show the evolution and expression of the conflict and any important connections to deeper patterns relationally, psychologically, and culturally? Does it seem to accurately portray the life cycle of the conflict from start to finish?

• Does their story help us understand the broader and deeper meaning of the conflict in their relationship? For example, it is obvious that this is a breakup story, but how does it convince us that this conflict is inevitable and even necessary for them, given the deeper divisions in their relationship? What details evoke the deeper meaning of their conflict?

These are some concepts to get you thinking about what a good story needs to do. We move on to share some additional criteria from the work in communication and related fields on personal narrative research.

Some Additional Criteria of a Good Personal Narrative

Carolyn Ellis (1997) has developed some useful criteria for evaluating the writing of personal narratives. Despite the obvious political issues associated with judging other people's stories, this set of criteria does allow us to think critically about how well the story opens up a conflict experience for us as researchers. So consider these criteria and related questions as you go back through the foregoing story one more time. First, Ellis points to several qualities of effective writing. Specifically, the story should be well written in that it effectively shows and evokes the scenes through which the conflict moves. The story should evoke the meaning and lived experience of the participants through their talk with each other, their thoughts, emotions, and bodily responses to the conflict.

- What specific aspects of the story content and how it is written do you think make this a good personal narrative from both of the relational partners?

Second, Ellis (1997) points to some important issues of the relationship of the story to its audience (researcher, readers) that makes a story good data. Specifically, a good story will describe the conflict as it unfolds and evolves over time through the patterns of interaction. Description should also be concrete and vivid enough that it is lifelike and believable as a real conflict. This believability should engage the audience members, and it should bring to life their own reactions to the story and similar experiences that they have had. A story is a communication event in that it engages the audience members and communicates the meaning of the conflict to them, but it also can include their interpretations (for example, your thoughts as the researcher).

- What specific details of the story make this lifelike, believable, and engaging to you as its audience?

Third, Ellis (1997) points to important criteria in terms of our assumptions in telling and collecting stories as data. Specifically, the story should be regarded as an open text, a work in progress, rather than a complete and final explanation or truth statement about the conflict. There is always room for more and even different interpretations. Also, the story should have a critical impact in that it questions, problematizes, or critiques something about the conflict. In this sense, the story takes risks and makes the storyteller vulnerable. As you share your own stories as part of the exercises in this book, you will probably feel somewhat vulnerable. For example, we ought to be able to examine the actions of the people in the story critically in terms of how they contributed to the conflict and how they might have done things differently.

- How does the story leave room for more interpretation and more questions for the participants in how they might have managed the conflict more effectively?

❖ WHY STORIES ARE GOOD STARTING POINTS FOR INTERPRETIVE RESEARCH

How do we collect the information about a conflict that allows us to dig into its layers of meaning? The answer is that there are lots of ways that you can do this. Some researchers collect great speeches that capture the meaning of social and political conflicts and their resolution. Some researchers collect conversations—whether natural or simulated—in which you can see the to and fro of a conflict in the microscopic details of how people talk together in conflicted ways. Some researchers like to collect broader social discourse that captures the role of conflict in protest, social movements, struggles, and so on.

For me, I have always found the collection of personal narratives— stories—extremely useful data for analyzing conflicts. This is particularly true when you can collect the various sides of a conflict as this will show you so much about the basis of what divides the people involved and how effectively they manage those divisions. When you can use these stories as a starting point for people to dialogue about their similarities and differences of meaning and experience of a conflict and perhaps more effectively negotiate those issues, then stories really become valuable artifacts for research as well as for the conflict management practitioner (mediator).

For narrative researchers, stories are revealing historical objects, much like great fossils are to a paleontologist. Conflict stories are in similar ways petrified or preserved pieces of communication—they are meaningful messages, people's efforts to communicate the meaning of conflict experiences to an audience, which could be themselves and you as the listeners (Fisher, 1987). They are, in this sense, objects that are richly packed with meaning that open a window into interpreting and understanding the way of life in which that story represents a real conflict. The interpretive opportunities that stories bring are substantial in terms of critical thinking about conflict behavior and exploring alternative ways of managing conflict.

Guidelines on Meaning for the Narrative Researcher

Some guidelines are important here about meaning and interpretation of stories and the need to be cautious and thorough in interpretive research. First, you need to recognize that stories that people use to represent their experiences are based on the truth of the experience for them, and this means that you may be getting a partial and perhaps unconsciously strategic representation of the conflict from that one account. People's conflict stories do not simply report the facts of a conflict but are meaningful as accounts that make sense in their life, for them, in particular ways (Denzin, 1997; Josselson, 1995). The stories you collect (and recollect if you are collecting your own stories) will represent the people telling them as well as the conflict they are telling you about. Stories will also contain clues the research subject is not telling you, so you will need to try to collect stories from as many of the people in the conflict as possible. These other people may fill in the gaps for you. You will also need to look for the meaning of the conflict between the lines that you hear and to some extent behind the stories that they do tell you. Look for what they are not telling you that your intuition tells you might be important to fully understanding the conflict. Look for the missing pieces of the story not told to you by one person that the other person in the story does reveal. These are important research skills for you to develop.

Second, you will need to consider the narrative characteristics of the story you are analyzing and approach it with due caution and ethics as a researcher. Besides including only particular aspects of the experience, stories blur the lines between fact and fiction; they are partly representations of the experience and they are partly stories as such (Langellier, 1989). Stories have particular forms and use particular plot, character, and motive archetypes. You are also probably looking at the story from a vantage point outside the conflict and from the perspective of your own ideas and assumptions about conflict and how it should be managed. You have to consider these characteristics as you dig deeper into the meaning of the conflict, as these characteristics of stories are representations that will have a deep effect on how you think about the conflict itself. Just like the paleontologist, you will also need to be cautious about the picture you create of the people; their conflict; and the communicative, social, and historical moment in which the conflict occurred, from the often small and partial clues you are given. We have to be cautious and recognize and acknowledge the impact of our own beliefs on our interpretation of a story. As Ellis (1997) points out, such engagement by the researcher-audience is fine, but we should note our own thoughts and perhaps biases as we engage with story texts.

Third, careful collection of the story and careful and thorough analysis are crucial habits if you want to get at the meaning of the conflict and base conflict management strategies on that meaning. We will come back to collection in more detail later, but for now, consider that the quality of your data—how good a story you collect—will partly be related to your skills as a researcher. You will naturally get partial and positional or strategic representations of the facts of the conflict in the reporting of what people did and said and why. You have to be effective in collecting what story or stories are available to you. You will likely only get as good a story as the questions you ask, so make sure you guide the storytellers effectively, with questions that enable them to give you the rich data you need. At the same time, you want the story to be as true to their experience as possible. They have to trust you and believe that you are listening without judging their actions and thoughts. People often tell me very personal and difficult conflict stories from their lives because I see the story both as an interesting specimen and as something deeply personal to them that I am privileged to hear. These two elements of my persona as a narrative researcher—clinical and empathic—allow me, as Chase (1996) suggests, to communicate to my research informants that I do not judge their conflict behavior and also that I appreciate the private and personal window that they open up into their relational lives for me.

Besides careful collection, you will need to be balanced and cautious in the interpretations you make about what you are told. Try to see the meaning of the conflict from inside it as it is lived by the participants as well as from your vantage point as an expert on the conflict principles you see happening in their story. Try to note you own suspicions as you listen to the story and, sort of like an investigative journalist, ask the questions that help you collect the missing pieces of the puzzle. Collect and then connect the clues that help you see the bigger picture of the conflict. That bigger picture—the relationship between all of the issues and the interaction that occurs in the conflict, as well as the possibilities for alternative approaches and where they might take the participants—*is the meaning of the conflict.*

Fourth, narrative is a starting point—a good one for sure, but the process does not end with the story told. Much depends on your ability to move beyond that story to explore and imagine and perhaps manage the conflict through the development of a new story. We will come back to this in much more detail in Chapter 2. Careful analysis and management is important as you examine the conflict for new possibilities and as you either develop advice for the people in the conflict or actually lead them through to a new story in the form of a resolution to the conflict. So the fourth caveat or guideline has to do with respecting the integrity of the story you are told, while looking for new opportunities for the participants, in the form of effective management or resolution of the story. At least you will likely want to help them to create a new understanding for themselves as they share their stories and learn about the perspectives and experiences of each other in the conflict (Pelias & VanOosting, 1987; Welker & Goodall, 1997).

You need to recognize that the story is a living and evolving account of the conflict that represents the participants' level of collaboration or division in the conflict. To do this, approach the story that is told to you, as in Antoine and Torise's account, as a good starting point. The participants may each think that his or her story is the whole truth and nothing but the truth and believe that the conflict and all its possibilities are accounted for in the telling. The story at this point closes down dialogue; it creates narrative closure. Your task as conflict practitioners, involved in conflict in your own lives, as well as researchers is to use the story as a way to open up the conflict from this point on. Telling the story should lead to understanding for the person narrating it. It is important to get the narrators to note and share with you their moments of insight into the conflict as they tell it—what are called *aha moments*. If the couple were to read each other's stories, what do you think they might think about that they had not thought about before? How might the storytelling bring to the surface aspects of the conflict that they had forgotten? What assumptions and aspects of their biography and culture were brought to the surface and perhaps led to questions that they had about themselves or about the conflict? What limitations of the conflict and opportunities for alternative approaches surfaced in the telling of the story or in listening to the stories of the other people in the conflict? For you as the researcher, it is useful to ask what you think are the aspects of the person's biographical and cultural background that are partly revealed in the story. How does Antoine and Torise's story have characteristics of a young African American couple in the southern United States? What is the moral of the story that each of them is trying to communicate and how do the plot and characterization choices they make reflect these interests? What underlying beliefs and assumptions are important in structuring the way the story is told and the way that the conflict is handled? These are some good questions to tap into the story and create understanding. We come back to all of these in subsequent chapters.

From understanding the meaning of the conflict, you can move to creating choices about change. How could the conflict move forward from here? How could they not repeat the same pattern in subsequent relationships in their lives? How could they have talked about their similarities and differences more effectively? These are questions that build on that understanding and provide a bridge to learning how to tell the conflict stories that you want to tell. At the heart of this process is what Richardson (1995) calls the "sociological imagination" (p. 216), in which constraints, opportunities, and change possibilities can become real (Earnest, 1992; Kohler-Riessman, 1992; Ochberg, 1992). This can take the form of moving forward the particular conflict being discussed. It can also mean developing strategies for not repeating the same type of conflict again. What can Torise do to ensure that she does not get into a similar conflicted relationship again, for example? This kind of imagination shows that the participants have learned from their story and are willing to try to tell a different story the next time a similar relational context seems to be emerging. This is what we mean by ending the process of analysis and management with a new story that reflects a new approach to conflict communication, where appropriate and possible.

Some important discussion questions follow, as you engage in uncovering meaning in Antoine and Torise's conflict story:

- Why is collecting Antoine and Torise's story a useful starting point in exploring the meaning of the conflict that they narrate for us?
- Are there any important limitations of narrative research into conflict that you should be aware of as you use it to analyze and manage the conflict?
- What do the narrative characteristic and qualities of the data mean for us as we use the story as the basis of our research into their relational conflict?
- If you had the task of collecting their story, what questions would you ask, and how would you be careful in the collection and analysis of that story?
- How does your reading of their story suggest ways that you might advise the participants to manage this conflict more effectively in their next relationship?

❖ THE CHALLENGES AND OPPORTUNITIES OF
MEANING FOR THE NARRATIVE RESEARCHER

As you follow the aforementioned guidelines and explicate the meaning of the conflict, you will need to be aware of some of the challenges
and opportunities of working with meaning. Being aware of these at
this early point will make you a better researcher of conflict and communication more generally. In terms of the *challenges*, first it is important to understand that meaning is a complex thing to grasp and
define. When people are in conflict, the meaning of the conflict is partly
in what is shared when people communicate. We will need to explore
meaning when we are analyzing a conflict in terms of the dynamic
interplay of the participants' talk, how this talk connects to what they
are in conflict about, how the conflict reflects underlying themes
between them, how they co-construct the conflict as they go, and how
the meaning evolves with the conflict. Meaning *is* in the people, but
it is also in their words, and it is also in what is not said and what the
conflict is really about—which may have only a symbolic connection to
the words used in the specific conflict and may even be only partly
conscious to the people involved. Meaning will be a complex thing to
capture and analyze for you as you analyze conflicts, but it is worth the
interpretive effort of stepping back and looking at the layers of meaning and the relationship between the behavior in the conflict and what
it seems to be really about.

Second, meanings can be different for the different people. Often
people in conflicts are arguing about the same thing but, because of the
deeper meaning for them, it may mean quite different things to each of
them. Many conflicts begin with misunderstandings and misinter-
pretations of information rather than with coordinated, rational, and
reasonable communication about oppositions or differences. This
achievement of shared meaning we call communication is often very
difficult to arrive at, but it is one of the main challenges that this book
sets for us. Do Antoine and Torise actually ever communicate about
their relationship? Working with meaning means that our job, as
researchers, is to accurately bring to light the differences as well as similarities of meaning for those involved in the conflict. Our job as conflict practitioners is to work to try to build shared meaning out of that
careful analysis. These are not easy tasks.

Third, it is important to understand that meaning has an analogue
character. You will be examining the relationships between the mentioned elements and layers of meaning in terms of how they combine
analogically (both/and) to create the meaning of the conflict. For

example, going back to the early definition of conflict, you will recognize that Antoine and Torise's conflict is *both* about being together as a couple *and* about their differences and oppositions. The meaning of the struggle is discovered in how Antoine and Torise balance both dialectics. In terms of the layers of meaning that you will work with, the conflict is *both* about the specific here-and-now conflict *and* it is also about deeper relational issues of compatibility and expectations. You will need to examine the layers and the connection between the layers for a full picture of the meaning of the conflict. The conflict is *both* about his perspective *and* her perspective and how the two clash. To get at the meaning of the conflict, you will need to read between the lines of the stories for clues about their differences. The truth of the conflict is usually somewhere in the analogue between the two stories. These are just some of the important analogic relationships you will start working with as you develop and apply your interpretive skills to explicating meaning.

Fourth, besides the analogue character of meaning, you will also have to recognize that meaning is inherently quite a slippery, often contested, often politically charged, and ambiguous thing to grasp. Meanings in conflicts are often not even completely accessible to the people in them. People often do not have a clear picture of what they are fighting about on a thematic or symbolic level. Those things are often much more accessible to outsiders, strangers—us—as we interpret the probable meanings. Perhaps we should approach meaning in terms of probability rather than assuming that we can definitively state what it is about. Remember that we are looking into other peoples' realities, and this is fraught with the possibility of making interpretive mistakes—seeing things that are not really there (often based on our own projections) and not seeing things that are there (often based on our own inability to empathize with the experience being studied). Much of what you will be doing as you examine the stories in this book is smart guesswork based on elusive clues and connections between clues. A further complication is that the meaning of the conflict for the participants can actually change as the process of doing conflict brings certain things to the foreground and as new connections between the conflict and deeper issues are brought to mind as the conflict evolves. So be aware of how the meaning, like the story itself, can change.

This slippery nature of meaning is actually where we find our hope for change and the resolution of conflicts, as resolution is based on our ability to create new meanings and new possibilities for conflicts through talk. As mentioned, meanings are also often contested and politically charged. It is possible to portray the meaning of a conflict in a particular way, and this portrayal—often based on the fact that we are trying to create our own story about other people's stories—is rarely neutral. Going back to our definition of conflict, often the perceptions of interference from the other creates the struggle to be defined as hero or victim in contrast to the villainous actions of the other. Because of the often competitive dynamics of conflicts, there is a rhetorical, persuasive dimension to the narratives that reflects these desires to be seen in a particular way and to portray the other in particular ways.

Fifth, it is important to neutralize the dangers of interpretation and embrace the characteristics of meaning effectively by attempting to voice and account for the various possible interpretations that could be made and by trying to work from within the lived reality of meaning for the people actually involved in the conflict. One of the worst things we can do in interpretive research is to appropriate the conflict experiences of others simply to affirm our own worldviews and theoretical viewpoints. Our job is to explicate how the people in the story lived through their conflict and explore the implications of their experience. One of the best things that we can do as interpretive researchers is to bring to light how communication and meaning interrelate and use this as the basis for discussing how new meanings might be shaped through communication so that people can live and work together more effectively and peacefully. This is the spirit in which we will approach our task of working with the meaning of the conflicts in this book and in which you should approach the application of the concepts in this book to your understanding and management of your own conflicts. The place to start is to carefully examine the connections of the layers of meaning.

We cannot assume that all people who find themselves in a conflict with a lover, loved one, or colleague will have the time and motivation to develop a fully articulated and charted account of the meaning of the conflict—even if a complete account were ever really possible. We recognize the reality of how people actually do conflict. What I am saying is that to study, apply, and practice the principles of working with conflicts at the level of meaning—often at a microscopic textual level—will improve your research skills as you apply them to studying conflict. What follows is a brief account of some of the *opportunities* of trying to work with meaning in conflict stories.

In terms of the benefits of working with narrative meaning, first, you will become more in tune with how actions connect to their effects in networks, cycles, and patterns of relationships. This will help you as a researcher and as a practitioner. We might refer to this as being *telesmatic*. This concept is based on the Greek term, *apotelesma,* which is defined as the "reflective intelligence that means we understand and take seriously the results of our communication" (Goodall & Kellett, 2004, p. 166).

Apotelesma is a temporal form of intelligence, as it implies an ability to see the past and anticipate possible future implications of conflict actions. This takes the form of developing reflective insight into what our talk accomplishes, what it limits, and how alternative talk might accomplish different things. Being telesmatic can also mean the ability to know when we have "been there" in terms of achieving dialogue and perhaps how to get back there. Finally, being telesmatic also refers to the ability to understand the implications and impact of our communication as it ripples through our lives and our relationships. Being telesmatic increases our ability and opportunity to revisit and repeat our effective communication experiences and not repeat the less effective ones. It also enables us as researchers to know how to portray interrelationships of factors and forces in conflicts that we are representing in story form.

Second, you will work with the multifaceted nature of conflict meaning. When a gemstone cutter cuts one facet of a stone to gain a clearer view inside it for imperfections and a better sense of its quality, this is called a *window*. It is literally a way to view the inside of the stone and develop an analysis or assessment of it. A single window can tell the stonecutter a lot. However, the true inner beauty of a stone is brought to maximum effect when it is faceted, which involves cutting lots of windows into the stone in symmetrical relationship—correlation—to each other. When the facets are in symmetry, the stone is much more likely to sparkle. To follow the analogy through, think of a single window as one perspective or insight into the conflict, and think of facets as examining the conflict from the multiple perspectives and meanings that the conflict probably contains. The research skills give you the ability to see the conflict from multiple angles, perspectives, even stakeholders, and to recognize that these are all part of bringing out the full meaning of the conflict you have before you.

Your skill as a researcher lies also in understanding how facets of the conflict relate to each other—specifically, in knowing how the story of one participant plays against or connects to that of another participant and how the truth of the conflict is somewhere between the different facets. These are research skills that you will develop. In terms of Antoine and Torise's story, my skills as a researcher depended on me recognizing that a fuller account of the conflict was to be gained by listening to and documenting the other facets or participants in the conflict.

- How would just having one side limit me as a researcher?

Third, when you develop a multifaceted sense of the truth of a conflict, you will develop tolerance as a researcher and as a practitioner.

Tolerance is the choice to try to understand in the actions of others the relationship between the choices they make and the choices that they do not make. You may not like the choices that people make and, in fact, as you examine the stories in this book, you might easily judge the participants. However, the more of a sense of why people act the way they do that you get from examining the meaning of conflicts, then the more likely you are to understand why they do what they do and why they do not do what they do not do. You will be much less likely to assign motives and characterizations (for example, as villains) as you deepen your understanding of why the conflict took the shape that it did. People will naturally fill in parts of the conflict story where they perceive gaps, and they will naturally fill them with things that reflect their own interests as researchers. This is particularly important to be aware of when you are a third-party mediator listening to the conflict of others and if you are trying to help others to manage their conflicts.

Fourth, a good narrative researcher will recognize and understand patterns. To understand is, to take the term literally, to come to know what is under what we stand on. Geologists practice this as they try to read back through rock strata to uncover a plausible story of how the land got to be how it is today. For our purposes, to recognize the patterns of the past that manifest themselves in a current conflict is to understand the moment in the present as it connects to the past or to other conditions and factors around the conflict. This is *systemic intelligence*, which is based on the idea that good narrative research is grounded in the ability to recognize patterns described or hinted at in the story and show how these patterns shape and help explain the meaning of the conflict.

Patterns manifest in several ways, and it is important to see the forms of patterning as they connect to a conflict. They can be more or less direct repetitions of something from the past—what might be termed an *echo*. When you are having the same conflict that you or your parents had in the past, this can be a *repeating* pattern. Patterns can be the result of things converging from different sources. For example, when a couple's conflicts are the result of a bad combination of habits from both of their family backgrounds that clash as they bring them to their relationship, this is a *convergence* pattern. As patterns converge to create new ones, they can throw *ripple effect* patterns into other aspects of a relationship or create new conflicts that spin off from the main one. Patterns can morph or distort and grow or shrink as they move through your life and are impacted by various factors as they do so. These might be termed *metamorphic* patterns. To seek part of the meaning of a conflict in the background of behavior and as a manifestation of underlying forces and factors is the basis of interpretive understanding.

- What patterns do Antoine and Torise seem to be repeating from their lives?

Systemic intelligence is also based on the ability to know what patterns might be changed and how to go about doing that. Such pattern changes create *transformative* patterns. How might you not repeat a pattern that seems consistent in your intimate relationships, for example? What would it take to replace it with a healthier pattern? Even more reflexive and deeper forms of pattern-based intelligence occur when we are able to see the patterns within and between our conflicts. What, for example, are the consistencies in the patterns that we see across various examples of our own conflict stories? Herein can be discovered a deeper understanding of ourselves. If Antoine and Torise were to sit down and examine how their two families converge in their own habits and patterns of conflict, then they would gain insight into why they have the conflicts that they do, and perhaps they might affect and change the patterns that they inherited and even create new ones that they desire to be part of their relationship. This form of intelligence can help us to shape the very meaning of being together in relationships.

Fifth, narrative research can hopefully connect understanding to learning. Understanding patterns and how they can and do change through our actions is the basis of conflict intelligence. Knowing how to take those insights and apply them to your actual relational communication is based on your ability to learn. Learning depends on your ability to see possibilities for change and know how to bring those possibilities into the level of probability (that things will probably happen a particular way). Generally, if you recognize that you are repeating a conflict experience across relationships or over time in a relationship, then there may be opportunities for learning. If you are working to improve, eliminate something, adopt something, or build on a particular strength, then you are learning to change; you are turning possibilities into probabilities. In the case of the relational conflict in the introduction to the chapter, the young couple might try to work with Mike's in-laws on improving the level of understanding of their long-term life goals that provide some context for his career choices. They might try several things and see which strategy seems to be making a difference in their relationship. This way, they are learning to be a family who is smarter at communication than they were when they were all just mad at each other.

Discussion Questions

Discussion Questions for Digging Into Narrative Meaning

- How is the meaning of the conflict and what it means to be in a relationship different or similar for Antoine and Torise?
- How are these similarities or differences in priorities, expectations, and values, for example, keys to understanding the perception of differences between them and their oppositional, conflicted relationship?
- In a nutshell, what do you think is really going on at a deep structural level of meaning that divides these two people and means that this couple experiences the ongoing pattern of conflicts that they do?
- How does seeing Torise's side of the story help you to see the gaps in Antoine's story and the ways that his story reflects his desire and motive to be seen in a particular way through the representational choices behind it?
- How do these selective and perhaps perspectival representations help you understand the politics of narrative representation for Antoine and Torise as well as for yourself in how you shape your conflict stories to achieve your representational goals? What do Antoine and Torise leave out, hide, include as true facts, or color the meaning of in some way that is guided by their interests?
- How can these representational choices be used to develop questions for them both? What would you most like to ask both of them or point out to both of them, based on the other person's story? How might these questions and comments that you have for both of them provide the basis of a productive relational dialogue?

Questions Related to the Challenges of Narrative Research

- What, if anything, is complex about the meaning of this conflict?
- How is the meaning of the conflict different for Antoine and Torise?
- What are some of the important analogues to consider as you examine both sides of this story?
- What aspects of the meaning of the conflict are slippery, contested, ambiguous, or unanswered?
- As a researcher, how might you take extra care as you interpret the meaning of the conflict? What might some typical interpretive mistakes be?

Questions Related to the Opportunities of Narrative Research

- What are the cycles, patterns, and interrelationship of behaviors in the conflict?
- How do both sides of the story present facets that compliment as well as oppose each other?
- How was your tolerance stretched as you read the story? How does having both sides help generate understanding for each person?
- What historical and cultural patterns do you see repeating in the story?
- As a researcher, how would you draw out of the conflict one or two valuable lessons for relationship partners more generally?

❖ HOW TO COLLECT A GOOD STORY AS RESEARCH DATA

Goodall (1996) urges us to "pay attention to the details. Ultimately they contain the whole story" (p. 24). He is right, although it takes a degree of interpretive skill to know what details to record and how to build them into a good story. We have also seen how moving from details to interpreting the meaning is quite a challenge. This part of the chapter outlines a step-by-step process of collecting the details of a conflict experience and building them into story form so that we can learn from them. This is exactly what Antoine had to do as he recollected his own story and collected Torise's. My students are often much more adept at telling good stories in the natural setting of a conversation than in knowing where to begin when sitting looking at a computer screen and understandably so. The following steps will take you from start to finish as you develop your conflict research skills.

The first step is to begin a personal conflict journal that focuses on recollecting the details of one or two important conflicts from your own experience. The beauty of beginning with journaling is that it takes off the pressure of sitting there with a blank screen and a paper deadline. Take on a detective persona, as Goodall (1989) suggests. This puts you in the mode of seeing details and clues in the conflict as if you were a stranger to the experience and you are trying to figure out what happened. Once in detective mode, my advice is to begin anywhere. It does not matter where because, as in a good mystery, the clues will eventually all fit together anyway. Begin by recalling the most memorable moments of the conflict. These will likely be the rich moments that are keys to the conflict, but they may also be a flood of memories that do not appear to be organized. For some people, what comes to mind first is actual talk, and for some it is their thoughts and feelings at the time of the conflict. For some, it is the lasting outcome of the conflict and its effects on the relationship. As fragments start to expand, write them into fuller events in the conflict. Then these fragments will naturally suggest others to be developed, and you are on your way with the journaling of the experience. Try to include the actual conversations if you can recall them. Include also the thoughts and feelings you remember experiencing as you lived through the conflict, the background information on the characters and their motives and actions, and anything else that pops to mind as you begin to recollect the experience. Pay particular attention to reconstructing actual talk and how it connects to the deeper thematic issues and meaning of the conflict. Make note of connections between parts of the story and how the conflict progressed chronologically. Start to think about how the fragments might be organized chronologically. The key at this point is to be honest. Do not censor the story but allow it to emerge. Real dialogue begins with narrative honesty.

Second, where possible, it is extremely valuable to collect the personal narrative of the other person in the story or narratives of other people's stories that you have no connection to. This task my students find much more difficult than recalling their own conflict experiences. To do this, you can adapt the steps of the journaling process and give the other person similar instructions to what you are getting here. I have found that students get the best stories from others when they give their informants clear directions about what they want the story to be about, what it should include, how long it might ideally be, and how much background to give. Then, if you can follow up with more detailed questions based on your knowledge of conflict and build those insights into the text of their story, you will likely have as good a story as one that you recalled yourself. It is crucial that informants be allowed to change the names of everyone in their stories. It is also crucial for you to get their permission to use the stories for your class and that they are able to revoke that permission at any time. This way, you are honoring the rights of your subjects and the ethics of personal narrative research.

Third, you will need to transform your journal notes into a first draft of the story. For this, you will need to think about your narrative voice in the text. Who are you in the story? Are you the main character, hero, victim, or narrator? Begin to clarify your persona and that of the other people. Begin also to organize your notes around a story plot, usually told in chronological order of some sort. This funneling (Agar, 1996) of your notes down to those elements and details that reflect the story you are trying to tell is crucial in realizing your goal of developing a thematically clear account that connects you and your experience to the audience for your story (usually your classmates). You may be working with several stories up to this point, and as you reflect on them, now one may seem to have a greater message or significance than the others. This is the one to continue writing about.

Fourth, you will need to refine and test the text. In terms of refining, it is important to make sure that you have taken great care with the language of the conflict. We will come back to this issue in Chapter 3, but the imagery, the metaphors and similes, and other literary devices you use to evoke and describe the experience are very important in making your story vivid, accurate, and believable to others (Atkinson, 1992; Langellier, 1989). In terms of testing the text or moving from your first draft to final draft, Hammersley's (1990) criteria of *naturalism*, *understanding*, and *discovery* are useful concepts. *Naturalism* has to do with the audience believing that you have been close enough to the events that you have captured the frame of reference and experience of the participants. *Understanding* has to do with your ability to convey the meaning of the event. You need to show that you understand the conflict enough to portray it accurately and clearly. *Discovery* has to do with the story communicating something more than itself in terms of a deeper or broader lesson about relational conflict. Bochner and Eisenberg (1997) add another useful story-testing criterion with their notion that personal stories should stimulate more questions and more dialogue. When you share your story, there ought to be more questions from the audience and more discussion as others connect the story to their own experiences and learn from them. When you are happy that your story is well written and that you have followed these steps of good personal narrative writing, then you are ready to share or perform your story for an audience. Think about how to improve the dialogue and negotiation in the conflict so that the story might move forward in productive ways. If it is the story of a well-managed conflict, then you are ready to learn about why it was effectively managed. These are questions we will take up in the next chapter. For now, a few final discussion questions for this story follow:

Discussion Questions for Examining Antoine and Torise's Story as Data

- How well do you think Antoine has documented and included the important details of the story? Which fragments or moments of the story are particularly vivid and well done?

- How well has Antoine collected Torise's story in comparison with his own? What are some of the challenges for him as a researcher in collecting her story?
- Is the plot structure and relationship between the characters clear and well defined?
- Why is Antoine and Torise's story worth telling? What meaning does it have beyond itself for people in intimate relationships?
- As you go back through the story and test the text, how refined is the story and how well does it live up to the criteria of naturalism, understanding, discovery, and dialogue?

❖ LESSONS FROM THE FIELD OF PRACTICE:
  AN EXERCISE FOR UNDERSTANDING
  AND SHOWING THE MEANING OF CONFLICT

The instructions for the following exercise are brief as it is a direct application of the principles and techniques from the chapter. The exercise challenges you to dig into your own relational conflict experiences and reflect on the challenges as both researcher and subject-narrator of the conflict. This will help you to bring together and use all of the concepts of this chapter.

Exercise: Personal Narrative Recollection and Reflection

Think of a significant event in your family or relational history in which people became conflicted over something meaningful and divisive. The conflict should meet the criteria of our definition given early in the chapter. Your task is to develop a three- to five-page personal narrative of your own that captures the meaning of that conflict for you. Try to interview another person in the conflict if possible and represent his or her side of the story. Consider and discuss the following questions:

- What were the challenges to you as both researcher and subject of the conflict?
- What did you learn about the conflict through the exercise of documenting it and making all of the choices in how you represented it?
- What did the conflict mean to you and to the other person, and how were the similarities and differences in your meanings important in shaping the conflict?

- What would you do differently in the actual conflict if you could, as you reflect back on the meaning in the conflict?
- What did the family learn from the conflict and how did the conflict impact the family over the longer term?
- What does your own conflict tell you about the importance of understanding and working on a conflict from the perspective of its meaning for all those involved?

❖ CONCLUSION

We have stepped into the relational lives of Mike and that of Antoine and Torise in more detail, and we have seen how their conflicts are about expressing and working with differences in meaning. You have also, I hope, paused to reflect on the meaning of your own conflicts and how the complexities of meaning in your relationships provide new insights into why they take the forms that they do. You should have gained a deeper insight into the process of collecting and examining narratives for insight into conflicts and for lessons about how to do them more effectively. Perhaps there are conflicts in your own relational or family experiences that have been particularly important turning points in the lifespan of your relationships and your family. Perhaps a conflict divided parts of your family, perhaps a conflict brought you closer together with an intimate partner in a romantic relationship, and perhaps you are still working on that one conflict that keeps popping up in one form or another, as much as you try to avoid it. The key to getting started as a narrative researcher of conflict is to appreciate the complex challenge of documenting, representing, and discovering the meaning of conflicts. It is a crucial process in which to have the care of a researcher and the vision of an effective conflict practitioner, as you will see in the next chapter when we move from meaning to dialogue and negotiation to create resolution to our conflicts.

I hope, also, that the achievement of actually sharing meaning—called communication—is all the more poignant and will remain less taken for granted as we navigate the complexity and joys of relationships. You have certainly seen in the conflicts explored in this chapter that effective communication is an achievement that is sometimes quite difficult but that often is not too far away. Perhaps a few small changes can make a big difference in all of our relationships.

We have focused in this first chapter on issues and techniques in the collection of conflict stories, as this is the first place to begin the research process of understanding a conflict. In the next chapter, we explore research-based techniques for analyzing the meaning of conflicts and practitioner-based techniques for developing conflict management strategies based on those meanings. To connect the techniques of conflict management to the meaning of the conflict is a key to producing meaningful and lasting solutions.

2

From Meaning—
to Dialogic Negotiation—
to New Meaning

❖   ❖   ❖

The struggle of our time is to build the practices of working together. This is the hope of a dialogic theory of communication.

—Deetz and Simpson (2004, p. 141)

Interpreting the lived-meaning of conflict—asking deeper questions about why it happens as it does—is a necessary precursor to determining how to act when you find yourself in a conflict situation.

—Kellett and Dalton (2001, p. viii)

To connect the two opening quotes, it is my view that meeting the challenge of working together more effectively is built on a foundation of inquiry in which we learn to question deeply for lessons about how to approach conflicts collaboratively. A brief example will illustrate the value of inquiring into conflicts in ways that promote collaboration. Latoya's high school relationship with Tee-Tee began like many relationships. Phone numbers were exchanged at the skating rink after many flirtatious looks back and forth and a conversation that felt full of promise and possibilities. After 2 years of dating, one day Tee-Tee revealed a secret that he has been keeping from her. He has a daughter who, he claims, was born 2 months before they met. Latoya was devastated and felt the pain of betrayal. Tee-Tee claimed he kept the secret from her to protect their relationship, and he vowed never to hurt her again. They reconciled, but in the back of her thoughts was always the suspicion that the secret revealed a network of his lies to cover things up: The baby seat in the back of the car was his mother's from baby sitting earlier that day; the person he was at the mall with was a friend's daughter, and so on. What other lies was he telling her? What other secrets was he keeping? Did she really know this man that well after all? The conflict that developed proved difficult for them to overcome, and the relationship ended.

If you examine for a moment the things that we have the biggest fights over in our close and intimate relationships, they often seem like things that would not end a relationship or cause a huge conflict. If Latoya and Tee-Tee were looking back on their conflict from a distance and from the viewpoint of a secure and loving relationship, their traumatic conflict over the secret child might not have killed their relationship of 2 years. It is quite common for people to begin relationships with others who have children from a previous relationship. It is also quite common to have secrets and topics that you do not want to discuss just as a relationship begins and progresses. It is also quite common to shade the truth and perhaps lie with the intent of protecting the relationship and not hurting the other person. The thing being fought over is often, for us, far less important than the symbolic meaning of the conflict. Latoya interprets the revelation as a betrayal and as a need to be suspicious, as a clue that she should question the very foundation of the relationship. This deeper meaning is largely why the relationship never fully recovered. If Tee-Tee had been more conscious of and sensitive to the possible meaning for Latoya or for the relationship of his behavior of keeping and then revealing a secret, he might have handled the conflict quite differently.

Sometimes conflicts are more about things, behaviors, objects, and so on, rather than what they mean symbolically. For example, it is quite possible that Latoya could have forgiven him his secret but then a conflict could have emerged about the mechanics and financial aspects of dating someone with a child. They may even have had a productive conflict about future rules for behavior between them. Most often, conflicts are about both tangible and symbolic meanings. This conflict is probably about both the tangible reality of the child and the tangible behavior of keeping a secret and lying—and it is also about the meaning of the revelation and related lies as a betrayal that calls the whole relationship and the person into question. Betrayal for her is paralleled with the secret having a protective meaning for him. He probably was not consciously betraying her but just did not want to face the likely conflict when she found out. He probably thought about telling her many times but could not find the right moment or way to tell her. They were teenagers, after all, without the wisdom gained from having had several long-term relationships. At the heart of their conflict is the fact that they had different and opposing meaning for the same behavior. This difference over tangibles and their personal meaning is the source of many relational conflicts. Knowing this and what to do with this insight is crucial for effective conflict management. It is, therefore, of utmost importance to understand the rich interplay of the layers of meaning in a conflict, both for understanding it and knowing how to manage it effectively, as it can often be a multilayered, multidimensional dispute with multiple meanings.

This chapter provides a rigorous approach to analyzing the meaning of conflicts as fully as possible. It also shows you how to build strategies for approaching conflicts as opportunities for collaborative exchange—here termed *dialogic negotiation*—as a way of managing conflict based on an understanding of its meaning.

Main topics and learning goals in this chapter:

- How to use research techniques to explicate the meaning of conflicts
- Some helpful theoretical background in sources of conflict
- How dialogue and negotiation build on and create new meanings in conflicts
- Skills for energizing conflict communication toward dialogic negotiation
- Lessons from the field of practice

❖ HOW TO USE RESEARCH TECHNIQUES
TO EXPLICATE THE MEANING OF CONFLICTS

The first part of this chapter illustrates the practical research techniques of explicating and analyzing conflicts for their meanings for the people involved. Of course, like most interpretive research or even detective work, if we view it that way, a big part of the process is smart guess-work. We have the luxury of placing the specimen story on the table—like a paleontologist studying a fossil—and really taking time over its dissection and interpretation. Recognize that as you engage in conflicts and try to figure out the best way to handle them in your real life, you may not have such a luxury of time and near-perfect hindsight. You can at least become smarter at looking for meaning, however, particularly similarities and differences of meaning between the people involved, and make strategic and ethical decisions about how you proceed with the conflict from there. We begin with a more fully developed story specimen for analysis. Then you will learn to connect conflict management strategies to the symbolic and tangible meanings of a conflict.

"Out With the Old and In With the New?" (Autumn)
A community and family conflict based around millennia of tradition is not easily resolved. A culture's proud bearers will often do almost anything to grasp tightly to what they hold dear: religion, values, customs, and a rich heritage. Try as they might, however, these proud people can expect to encounter a host of inevitable conflicts when they leave their comfort zones and become minorities in a new land. This is the story of an Indian family who made that change. Though their move was beneficial, it introduced them to new conflicts between the young and the old generations of the family and community in their small American town.

In the 1980s, a young couple, Shashi and Manju Patel, left their places within the highest caste in the Indian province of Gujarat. With their three young children, they immigrated to the United States, taking residence as hotel managers. They had willingly become poor in hopes of creating a more promising future for their family. Over the years, their children flourished, all the while becoming fluent in English while retaining their fluency in Gurarati. They thrived in their town's Indian community, yet branched out to their own American circles at school. They were popular with their friends, active in sports and clubs, and brought home exemplary report cards.

Shashi and Manju were very pleased with their children's success. Yet as the children became more and more Americanized, the parents immersed themselves totally in their town's Indian community. Their entire identity remained wrapped up in the expectations and approval of other Indian immigrants living nearby—so much so that Manju never felt it necessary to learn English and Shashi never learned to drive. Neither grasped written English enough to function independently. They remained legal aliens while their children became bilingual U.S. citizens.

Even though the Patels brought their children a world away, they made great efforts to pass down their Indian heritage. They instilled them with Indian customs in everything from dating and marriage to the devoted practices of their staunch Hindu faith. The parents had strong memories of life in India. But as much as they desired their children to carry on their unaltered traditions, the younger generation did not share the idealistic memories of their parents. While they respected their strong Indian heritage, they knew they were Americanized—with Western ideals and values. The pull between their Indian and American identities would manifest in a host of conflicts between the family generations.

One conflict in particular, surrounding the second daughter, Tejal, illustrates these family and cultural tensions. Tejal was only 3 years old when her parents brought her to the United States, so she quickly adapted to her new surroundings. She became fast friends with a large group of girls who have remained close all the way through college. At times, her friendships caused family conflicts because of her parents' insistence that she abide by a strict curfew, even when she visited from college. However, a life-altering decision at the age of 17 caused the biggest conflict between Tejal and her family. At that time, Tejal made a decision to convert from Hinduism to Christianity. She became the first Christian in a community of hundreds of Hindus and 5 years later remained the only Christian. Tejal's family waited for her to pass through her fleeting stage of rebellion in her new religion. But her faith only grew into an essential aspect of her life, ultimately defining her personal values and beliefs about her reason for being.

This conflict heated up considerably when Tejal was 22. Her uncle Akhir—one of the wealthiest and more prestigious members of the community—hosted the biggest event of the year for their community and family. His daughter Swati was getting married, and over a thousand Indian friends and family members were coming in for the 3-day event. Tejal was excited to be part of her cousin's wedding. She and her sister would be bridal attendants, which meant rarely leaving the bride's side throughout the entire wedding process. For days, Tejal and the other girls underwent extensive beauty rituals to prepare for the event, including elaborate Mendhi henna paintings on their hands and custom fittings of ornate Indian gowns.

Tejal felt so exhilarated to stand next to Swati's side throughout the wedding process, though she had feelings of dread as well as joy. She knew that the wedding would include a high degree of Hindu god worship and that the wedding party would be expected to perform several symbolic Hindu rituals. Her uncle Akhir would not approve of her avoiding the Hindu rituals. But as a Christian, she strongly believed that she should not sacrifice offerings or show reverence to other gods.

As much as she wanted to avoid the conflict and controversy that would come if she avoided worshiping their gods, Tejal knew that she could not allow herself to compromise her deeply held beliefs. As she stood debating her choice, Akhir approached the large crowd of cousins who had gathered in preparation for the first worship rituals.

"Namaste," he said to his eldest son.

"Namaste," the son repeated.

Tejal closed her eyes, wishing her uncle would not come to her. She knew that the word meant, "The divine in me salutes the divine in you."

As a Christian, she did not feel comfortable saying this.

Akhir did come to Tejal.

"Namaste," she heard, her eyes still diverted.

"Namaste," she near whispered in return—immediately sensing her own internal defeat as she did so.

Akhir knew that she was a Christian but tested her in public to show her that the community values of being Indian were in effect. Taking a deep breath, she prepared for the next ritual—a time for the group of cousins to enter a room in which they were expected to meditate and lay sacrifices at the base of a large shrine.

Tejal felt numb as she entered the room. "God give me strength," she prayed as she made her way to the back wall. While her other cousins kneeled in meditation before the Hindu gods, Tejal separated herself and discreetly prayed alone. Akhir watched from a corner with flames in his eyes. How could Tejal do this to him, he wondered? He had sponsored her family's immigration to America. He paid for Tejal's college education. Yet she was humiliating his family in front of the community. Tejal felt the disapproving gaze of many people as she trembled with fear and fought back the tears. Akhir decided to let go of the conflict for the moment, but soon her younger brother approached her and pulled her aside.

"Why did you do that?" Abhi asked, "I know you are a Christian, and I know you decided it because of your friends, but we're not like other people, Tejal. Your friends don't understand what goes into our culture as Indians. We have to all work together and stay committed to each other as family and as Hindus."

Tejal was grateful for his loving reproach but wished that she could explain Christianity to him and that it was not about fitting in with peer pressure from her Western friends. She remained silent and nodded in reply.

When they returned home that night, Tejal's mother was not so gentle.

"You have disgraced the family by this!" She screamed, opening the gates to a stream of criticism. Manju was angry and embarrassed by Tejal's inappropriate behavior, and she was not afraid to let her know. What was Tejal thinking, to shame her mother by avoiding the sacred time of meditation and sacrifice? Tejal would be able to leave soon and return to college, but Manju would still be at home, in the midst of the judgment of the Indian community. She knew that the other women already looked down on her, silently blaming her bad parenting as the cause of Tejal's shameful rebellion. Tejal cried, knowing that the day's events had only been a piece of the conflict and that it was far from over.

❖ SOME HELPFUL THEORETICAL BACKGROUND IN SOURCES OF CONFLICT

Families are often the special people we most rely on as we grow up and as we move through life's ages and stages. Ideally, loving bonds and mutual care unite their members. Families are also complex systems of people across generations and across time, within cultures and historical periods, often with differing needs and expectations and evolving identities and goals. Families are also increasingly the result of merged parts of other families, as parents divorce and remarry, with "step" and "half" relationships being much more common. It is little surprise that conflict results in the to and fro of the life and times of families with such complexity and change. Conflicts in families express the tensions and frictions that arise in the to-ing and fro-ing of being together. Conflicts are also the process by which the changes occur that are necessary to hold the system together and evolve so that the family adapts and can endure the to-ing and fro-ing. The key for us is to examine the way that the meaning of being in a family and all of the assumptions that connect to those meanings sometimes differ and may conflict. Another key is to recognize how differing meanings can be sources of deeper understanding and possible change in family communication and conflict, as complex and difficult as family conflicts can be. What follows is a summary of some of the important concepts and dynamics that are associated with family conflict. As you examine and analyze the story of Tejal and her family conflict, use these concepts and questions to enrich your analysis and understanding.

Common to many conflicts are dynamics and causal factors that are useful to consider as a background to discovering the meaning of conflicts. We need a theoretically grounded vocabulary to explain conflicts. The underlying dynamics can be accounted for through theoretical constructs, such as dialectical tensions (Baxter, 1988, 2004; Baxter & Montgomery, 1996; Stueve & Gerson, 1977), perceived violations of expectations (Galvin, Byland, & Brommel, 1992), and so on. To expand on these dynamics, we examine the following main factors that are often integral to conflicts. For additional background to understand relational conflicts, see Baxter (2004) and Kellett and Dalton (2001, pp. 162–183). For additional background in understanding dynamics more specific to workplace conflicts, see Cheney (1995), Constantino and Merchant (1996), Mumby (1993), Nicotera (1995), and Smith and Eisenberg (1987). For background specific to understanding community conflicts, see Kellett and Dalton (2001, pp. 103–119).

First, family expectations and goals, including expectations of life scripts, roles, and goals, can create the conditions and the substance of a conflict. Expectations for things following particular norms are powerful setups for conflict, because people do not always share them, although we often assume that they (and we) do. Also, most of us are largely unaware of how our expectations shape our actions and judgments and affect our relationships with family members. We are also almost always of the belief that our expectations are reasonable—even right. So if our expectations are often different but we believe ours are right, then there will be family conflict. One of the most powerful expectations that leads to conflict in families has to do with the life scripts or life stories that people expect for their own and other family members' lives. Parents will often have scripted stories of their children's lives before the children have a chance to make their own choices: What type of persons they will be, what they will do for a living, the type of persons they will marry, where they will live, and so on can be quite firm if sometimes unconscious expectations. When children make choices that contradict those expectations, then there will emerge what might be called *life script conflicts*. Try to imaginatively reconstruct the life script that Tejal's parents may have held for her and that of Tejal herself. Explore the following questions to help you:

- How are Tejal's and her parents' expectations for family norms of behavior different, and what factors created these differences?
- In what ways does their family conflict move beyond differences to show a clash—a conflicted opposition between life scripts?
- How does their conflict provide an opportunity to examine their different life scripts, and why is this opportunity not taken?
- What life script conflicts have been important in your life?

Linked to this script-based sense of expectations are conflicts that emerge when there are tensions in the meanings that people attach to roles and responsibilities in families, particularly when these expectations impinge on issues of their members' own identities and life choices. For example, if there are conflicted meanings associated with roles such as "son," "daughter," "father," "mother," "uncle," "first born," and "middle child," this can create conflicted tensions, rebellion, disappointment, and often volatile arguments in families. Families often experience these tensions when role expectations change socially and culturally over time or across cultures if the family moves.

- How do role tensions feed into the Patels' family conflict?
- Where do these role tensions come from in the culture of origin and personal history of the family?
- How does the conflict affect role identity and tensions in the aftermath for Tejal, her mother, and her uncle in particular?
- How do role tensions figure into the conflicts that your family has experienced over the years together?

Families will rarely set out specific goals like a corporation, but there are often implicit or partially explicit goals that the family is directed toward. This has to do with the basic function and meaning of being together. Asking the questions, "Why are we together?" and "What are we oriented toward achieving?" will usually reveal these goals. Asking these questions may also reveal major differences in members' expectations about the meaning of being together, and it may reveal a lot about the conflicts experienced as a family.

- If Tejal and her family answered these questions, what do you think they would say?
- How might similar or differing perspectives on life goals be linked at a deeper level of meaning (do they have common goals)?
- How might this connection be an opportunity to share perspectives rather than simply clash?
- How might differences over goals explain some of the conflicts that your family has experienced?

Second, family dynamics, stages, and cycles can have a great deal to do with the meaning of a conflict. For example, how do you think the internal dynamics of the family, including cycles and repeating patterns of conflict as well as structural and stage issues at this point in time, account for the conflict in the Patel family? As families navigate the long-term life cycles of families, from marriage and family formation, through childrearing, teenage children, possibly divorces, merging, weddings, ageing parents, and spatial distance, there will be conflicts that center on specific issues along the way. These issues may include (1) negotiating duties and responsibilities so that members of the family come to know who does what and how those mutual responsibilities fit together to achieve the things the family needs to achieve, (2) maintaining unity so that there is a sense of working together despite conflicts along the way, and (3) distributing power and resources so that the structure of the family is maintained and people know what they can and should do for themselves and for the family.

- In what ways is the Patel family conflict partly explained as the family navigating a specific issue at a specific point in their common history? Do not underestimate the power of naming things. To be able to define and point out the issue is a good starting point for addressing it and collaborating on common perspectives on it.
- How might the Patels become more effective in working with their conflict at the point in their family life that they currently find themselves?

- How does the Patel family conflict resonate with your own family conflicts?

Often overlaid onto the previously mentioned life cycle of families are repeating patterns of familial conflict. As conflicted issues flow through one generation of the family, they are likely to reflect a similar pattern from a past generation and the coming together, interrippling, or clashing of patterns from the different sides of the family (usually the mother's side and the father's side) from previous generations that are continued in the habits and the culture of the family. Unresolved conflicts, dysfunctions, and built-up resentments in families also tend to create repeating patterns of conflict.

- How might the Patels' situation be linked to repeating patterns or unresolved conflicts that have created cycles of conflict for them? We often do not get a full picture of the family history or of previous conflicts as they might connect to and fuel the current one, so the emphasis is on thinking about how they *might* be connected.
- Can you identify conflicts that appear and reappear in your family as repeating and perhaps unresolved patterns? If so, how might you map out the life cycle of such conflicts? Indicate on your map what factors drive and maintain the cycle.

Other related dynamics that create conflicts might include intergenerational attitudes and beliefs, birth order, changing cultural and social practices and norms, family habits of avoiding conflict, and so on. Many of these issues may figure into explaining Tejal's family conflict and perhaps even some of your family's conflicts. How might these factors help explain the meaning of the Patels' conflict? How might these dynamics help explain the meaning of some of the important conflicts that your family has faced? Having explored some of the important dynamics that help explain the meaning of a conflict, we will explore the methodology we will use to explicate meaning.

❖ HOW DIALOGUE AND NEGOTIATION BUILD
    ON AND CREATE NEW MEANINGS IN CONFLICTS

The following three-part process—analysis, dialogic negotiation strategy, and building lasting skills—integrates negotiation technique, dialogue theory, and communication skills. As you develop the process for helping manage the Patels' conflict, you will develop an understanding of the important theory and principles of dialogic negotiation that are at the basis of each of the subsequent chapters.

Part 1: Analyzing the Meaning of the Conflict

The technique for analyzing conflicts is drawn from a combination of narrative analysis developed for analyzing conflict narratives (Kellett & Dalton, 2001) and the interpretive technique developed for explicating and understanding the meaning of communicative experiences more generally (Kellett, 1995, 1996, 1999; Lanigan, 1988). We also integrate negotiation analysis. You will use these steps of analysis and techniques as you analyze different aspects of conflict narratives throughout the book. These steps and techniques are designed to enable you to complete what is often a difficult and confusing task of systematically examining the stories for their underlying meaning. Like a good anthropologist or paleontologist, you need to be cautiously systematic as well as creative and insightful in imagining the reality that lies in the white spaces between the lines of the clues you are given and the ones you do not have access to. We only have Tejal's side of the conflict, remember, so the responsibility is to be analytical and also fair to the various people in the conflict. This is not a responsibility you should take lightly—rather, you should be as thorough and careful as possible. This is particularly true when you consider that this chapter suggests that we approach the management of conflicts from an understanding of their meaning and origins. You will want to develop change strategies for your own conflicts and suggest change strategies for others that are based on the real root causes and systemic reality and manifestations—*the meaning* of the conflict you are studying.

I begin this part of the discussion by explaining the steps of analysis that you will use to create the dialogic negotiation strategies.

Step 1: Description of the Specific Family Conflict

Before analyzing the conflict through the stories of the participants, you need to collect the stories. It is important to capture as much as possible of the details, background, and actual talk and behavior that occurred in the conflict, as these are the data that you will be analyzing. It is important to begin with good data (Kellett & Dalton, 2001, pp. 27–48).

Using the Patels' story to practice on, have a good read through of the story and note your initial reactions and questions that indicate what you would like to know more about. Then you go through the text of the story again and carefully identify and describe all of the details of the story that show you that the people involved are experiencing and expressing their conflict through their communication. List and describe the manifestations of the conflict in specific behavior and communication. These behaviors and communicative expressions cluster together to express the wedding conflict as it is experienced by the family. Identify the communication and behavior as told by both or all sides of the story where possible.

So at this point, go through the Patels' story and highlight and describe the conflicted expressions at and around the wedding. What is being said and not said that shows you there is a conflict between these people? What details of the scene and the action support the understanding that these people are divided on an important aspect of their relationship? Continue through the story describing each moment where their conflict gets expressed, verbally, nonverbally, or even by moments of silence and what people are thinking in those moments of silence.

The second part of the description is where you start to dig to uncover the layers of meaning that form the structure beneath the surface you have just described. You need to identify the more enduring aspects of the family relationship that the wedding conflict seems to connect to. For this, ask "why" questions about the communication you have described so that you can start to make sense of the conflict. Why did the conflict blow up at the wedding? What was brewing in the background and history of this family that found its way out through the wedding conflict? Go back through the story again, and this time look beneath the description of expressions that you have completed and look for possible deeper, more enduring issues that are being expressed through the wedding conflict. For example, you may start to see elements of the conflict connect to deeper issues of differences in the definition of commitment to personal identity and family and cultural membership, power issues related to expectations that are based on historical financial relationships, and so on. This step should give you a list of deeper issues that seem to be being worked out, expressed at the wedding, and through which the participants are dividing perhaps more generally in their relationships. Do not jump to conclusions in trying to get the complete big picture that explains the conflict. You will uncover much more interconnection and relationship of themes before you have a complete analysis. You are still describing the conflict rather than coming to conclusions about its meaning, but you are probably starting to see hints of the bigger picture of the meaning emerging.

Step 2: Reduction to Central Themes

Using the theoretically grounded concepts and principles of family conflict, try to reduce the list of symbolic, deeper issues discovered in your description to the essential oppositions between these people on central themes that are under the surface of this conflict. Also identify issues and themes you think the family may be connected to more than this conflict illustrates. Do they all share a love of their Indian heritage and their lives here in the United States, for example? Perhaps they just have different expectations about what that love means and how they express it in their own personal lives. Do you think they also love their family and enjoy their membership in the Indian culture? Here you are engaging in what we define as *explication* (Kellett & Dalton, 2001, p. 94). You are asking good questions to try to explicate or bring to the surface the meaning of the conflict as a systemic picture of the oppositions, patterns, and interconnections of the people just under the surface of the conflict. Express these as thematic oppositions and so on. For example, by stating that Tejal's uncle expects loyalty to him and the traditions of the Indian community at the expense of personal expression and that for Tejal, the expression of her identity takes priority over loyalty to her uncle and what he stands for—you have begun to explicate the oppositions that are the driving force of the conflict. So you are essentially looking beneath the conflict for the essential basis of the things that divide them and that explain the existence of the conflict as it manifests in communication. How do you think their conflict is a sign that expresses deeper thematic issues that they may not even be consciously aware of? Here you are delving deeper into the systemic picture of the conflict that will help you dig down to the core meanings for the people in the conflict.

Step 3: Interpretation of the Meaning of the Conflict and the Implications for Negotiation

This step takes you through the understanding, questioning, and changing parts of the stages of systemic analysis (Kellett & Dalton, 2001, p. 94). Here you are looking for the meaning of the conflict that connects all of your descriptive and interpretive insights together into a plausible account of why the conflict happened and why it happened as it did. This will naturally lead to questions such as "Do we now have a better understanding of how and why these people behaved and communicated as they did, based on the context and lived reality of their conflict?" "How could it have been more effectively handled?" "What can the participants do from here on to manage the conflict more effectively?" and "How might they change aspects of their family communication in the future so that they do not repeat the same conflict the same way?"

As you piece together your interpretations that form the answers to these questions, you are starting to arrive at a fuller account of the meaning of the conflict in terms of why it happened as it did and why it did not happen in other possible ways that may have been more or less effective than what did happen. When you reflect on these relationships of what happened, why it happened, and what could happen, you should arrive at statements that reveal the big picture of the conflict. For example, we might make the interpretive statement that this family is having a specific wedding conflict because they realize they have more enduring fundamental differences (themes) that are not being effectively expressed in the family culture up to this point. The conflict surprises and enrages family members because they do not discuss differences effectively in everyday life and because they are tied together by cultural expectations that are different for different people in the family. The community judges the family harshly because their specific conflict (the wedding) and its connection to deeper themes (traditions and loyalty) are archetypal for them living as a community here in the United States. They are all probably struggling with the dialectical tension of living as Americans in the United States but with a close respect for the traditions and expectations associated with being Indian. These tensions are probably particularly poignant as Tejal's generation becomes more integrated into the United States (Westernized).

These statements could be one component of your interpretation. Develop as much of a plausible account as you can that enables you to capture the meaning of the conflict. This meaning will then form the basis of your questioning and working on ways to manage the conflict. What additional questions are generated about the family and about their conflict from studying this particular conflict? Ask questions about the additional choices and possibilities that might be explored for doing conflict more effectively. Finally, begin to imagine the ways that following these options might impact their conflict and their relationships more generally, if they want to keep alive this ongoing set of relationships.

Having developed your analysis technique that provides you with a working theory of the meaning of the conflict, we move on to the management part of the equation. In this next section, you will learn how the method of intervention into a conflict—the management strategy—is most effectively based on your careful analysis.

Part 2: Developing Dialogic Negotiation Strategies

Your task is to take the key findings from your analysis and develop the strategy for communication that will best manage the conflict. To do this, we will outline some of the main theoretical assumptions and practical techniques of dialogic negotiation, along with the necessary questions for your analysis. As we look at the Patel family, I can't help thinking that this whole conflict might not have been necessary if Tejal had clearly expressed her religious identity and why this meant that she could not make a sacrifice at the wedding. At the same time, within the culturally rigid confines of her family, she did not feel able to do that while maintaining the perception of others as being someone who respects her cultural heritage. So perhaps there are shared responsibilities for the conflict, and perhaps the family members also have a shared responsibility to express ideas more honestly and to have an atmosphere in which this is possible. As you imagine working with this family through the process of dialogic negotiation, bear in mind the deep connection between the members of the family.

There are several core characteristics of how to talk dialogically as one engages in the exchange of negotiation (Goodall & Kellett, 2004; Kellett & Dalton, 2001). These characteristics are based on thinking strategically about how to achieve the dialogic goals of getting the people in the conflict to engage with each other's perspectives in meaningful ways and that they allow the process of talking to generate both their shared understanding of their personal meanings of the conflict and the most collaborative solution that is possible for them (Cissna & Anderson, 1998). As such, dialogue is a focused yet creative form of communication that respects relationships and promotes shared solutions within difficult contexts where such values might not be explicit goals (Arnett & Arneson, 1999; Pearce & Pearce, 1999). (For excellent and somewhat parallel discussions of dialogic communication and conflict resolution, see Isenhart and Spangle, 2000, and Littlejohn and Domenici, 2001.)

First, dialogic negotiation *begins with an understanding of the meaning of a conflict and also with a clear, working model of how the parties might negotiate the things that are important to them (exchange concessions and demands).* The basis of collaborative negotiation is that negotiators approach differences as opportunities to engage in reasoned discussion that focuses on developing shared understanding that serves as the basis for agreements (Deetz, 2001; Spangle & Isenhart, 2003). The basis of negotiation is the movement through issues based on the exchange of demands and concessions (Fisher & Ertel, 1995; Johnson, 1993) based on the things that each of the people in the negotiation find important.

The things that people find important will form the basis of their ideal solution. So for example, Tejal's uncle might ideally demand a public apology and an agreement to maintain strong Indian cultural ties through the next generation. Tejal might want to recognize that she is proud of her heritage but that she prefers to become more Westernized and wants to openly express her evolving identity. This is the basis of their conflict and also a possible point of beginning negotiation. The questions become, What will each trade as concessions to get close to their own ideals? What will they actually settle for in order to replace their family fight with peace? This negotiating room between ideal and acceptable provides the focal point of the other dialogic negotiation principles described in the discussion to follow.

I have read through the story for possible concessions and listed them. These should help you get started in mapping the relationship of tradable concessions and demands between them and in deciding what you think is particularly important to each family member.

List of Possible Concessions

- Tejal could recognize and acknowledge all of the sacrifices that her family has made for her and her siblings.
- The parents and the uncle could recognize that they thrived as part of the Indian *and* American communities and that it does not have to be an either-or choice.
- The parents and the uncle could recognize the academic successes of Tejal.
- The parents could recognize that there are inevitable generational changes happening and not see this as a threat.
- Tejal could make greater efforts to recognize and continue participating in the aspects of Indian heritage that are important to her parents and uncle.
- Tejal could deny her Christian faith and return to Hinduism.
- The parents could acknowledge that their children do not have the same idealistic memories that they do.
- Tejal could make more effort to respect her parents' rules, such as the curfew.
- The parents and uncle might see her faith as not necessarily a denial of their heritage.
- Tejal could have taken greater care not to shame her uncle publicly, given his prominence in the community.
- Tejal might acknowledge more actively all that her uncle has done for her family.

- Tejal could apologize for shaming her uncle.
- Tejal could have expressed her discomfort with specific parts of the ceremony and allow them to redesign the ceremony accordingly.
- The family could be better at allowing their children to express themselves and not see it as a threat that they are evolving into Asian Americans.
- Tejal could be better at compromising her beliefs for family peace and so could her parents and uncle.
- The parents and uncle could agree not to test or shame Tejal in public because of her beliefs.
- Tejal could more actively recognize her uncle for his support and acknowledge that he did not deserve to be humiliated.
- The family could all better manage its public image and be more cohesive publicly so that disgrace is not a recurring issue.
- The family could work on ways to stick together through the community judgment, rather than fall apart.
- Tejal could help her mother not to feel like a bad parent.
- The family could change its definition of Tejal's behavior to reflect the fact that she is searching for her own identity, not just rejecting the one they expected her to have.

The following questions will help you organize this list so that you can examine the Patel family's conflict for negotiation opportunities.

- What would be an ideal solution for each member of the family in terms of what each gets out of the conflict (refer to the foregoing list)?
- What would be an acceptable lower limit for an agreement to evolve—the minimum that each of the participants wants?
- What unites and divides the members of this family around the themes and issues hinted at in the list of concessions?
- What concessions might each of the family members most likely seek from the others in the form of demands?
- What concessions might each of the family members be most willing to trade or make to see progress in the conflict?
- How might these elements of negotiation form a basis for the dialogic negotiation between the family members?

When you have mapped out the negotiation possibilities for the conflict, you should have a good sense of what they will need to dialogue about in order to bring about progress in their family.

Second, dialogic negotiation *focuses on shared and open questioning of the conflict and of each other's needs.* Dialogue is, by definition, a "moving through" to a new understanding through talk. Good questions are essential to doing the work of explicating the issues and examining similarities and differences between the participants on those issues. Good questions are those that are designed to get *all* of the people in the conflict to think critically about *their own* behavior and related meanings in the conflict and to promote open and equal discussion between them. Questions should also stimulate recognition of the needs and negotiation goals of the others.

- What are some good questions (as defined earlier) and issues that emerge from our analysis of the meaning of the story that you would want the people in this family conflict to think about and talk about?
- What underlying themes on which they seem to be divided would you want them to address and discuss? How would you get them to discuss the relationship between personal, family, community, and cultural aspects of these issues?
- What questions might you develop to enable them to discuss the relationship between the meaning of the conflict and the form it has taken so far?
- How might these discussions about mutual desires and oppositional issues potentially lead them to recognize and perhaps work from their diverse and oppositional perspectives to develop a better, less destructively conflicted approach to their family?

Third, *dialogic negotiation integrates diverse and oppositional perspectives as a way to achieve win-win solutions.* We have conflicts because there are perceived oppositions between people that have real meaning for them. For example, sometimes we believe that if the other person wins, then we lose; or we might believe that the other person is in the way of our ability to achieve our goals. These meanings lock people in conflicted opposition until they are able to see how these meanings limit their communication with those people. Getting to this more dialogic understanding involves the participants putting their different experiences, perceptions, and meanings related to the conflict on the table and then negotiating from that point of open exchange. Hopefully, as they negotiate, they can integrate those perspectives into a new, more commonly shared account. Of course, all parties must be willing to approach communication with this spirit of collaboration, which is created when each of them shows willingness to make concessions that the other persons value.

- Based on our analysis of the meaning of the conflict, how would you show the participants in this conflict that they have specific perspectives on it that are grounded in their viewpoints or standpoints?
- How would you convince them that their perspectives are both valid and partial at the same time?
- How might you get them to listen to and think about engaging the perspectives and interests of the other parties in the conflict?
- Would it be helpful to get each party to verbalize the perspective of the other as a way for them to acknowledge each other's perspectives and accurately represent the experiences and viewpoint of the other in the conflict? Allow the people they are paraphrasing to correct their accounts where necessary.

Fourth, *dialogic negotiation moves participants beyond argumentation and competitive negotiating*. As we have discussed earlier, dialogue promotes the fusion of ideas and the energy that is associated with those ideas and our commitments to them. This may necessitate the opening up and expression of differences through arguments. However, dialogic negotiation moves people beyond polarized arguments. At some point, an engagement rather than an oppositional stance has to come about, and there is the assumption that both parties create a common understanding rather than simply agreeing on who has the better argument for a particular solution.

- Why might there be a tendency for the family members to want to argue and point fingers early on if you could get them around a table on this conflict?
- Why would arguing limit their ability to reach a resolution to their conflict that is meaningful for the family and the community?
- How would you move them beyond arguing to more dialogic communication?
- Under what circumstances might arguing be the realistic or even desirable way to communicate about this conflict? Might it, for example, get their differences out in the open and on the table early on?

Fifth, *dialogic negotiation is based on systemic analysis and leads to plausible scenario building*. A plausible scenario is a more or less agreed upon summary version of the conflict based on the deep or systemic analysis of the conflict—particularly the meaning part of the analysis. This can be a good starting point for change. A systemic analysis can lead to a more commonly understood version of the conflict: The various parties focus on the summary of the meaning of the conflict and position themselves in relation to your summary. The conversation can then be one of open exchange that shows enduring differences as well as any newly found commonalities as they think about that meaning. Thus the plausible scenario that results from engaging each other's perspectives provides a starting point for building dialogue that takes them beyond the current conflict.

- What plausible scenario would you begin with as you present the participants with your analysis and diagnosis of the conflict?
- How would you encourage them to renegotiate a shared and agreed upon plausible scenario of the conflict origins and effects? Engage the various parties in a point-by-point analysis and revision of the plausible scenario you developed. Expand and change the plausible scenario until everyone can live with it as a working story or theory of the conflict so far. Recognize and acknowledge this agreement as an important turning point in the conflict. Note the points over which you cannot get agreement and move on with what you do have.

Sixth, *dialogic negotiation integrates the surface and deeper issues in conflict management practices.* As we have seen from our approach to analyzing conflicts, various facets and layers are present in conflicts. Meanings are complex. They can also be quite simple. It is important to build the process and possible solutions based on those various meanings.

- How do the different layers and facets of meaning from the perspectives of each person combine to create the meaning of this event as a conflict?
- How do these meanings differ and connect each person in the conflict?
- How would you use these differences and similarities as a starting point for their dialogic negotiation?

Seventh, *dialogic negotiation develops conflict discourse that explores shared and different meanings and points of possible new meaning.* Dialogue may not be a perfectly linear process of progression through negotiating concessions and demands toward a shared and equal solution.

There may be cycles and twists and turns in the story. There usually are. However, dialogue is usually marked by emergent meanings that may not have existed or been conscious to the participants before the talking began. Dialogic negotiation is tool for the communication alchemist—it points to and helps achieve a new substance and form of communication between people.

- From your analysis, what are the points in the perspective of each participant at a deep level of meaning where they may share more common ground than they thought they did? Might there be important connections between the members of this family that could form the basis of building a better relationship?
- How would you develop each of those possible points of similarity into a topic of discussion that the family could build concessions and demands around?
- What are the points on either symbolic or tangible issues on which they seem to fundamentally differ?
- As you compare and contrast their perspectives, identify areas you think have the best chance of being used to build new meanings that connect the participants in new understandings of their conflict and in creating new directions or new options for how to behave and communicate in the future.

Eighth, *dialogic negotiation embraces narrative as the structural form of communication for promoting emergent or new meanings.* In approaching dialogic negotiation as the process of doing collaborative conflict, you will also need to recognize that narrative is the dominant form that a conflict takes. What you are doing as you bring people together to solve conflicts is (a) inviting each of them to present the story of the conflict that represents his or her version of events; (b) encouraging them to question their own and each other's stories of the conflict; and (c) developing a new story from the exchange of demands and concessions that are based on their ideal and acceptable solutions. Approaching the conflict this way reframes it and points to a more collaborative future or at least a solution to the conflict.

- Why would getting these people to share stories of the conflict and of what they most want for the future as a family be a useful narrative exercise?
- How might this approach to the mediation process as a narrative enterprise shape your understanding of how and why you are helping them?

- How might such narrative mediation help to move the conflict through to new understanding for the participants?

Ninth, *dialogic negotiation broadens options for preconflict and postconflict management:* The dialogue should, ideally, lead to better relationships, more clearly defined ways of communicating with each other, and better mutual understanding. There should be more options for negotiating future family relationships than existed before the dialogue began. At least the dialogue should bring out the possibilities that they might know themselves but cannot see because of their conflicted relationship. Remember that a solution or an issue may be perfectly obvious to observers into their conflict from the outside. It is much more difficult to see opportunities when one is locked into the conflict and focused on differences and oppositions.

- As the mediation process evolves, how might it provide the participants with more opportunities for managing this conflict than they thought possible and than they practiced in the past?
- How might they make smarter choices from among the various options, such as avoidance, aggression, competitive arguing, and collaborative dialogue?
- How might this communication intelligence help them build more collaborative family relationships in the future or at least encourage a deeper appreciation for their ability to choose their won identity and behavior within the family culture and how they approach a conflict more effectively?

Part 3: Using Meaning to Build Lasting Conflict Communication Skills

The foregoing are the specific techniques and skills of doing dialogic negotiation. What follows are some important skills in managing conflict communication that are based on an appreciation of how to use the meaning of the conflict itself as a source of energy for using the techniques. As you think beyond Tejal's situation to subsequent conflicts in the Patel family, these skills can enable the participants to build the communication skills that will help them be more proactive about exploring the meaning of their conflicts and perhaps be more effective, whatever the conflict is that they face together. These same skills apply to your own conflicts as well.

❖ SKILLS FOR ENERGIZING CONFLICT
    COMMUNICATION TOWARD DIALOGIC NEGOTIATION

It is often quite a difficult job to manage the energy of a conflict (redirect, diffuse, focus, refocus, release, slow down, speed up, etc.) through your communication. Conflicts are complex systems of energy exchange that are often quite difficult to map and explain—sort of like storm systems—and the management of a conflict depends on the ways that the other person or persons are handling their approach to this energy. It is difficult enough if all parties are pulling the energy toward the fusion of dialogic negotiation and away from the fission of argumentative talk, but it is an enormous task to push toward fusion when another is focused on the divisive tendency of argument and fission. These competing or opposing forces of energy can lead to enormous turbulence, volatility, and changeability in the communication climate. Imagine how difficult it might be to get productive discussions going in the Patel family. It will not be smooth at first as there are lots of hurt feelings and strong opinions. Recognize that you cannot engage in dialogue with another person who simply wants to argue that they are right and that you are wrong. And they cannot argue with you if you are focused on addressing the conflict as a common problem. The frame guides the forms and directions of energy produced.

One useful strategy for energizing conflicts toward dialogue is to use both the deeper symbolic issues of a conflict and the more tangible aspects of the dispute to help manage the flow, direction, and forms of energy. *This way, you are using aspects of the meaning of the conflict to manage the conflict itself.* It is possible to use specific and concrete tangibles to energize the talk toward collaborative dialogue. For example, if the energy of a conflict is dissipating or flowing over into a separate issue that is leading to escalation of the conflict, it is possible to use a tangible issue to bring it back to focus. Tangible issues can be things such as specific exchanges in the negotiation or points of agreement that can be reiterated and affirmed; specific behaviors that are central to the conflict, clear to the other person, or central to changing the scope of the discussion if it is too general or unfocused; and specific possible changes that might make a big difference in the flow and energy of the conflict.

It is also possible to energize the talk toward dialogic negotiation through the deeper issues of meaning. For example, if a conflict needs to move beyond the surface dispute to connect to the deeper family or community issues that it connects to, this redirection can rapidly energize a conflict and focus it on the deeper meaning. This is a risky move as it will often speed up and intensify the conflict, but it can help focus the participants on the real meanings that are at the heart of the divisions between them. For example, it may be important at some point to move from the wedding behavior as the more surface dispute to the issues of personal versus family identity, loyalty to tradition versus faith, responsibility as an Indian and freedom as an American, and so on, that are under the surface of the Patels' conflict. The symbolic issues that can energize a conflict can be underlying themes over which there is meaningful division; values, goals, and expectations; and the personal meanings of the conflict.

It may also be a useful skill to be able to move between more surface and deeper levels of meaning in the conflict and be able to explicitly identify them and discuss them as such. This way, the energy is clearly focused on one issue or level at a time, and intensity and volatility can be managed by moving nimbly between levels. Both surface and deeper levels of conflict meaning can provide focal points toward which conflict energy can be directed. They can also provide starting points for conflict energy to be released or points at which the conflict can be reframed and redirected in productive ways. Understanding this means that you can work productively in the ebb and flow between levels of a conflict and in the flux between cyclical states of dialogue (fusion, resolution) and argument (fission, escalation) that are typical of conflicts. Skill at managing these forms of energy will enable you to understand the relationships between energy and patterns of emotion, communication, and conflict behavior, and such skills will also enable you to choose the direction of a conflict to some extent.

A second main strategy for managing conflict is to focus energy on opening dialogues about the very relationship between the surface and deeper symbolic levels of the conflict. This will naturally generate more complexity in the discourse as the flow between levels will be less clearly defined. However, to discuss the relationship between the dispute and the personal meanings of the dispute for all concerned offers the most likely conversational scenario for substantial and meaningful dialogic negotiation in which the parties understand each other, can engage and appreciate each other's perspective, and understand what divides them and in which the meaning of the conflict forms the basis of the conflict dialogue. This focus on multiple layers of meaning will likely create a desire for fusion-based dialogue in which there is an approach to the conflict as opportunity to bridge differences and move forward together to a mutually agreeable solution. If the parties involved can become conscious of and appreciate the tangled interconnections of layers and issues by which they have created this conflict, that will go a long way toward their understanding each other, and this will take them a long way toward working together and hopefully negotiating. The following discussion questions will help you explicate the possible role of meaning in energizing the Patel family conflict.

Discussion Questions

- At key points in the evolution of the conflict, how might Tejal and her uncle redirect or reshape the energy of their conflict by moving to more surface issues, such as how people should behave?
- Similarly, how might they more effectively integrate connections to the underlying symbolic issues, such as cultural assumptions that may be at the core of the conflict, and which they may not even be fully aware of until they engage in dialogic negotiation?
- Are there moments in the conflict, as we are see it through her story and as we might imagine it happening, when they might have switched between levels of meaning in order to shift the energy level, type, and direction?
- How might an opportunity to discuss the relationship between levels of meaning emerge between these family members? How might they benefit from this level of honesty in shaping the direction and flow of the conflict?
- What would it take in terms of communication energy to stimulate and reach levels of understanding and even appreciation for the differences between Tejal and her uncle?
- Choose a point in the story and imagine how Tejal or her uncle might redirect, diffuse, focus, refocus, slow down, or speed up the release of the energy of their communication more strategically so that the conflict takes a more productive form. How might this change help to redirect the energy and flow of the conflict?

Important Dialectical Skills in Stimulating Dialogic Negotiation

Tejal's conflict was by no means something we would think of as having stimulating dialogue between the parties at this point. In reality, we might say the energy of the conflict fizzled, ran off in different directions, spread to other members of the family and community, and ultimately left more confusion than clarity in its wake. It also left behind a climate in the family that is fragile and tense, to say the least. Perhaps it is completely unrealistic to expect there to be a happy ending to this particular conflict. If that were even possible, it may take many years to get there. The following section moves you to discuss Tejal's future relationships, because she clearly has some work to do. It also gets you to reflect on your own dialogue skills and to evaluate how effectively you organize your conflict communication energy for dialogic negotiation. The overall questions I want you to consider here have to do with Tejal becoming more effective in organizing her communication for conflict management than dialogic negotiation can sometimes bring. In order for you do this, examine Goodall and Kellett's (2004) framework of three dialectical tensions, which follow. When effectively balanced, they naturally create the communicative context for fusion energy and dialogic negotiation to emerge.

The first dialectical tension that generates dialogic energy for transformation of a conflict involves your ability to balance (a) the important skills of being free and open enough to be able to get in the spirit (*ethos*) for dialogue to emerge and (b) the more intellectual ability to know that you have been there, how you got there, and how you might try to get back there again, perhaps in a different conflict situation. This skill we have defined earlier as being *telesmatic*, after the Greek word *apotelesma*, meaning "knowing where your ideas and speech travel to" (*telesma*) and what impact they have after (*apo*) you have spoken them. To move a conflict toward dialogic negotiation, it is important that you create the mood and context for it through the spirit of dialogue that permeates your approach to the conflict. This approach involves making the effort to take the perspective of the other people, genuinely engage with them on their perspective, and allow the talk to evolve and take on a life of its own as the synergistic expression of collaboration. Being telesmatic is the reflective form of intelligence that allows us to recognize, after the fact, those moments when the ethos worked to create dialogic negotiation, to be able to describe the consequences of our conflict ethos within the conflict, and understand how to do the work of getting back there again.

The second dialectical tension in creating the conditions for dialogic negotiation has to do with (a) balancing the techniques of dialogue and negotiation (*techne*) with (b) the ability to surrender to the mystery of it—its synergy—that is often far beyond the sum of the technical things that the individuals are doing with communication (*mysterion*). The strategies and tactics of creating a space and time for open and honest talk, asking systemic questions that get at the heart of each person's perspectives and experiences in the conflict, and using that to create real exchange are necessary techniques for generating dialogic talk. At the same time, dialogic negotiation will pull you into the more boundaryless, more fluid relationship with the other, and a more flowing state of talk. It is in this skillful yet mutable state that both profound connections and transformational learning can happen, as the place where technique and mystery meet is highly creative. It is the place where deep things get expressed and new possibilities emerge, and often the boundaries of self and other melt away.

The third dialectical tension has to do with (a) being playful and even mindless in the moment of the talk (*paignion*), and yet (b) remaining open to the vastness of communicative and even spiritual possibilities that lie beyond the current moment (*vathis*). This tension has to do with allowing yourself to be in the moment with the conflict dialogue and to take risks and be creative on a moment-by-moment basis. At the same time, the notion of *vathis* implies that as we engage another person, we are open to the fact that the current moment may exist within a much broader and more profound purpose, such as in moving a relationship forward or addressing long-held perceptions of injustice or unfairness in a relationship that bring about transformative change, and so on. This dialectic is balanced when the moments of talk connect to a deeper moral or plot line in the broader relationship of the people in conflict.

Tejal, her uncle, and her parents have lots of potential room to grow in their qualities and balances of dialogue. We likely all have some changes we could work on in our families. The following questions will help you to explore the implications of these skills and tensions for communication in the Patel family conflict:

- What are the cultural, gender, familial, and community constraints that limit Tejal's ability to employ these dialectical tensions in her relationship with her uncle?
- What is out of balance or missing from these dialectical tensions in her family that you would advise her to work on?
- Which of the balances need to be worked on within her family as they navigate their identity and place in the community?
- How and why might you have been similar to or different from Tejal in how you might have handled that same context if you were to find yourself in it?
- How do you account for the similarities and differences in the context that Tejal found herself in, and how are these similarities and differences related to your ability and expectations in working with energy and communication?
- How might she work on each of the skills and on the balance of them from this point on in her relationships?
- What would it take in terms of communication, energy, and change to achieve effective conflict management in the family

around this conflict? Work back from that end point and try to imagine all of the details of the story that would have to be different. Develop these differences into an ideal plan of change for her family communication.

- Which of these dialectical tensions and skills do you still need to work on in your life as you create and face its inevitable conflicts?

Having examined the Patels' case and applied the principles and techniques of dialogic negotiation, we move on to examine some additional cases and their implications for managing conflicts through their meanings.

❖ LESSONS FROM THE FIELD OF PRACTICE: AN EXERCISE FOR FURTHER ANALYSIS OF DIALOGIC NEGOTIATION

Exercise: Negotiating Based on the Meaning

We have discussed in some depth the techniques for analyzing a conflict for the meaning for the various participants and then building dialogic negotiation strategies based on that meaning. I would like you to follow the process through from start to finish based on a significant conflict in your own family. Try to imagine the various perspectives and stakes in the conflict if it is too difficult to collect the stories. Examine the perspectives of the people as if you were an outsider; try to be an external observer of your own family just like we were for the Patel family. Develop some strategies for how you might help move the family conflict forward. List and discuss with the class all of those barriers that might get in the way of your family embracing dialogic negotiation. Remember, this is an ideal form of communication, and it is worth noting how difficult it might be to achieve in the context of your own family. How might your recommendations for dialogic communication also result in long-lasting improvements in how your family communicates, particularly about conflict?

❖ CONCLUSION

In this chapter, you have been invited into the complexity of the multiple dimensions and multiple layers of meaning in the relationships of the Patel family. You have learned that through carefully examining the story in a rigorous, research-based manner, a clearer and deeper picture of the inner workings of the meaning of the conflict can emerge. You have also learned that approaches to managing conflicts are often more effective, long-lasting, and more meaningful if based on the meaning of the conflicts for the people who happen to be in them. Of course, finding meaning is by no means an unproblematic or simple task of arriving at a fixed, unitary, and definitive statement of truth about the conflict. Meaning can be fluid, flexible, changing, and multi-faceted. Neither is the process of managing a conflict based on those interpretations of meaning a simple task. Interpretation of the conflict and management based on those interpretations is itself fraught with important issues and caveats. Yet with these issues in mind and well noted, it is possible to improve your chances of understanding and managing effectively by embracing the techniques of dialogic negotiation outlined in this chapter.

This chapter has illustrated for you the strategies for managing conflicts through dialogic negotiation that work with the complex relationship between the layers of meaning in conflicts. You may not become a conflict management professional, but nevertheless, I hope you think carefully about any conflict you are in or that happens around you. Try to have a positive impact on that conflict from a deeper than everyday sense of what it means to engage in conflict as oppositions at the level of meaning between people. Try also to think about the dialogue and dialectical skills outlined at the end of the chapter as ways that you can build lasting skills for managing conflict effectively.

3

Language as the Fabric of Conflict—and the Foundation for Dialogic Negotiation

❖   ❖   ❖

My speech surprises me and teaches me my thoughts.

—Merleau-Ponty (1962/1979, p. 178)

As the opening quote suggests, there is much we can learn about our conflicts and about ourselves from listening carefully to our own speech as we engage in conflict. In fact, Merleau-Ponty (1962/1979) recognized that it is only in speaking that we fully understand how we feel and what we think about a conflict. The language we choose during conflict is crucial in both forming the basis of our conflict stories and in moving those stories forward strategically. Effective conflict management relies on this ability to listen to and analyze the language that you use in conflicts and your ability to imagine and choose language that helps you achieve your goals for that communication—for example, a competitive or cooperative conflict.

There is something about choosing language that is crucial to actively constructing the dynamics and meaning of the conflict as dialogic negotiation, heated argument, or whatever our goals for the interaction might be. If our talk can surprise us, as the quote suggests, then perhaps we can make choices that have surprising and constructive results for all of the participants in the conflict.

Let's begin with a quick example that we can probably all relate to. Recently, a friend of mine described a very current, turbulent time in her relationship with her live-in boyfriend. She wanted to know what I thought about the possibility of breaking up with him. She explained that her attraction for him had dwindled and that they were in a rut. Their sex life was minimal, and they were not having fun anymore. Coupled with this, she was afraid to raise the topic for fear that he would be terribly hurt and that things could get very difficult in the home context. At the same time, she feared that he was making plans to propose marriage and go to the expense of a ring and a foreign vacation as a graduation gift. Graduation was just a month away. She did not want to wait and risk this embarrassing and awkward scenario, yet she could not face breaking up with him and all of the conflict that might well go along with that. Working on scant information and recognizing that her description may have been tied to the emotional low point of the moment she was talking to me, I was reluctant to offer direction one way or the other—to break up or not. So instead, I asked her to describe what the relationship felt like. She paused and then said that it felt like being on a rollercoaster with too many ups and downs, extremes of feelings, too much uncertainty, and seemingly no safe way off until it came to its own natural end. This seemed like a pretty accurate metaphor in terms of capturing her experience. My next questions were, What do you want a relationship to feel like if you do not like the rollercoaster experience? and Can you get from rollercoaster to that other type of experience with this particular man? More important, perhaps, I asked, Do you want to do that kind of work *with him*? It is in moments like these when you know that the very language of how conflict is thought about and how it is done matters a great deal. You can certainly over-interpret language imagery and approach metaphors too mechanically and simplistically, but that central image allowed her to better articulate where she was in the relationship, where she would like to be, and how the conflict she was experiencing was an expression of the gaps between her desire and the lived reality of their relationship. Last, it provided a means of talking with me beyond the current conflict, and potentially with him, so that they could renegotiate the characteristics of the relationship or get off the "ride" and look for a different experience. Might her use of that metaphor be a place where they could dialogue openly as a couple about their relationship and negotiate effectively about what they want the experience to be like? I think that such a discussion might surprise both of them in some important ways.

Besides the overarching images and metaphors of conflicts like the one in my friend's story, the finer details of the language—how we talk in the midst of them and how we talk about them as we remember the experiences, as well as all of the nonverbal communication that we use to express conflict and communicatively construct it *as conflict*—make up the symbolic fabric of conflict. Also meaningful is the language not chosen or the language that could be developed to approach a conflict—more like dialogic negotiation, for example. In this chapter, we examine the relationship between the language that is used to express and engage in conflicts, the connection of that language to the meaning of the conflict, and the impact of language on their dynamics and results. Our objective is to become self-conscious about language so that we are able to understand the complex and multifaceted relationship between language choices and conflict processes and outcomes. Specifically, we will become conscious of the choices of language in conflict and the choices that might be made to manage it. I want you to apply the specific principles of dialogue and negotiation from the previous chapters to each of the stories and exercises in this chapter, wherever possible. The resulting sensitivity to language will provide a foundation for your analytical and creative skills for working through the concepts and exercises in the upcoming chapters.

Main topics and learning goals in this chapter:

- Language, intensity, energy, and meaning
- Metaphors, imagery, and symbolic fabric of conflict
- Speech, silence, and the possibility for dialogue
- Dialogic negotiation as conversational scripts
- Lessons from the field of practice

The following story helps illustrate the relationship between the meaning of the conflict and the form and content as well as the intensity of the communication. It also illustrates well the relationship between the language of the conflict and its broader familial, relational, and community context. This is an archetypal "barking dog story," but it is a barking dog story with a twist in that you are given access to the deeper meaning of the conflict and the relationship between this deeper meaning for the participants as they communicate.

❖ LANGUAGE, INTENSITY, ENERGY, AND MEANING

As you do your initial read through of the following story, try to imagine the reality of the everyday relationships within the seemingly tight-knit community of families. How can an old dog who barks a lot seemingly divide these people and lead to some quite intense episodes of conflict? How can such an incident lead to long-lasting distance and animosity between people who seemed so close? Perhaps there are clues to the intensity of the conflict language in the meaning of what Puddles, his behavior, and their reactions to that behavior represent symbolically. The behavior of barking too loudly is certainly annoying, but is it enough to account for the intense language of the conflict? If not, then you are obviously seeing clues to a deeper and more intensely meaningful conflict. In your read through, try to examine the clues to the intensity of the language and the relationship between that intensity and the meaning of the conflict for the people involved.

"Puddles" (Megan)

(Background)

The community I grew up in is a very small, very close-knit place. My neighborhood consists of only 10 houses. All of the neighbors know each other, and they are all very good friends. Two years after my family moved into the neighborhood, a man named Jerry and his family began building a house behind my family's house. In the beginning, Jerry and my father were very close. They shared secrets about lawn care and gardening and discussed issues concerning the neighborhood. Jerry began to tell my father about his particular problems with the family that lived next to him—the Brown family. My father is good friends with the Brown family, and the situation with Jerry got very uncomfortable for him. Jerry ended up taking the Browns to court for the problems between them, and my father felt that it was completely unnecessary for him to do that.

After this incident, my father began to distance himself from Jerry. He also began noticing some of Jerry's quirks as a neighbor. For example, Jerry building his fenced-in garden on our family's property and his constant complaining about all of the other neighbors. The conversations between my father and Jerry became more like Jerry lecturing to my father. He began telling him how to take care of his garden, how to cut his grass, and even how to keep his pets. This caused a strain on the relationship between Jerry and my father because my father was friends with all of the other neighbors and because he is an adult and does not feel he needed someone telling him how to take care of his property. The situation created a lot of tension between them.

(The Conflict—Dad's story)

It began one morning about 8 a.m. My wife had let out our 17-year-old Bassett hound—Puddles—outside and he began to bark. Being 17, Puddles had

ODD (old-dog dementia). This caused him to bark a lot and often for no reason. When Puddles was let outside, he began to bark. After a couple of minutes of barking, our phone began to ring. Our neighbor Jerry was on the line.

"Bring your damn dog inside! He's waking Esther up," he snapped at my wife, without even greeting her.

My wife knew that Puddles was very loud, but because he was old and senile, she had no control over his barking. The other neighbors were very kind to Puddles and dealt with his barking because they knew how fragile his state was. When my wife told me about Jerry's phone call, I was furious. I didn't want to see or hear anything from Jerry anymore, and I hoped that he would not have the audacity to approach if he saw me.

Sunday morning, I was mowing my lawn, and Jerry came over to talk to me. As we were talking, I was not going to mention anything about Puddles, but then it happened. He began to talk about the animals in the neighborhood, and I knew what was coming. Jerry said,

"You know, Stuart, Puddles has been barking a lot lately; you need to pay that dog a little more attention."

I replied, "Well, Jerry, he is an old dog; he is 17 years old. When we let him outside, he barks; we pet him and he barks. We are trying, but sometimes he has spells where we just can't stop him barking. The vet said it was part of the ODD."

"You know, if you really loved that dog, you would put him to sleep," Jerry snapped back.

That was it. I exploded. I told Jerry everything I had been hiding inside since he built his garden on my property. When he told me to put my dog to sleep, it was like someone had just stabbed me through the heart with a knife. Anyone who knows me and my family knows how much I loved my pets, especially Puddles. We had a special bond. The only thought that kept running through my head was, who does he think he is, telling me that I should put my dog (who was like a son to me) to sleep. How dare he accuse me of being a bad pet owner? I began tearing into Jerry, berating him about having no right to tell anyone what was good and bad and how pets should be raised. When I had finished giving Jerry a piece of my mind, I stormed off, leaving Jerry with his jaw dropped in disbelief and an unfinished lawn. I stormed into my house, slamming the door behind me so hard that I saw my wife jump when I came in.

She looked up from the desk and said, "What's happened, what's wrong?"

I explained the whole story. We decided that it was no longer necessary to converse with Jerry or Esther, his wife. We even discussed moving to get away from the two of them. But we decided in the end simply to ignore them.

A few months later, Puddles's health took a turn for the worse. He began to have trouble even standing up by himself, not to mention the fact that he was almost completely blind and deaf. In the end, after a long discussion with our vet, we decided that it would be best for Puddles if we let him go. It was the hardest decision we ever had to make. I was losing a family member, and it was my decision that was causing the loss. A couple of weeks after we put Puddles down, I was in the yard doing yard work when Jerry approached me.

"Stuart, I haven't heard Puddles barking lately," he said.

All I could say was, "That's because he's gone, Jerry. We had to put him down a couple of weeks ago." I walked away.

Jerry and I keep our distance for the most part. We rarely speak to each other. When we do speak, the conversations consist of hellos and goodbyes. We are no longer the close neighbors we used to be.

Use the discussion and questions that follow to complete the three interpretive steps described.

Step 1: Description of the Conflict Language

Go through the story and identify and describe each of the examples of intensely conflicted language between these people.

Step 2: Reduction to Essential Themes

Try to identify the underlying divisive theme for each intense language exchange as an expression of their conflicted relationships over Puddles. For example, which exchanges or outbursts are linked to themes such as intense dislike, anger, distance, lack of reasoned verbal expression of differences, or combinations of such themes? How do the various events in the conflict connect around those core meaningful themes?

Step 3: Interpretation of the Meaning of the Language

Interpret how the intense language and the underlying themes fit together to create a divisive and argumentative conflict that has layers of meaning. How does their talk connect to deeper relational or contextual themes, such as "insider" and "outsider-newcomer." How do their styles of communication result in specific unproductive dynamics and patterns in their conflict? How might they have negotiated their conflict more dialogically and effectively, and how would the talk of the conflict have been different with that approach? The following theoretical discussion of intensity and conflict and related questions will help you to flesh out this interpretation and think about your own conflict language more broadly.

One of the things that marks communication as conflicted is the presence of unusual levels of intensity (Jones, 2001). Intensity can manifest in many ways, both verbal and nonverbal (Frijda, Ortony, Sonnemans, & Clore, 1992; Jones & Remland, 1993; Noesner & Webster, 1997). For example, conflict is often marked by emotional language of various sorts. Such emotional language can actually be productive for the conflict. People will often not realize that you feel strongly unless you demonstrate that feeling through intense language that shows you have strong feelings. So language that expresses perceived division, personal experiences and emotions associated with the conflict, and personal wants and needs from the conflict can be very healthy—even if it is intensely expressed. Intense language can still be dialogic if it opens up communication and makes issues and topics available for negotiation.

The key is that the intensity of language ought to reflect the intensity of the meaning of the conflict. At one extreme is language that does not reflect true feelings; at the other is angry talk that can lead to incivility and even hate (Ellis, 2001; Whillock, 1995). Accusations, personal attacks, blame statements, profanity and name calling, angry outbursts, statements that focus on "I" as an expression of personal needs or stakes in the conflict, crying, screaming and shouting at the opposition or at members of your own side of the conflict, and so on are all ways of expressing that you are conflicting with that other person. These are usually examples of less effective forms of expression because they typically undermine dialogue, limit negotiation exchanges, personalize the conflict, and highlight divisions between people (Leets & Giles, 1997). Conflict is also often marked by the presence of intense nonverbal expressions of division and the frustration of being in conflict with the other person. For example, dramatic nonverbal and paralinguistic expressions, such as door slamming, shouting, glaring, gesturing rudely, and even ignoring people, are all expressions of intense conflict. These nonverbal expressions are ways of working out the energy of intense feelings that the people are not expressing verbally. They are good ways to let off steam. Sometimes they are used to stand in place of what might be much more effective and less ambiguous verbal communication.

Less dramatic forms of nonverbal communication may also show the intensity of feelings in a conflict. Avoiding people, ignoring them, reestablishing nonverbal and territorial boundaries, spending less time with the person, and so on are all nonverbal ways of showing conflict with people, such as the neighbors in the story, and the level of intensity of the conflict. If you suddenly decide to build a communicative fence or wall between you and the other person, you have symbolically marked your distance from them in ways that might not necessarily show how you feel, but they show that you feel differently about them and conflicted with them. They may also be ways of showing the other that you have intense feelings that you are not expressing verbally but that if something triggered you, you might, like prefight displays. They may also be ways of avoiding confrontation while showing a sense of conflict. This is a safety issue in conflict. People instinctively wish to avoid dangerous confrontation that might lead to injury or death and yet they want to express their desire for a confrontation. These forms of intense expression allow that balance to occur and sometimes can actually invite the conflict to open up. How often do we show the other that we are conflicted with them nonverbally—drifting away, not responding to them as we might, and so on—as a way of inviting them to ask us what is wrong? Go back through the story and identify as many of these dramatic and less dramatic verbal and nonverbal ways of expressing the conflict and try to identify the thematic function that these expressions served.

Conflict language that expresses anger, deep dislike, hatred, or threats to take the conflict toward violence are particularly important to examine as these show a vibrant intensity in the perceived opposition between the people in conflict. This is the notion of interference that was part of our definition of conflict in Chapter 1. These forms of talk are usually clues to a double-bind relationship between the people in which they perceive the presence or even existence of the other as fundamental to the conflict. "It is the other person's fault," and "that person is in my way," are typical sentiments during such conflicts. They may also be clues that the meaning of the deeper thematic differences between the people are not being effectively negotiated. Examine the story in particular for these especially intense expressions. How might these expressions reflect the deeper conflicts between the families in that particular neighborhood?

Such intensity is usually generated by the meaning of the divisions between the participants of the conflict. Of course, intense language can be a manifestation of psychological issues or personality. We have all probably known people who are volatile and ready to take a conflict to an intense level without much provocation. This is not what we are exploring, although it is an important issue to consider when the meaning and the intensity do not seem to match. The more personal and deep the meaning of the issues people are divided on, then the more intense will be the language that they share. Intensity can evolve as the participants perceive difference and opposition to be growing. As a conflict escalates, the intensity can take on a life of its own and grow along with the escalation of differences.

Intensity can also be mediated by family and cultural contexts. There are families in which intense language, even profanity, is a common way of expressing their conflicts. This can be good if they are able to channel this intensity into clearly expressing conflicted issues. It can be bad if the volatile expressions are used to repress communication or abuse people. There are families in which the expression of emotions, even associated with conflicts, is much more subdued, muted, or even avoided. This can be good if it means that conflicted issues are placed on the metaphoric table in reasonable ways. However, passive-aggressive forms of intensity can predominate in such families, and this typically leads to cycles in which intensity is displaced and redirected into such things as sabotage and behind-the-scenes wrangling. The energy of the conflicted meaning has to go somewhere.

There is a balance between intensity of emotion and reasoned discussion that, if done well, is ideal dialogic negotiation. It is ideal because you need the intensity to help express and communicate differences and you also need reasonable discussion to then negotiate the issues in the conflict. As you look beneath the story of Puddles, what clues do you get that there is a lot more going on in this little neighborhood and between these families than a dispute over a barking dog? Of course, for Puddles's owners, he is not just a barking dog, he is a member of the family. Perhaps this aspect of meaning—what Puddles represents—and how the other family relates to that meaning might be at the heart of this conflict. I think it is, but you will need to untangle the interrelationships of intensity and meaning as they all connect together in the conflict story.

Intensity is also important in accounting for the evolution and dynamics of a conflict as well as its outcomes. For example, if the conflict starts to center around one meaning, this focus will move the conflict in particular escalatory spirals that will reduce the level of reasonableness between people. Such a move will also make the motives of others seem darker and more personal, reduce the perspective taking and negotiation that allows dialogic progress on the conflict, and means that much of what could be said that might actually be very valuable in propagating understanding and that might show connections and similarities between the people is lost. When the conflict takes on the form and content that it does, the meaning is led in particular directions *and not in others*. Intensity of language breeds intensity of the expression and meaning of conflict between the people in it. For example, threats often lead to more threats, and so on. What is *not* expressed when the intensity takes the conflict in a particular direction is important for us to consider. For example, we do not know if there is a particular reason why Esther being woken up is a particularly deep issue for the neighbors. Might there be a good reason why the neighbors are so upset, that the other family never considers? How does the communication between them ensure that such personal experiences that might be very important are never discussed and therefore never make it into the story? The following discussion questions will enable you to examine the relationship of intensity, meaning, and the conflict over Puddles. Use your answers to these questions to complete the three interpretive steps given earlier.

Discussion Questions

- What intense verbal expressions are productive or effective in expressing strong feelings in this conflict?
- How well does the intense language express divisions, personal experience, emotions, and personal wants and needs?
- What less effective forms of intense verbal expression did you notice happening in the conflict? What impact did each of these have on the conflict in terms of undermining dialogue, personalizing the conflict into an us-versus-them form, and highlighting division?
- What dramatic forms of nonverbal communication did you witness in the conflict? Are there other examples of this that you might expect to occur in this conflict but that we do not see directly reported in the story?
- What functions do these dramatic expressions perform: Are they letting off steam, replacing much needed verbal communication, or both?
- What less dramatic forms of intense nonverbal communication are evident in the conflict?
- What function do these less dramatic expressions perform in either escalating or helping to move the conflict forward?
- Are there any particularly vibrant and divisive verbal and nonverbal expressions, such as of anger, hate, and so on? How do these expressions relate to the underlying thematic division between people?
- What are the more fundamental divisions between the two families, and how do these differences fuel the intensity of the specific conflict over Puddles?
- How does the way that the conflict progresses show that the important perceptions and experiences and facts are not expressed or understood, and how does this affect the outcome and level of satisfaction with that outcome?
- How might the participants have handled the language of their conflict more effectively in expressing and negotiating the deeper thematic differences between them as well as with reference to the more specific example of the conflict over Puddles?
- How might you have acted and spoken if you found yourself in a similar conflict? How much would you follow the advice you might give these two families, and how much might you do the same as they did?

It is clear from this first story that there is a close and multifaceted relationship between the language used in conflict and to represent conflicts and the personal and contextual meaning of the conflict itself. The meaning of a conflict structures the language and the intensity of the language that is used in it. At the same time, the language that is available to us and that we habitually choose to engage in conflict with also structures the dynamics and end result of those conflicts. The next story illustrates how a deeper understanding of this twofold relationship of language and meaning can be understood and learned from.

❖ METAPHORS, IMAGERY, AND SYMBOLIC FABRIC OF CONFLICT

Much has been written about the role of metaphors and language imagery in communication (e.g., see Koch & Deetz, 1981). When thinking about such language devices specifically in terms of conflict discourse, you should recognize that metaphors and imagery do not simply add adornment and beauty to the language (Black, 1979; Davidson, 1978; Ricoeur, 1967). They certainly do add beauty to what you say and how it sounds, and they certainly help with bringing to life the stories of our conflicts, but that isn't all they do. The following poem was submitted as part of a writing assignment in which the student was directed to consciously use language devices to bring to life the meaning of the conflict experience. Recognize that this is not necessarily how we typically talk about and engage in our conflicts. Much of the time we are actually more or less unconscious of such image choices. This is the point I am making here: The language we use to engage in conflict and to represent those processes and experiences in narrative form provides a concrete way of expressing and perhaps guiding the meaning and dynamics of the conflict (Kellett, 1987). Hence, language provides the symbolic fabric of conflict. Creative language devices, such as metaphor, may be quite fundamental or archetypal to the practices of doing and representing our conflicts in ways that are important to reach our goals to openly express ourselves and negotiate from that standpoint.

First, as you examine the poem, I want you to consider how the creative language devices enable the poet, Jen, to express the depth and intensity of her experience both for her and for us, as the audience for the communication. This is a crucial dialogic skill. Consider each image and what she is specifically trying to communicate through it. Consider also what the story might have been like without some or all such devices. How could she have portrayed her experience and communicated it to you *as her experience* without such language? To help you to address these questions of language expression and meaning, I have highlighted as many of the more obvious poetic and vivid language devices as I could see. Go through each of them and reflect on how the choice of the image enables her to bring to life some aspect of this specific conflict or some aspect of the more deeply conflicted long-term relationships with her mother, with herself, and with the men with whom she has intimate relationships.

Second, at the same time that language provides a vivid and evocative fabric through which to create and represent conflicts, it may also limit her expression and perhaps even structures her experience of conflict in important ways. Read through your ideas about how the language enables her expression and think this time about ways that these images have implications for how she sees herself, how she continues to have a particular kind of relationship with her mother, and how her relationships with men connect to her conflict language habits. One of the discussion issues we engage through this exercise in my conflict class is the way that the structure of a poem and the need for vivid and poetic language creates structural constraints on how the experience is expressed and portrayed—how the story gets told. Students talk about how the need for rhyme and rhythm and consistent imagery in their poems sometimes structures the very ways that they are able to represent their experience. This vivid experience with language often leads to important reflection on how that is also true of more everyday and less poetically driven representations. How does the language of how we do conflict in our culture impact how we engage in and represent it? How does your language affect how you do it? This is an enormously important question as it has implications for examining the way that our culture and its predominant language forms structure how we see and how we engage in conflict. It also has implications for each of us as individuals or from the perspective of particular relationships to examine the habits and taken-for-granted ways of seeing and doing conflict that are predominant. This in turn sparks the question of how such habits of language limit us in ways that we can address and learn from. It also, perhaps, brings up the question of how our symbol systems provide ways of seeing and doing conflict that we are not even conscious of but that are important in structuring how humans do conflict and certainly how conflict is culturally mediated by language and personal habits.

Third, it should be possible, once you have explored some of the enabling and constraining functions of language, to reflect on the ways that Jen and her mother might examine and question the language practices of their conflicts together. There may be ways that the language Jen used to represent her relationship might be questioned for their effects on their relationship—likewise with her relationship to men, and how she does conflict more generally in her life. It would be useful for her to reflect on how her habits of language and representation enable and limit her. How do her habits reflect or differ from our discussion of dialogic negotiation? It would also be useful for her to examine how her cultural and family background has impacted her language practices and representational choices (how she talks during conflicts and how she portrays and remembers them through conflict stories, respectively). It may be possible to use key elements of her representation of her conflict with her mother as a starting point for dialogue between them. It might be useful, if extremely difficult, for Jen's mother to read the poem. Perhaps she could respond with her own account of their relationship. This might be the basis of some productive and even transformative dialogic negotiation between them. It might make things worse, too, at least in the short term, but at least they would have some deeper understanding of the long-term and dysfunctional cycle they are maintaining through their language practices. For Jen, this understanding seems particularly important, in that her conflict with her mother seems to be central to her sense of identity and the source of issues in her relationships with men.

Finally, it might be possible to use vivid and evocative language to create alternative visions for her relationship with her mother, herself, and with men through changing the habits and practices of how she engages in conflict and how she represents conflict. Think about what some alternative images for her conflicts and her relationships might be and what it would take for her and her mother to create alternative images and then stories. For example, instead of using the story archetype of her overcoming the villainous actions of the mother, might it be possible for them to work toward a new story that moves the relationship forward? Look for the seeds of such images in the images she does use. Very often the images used also contain or connect to the desire for a different or oppositional image. This creative function of language can enable new relational stories based on new images and metaphors and different communicative practices. These might be idealistic goals, but they are worth exploring, if only to understand the power of language as the symbolic fabric of your own conflicts.

Here is some important background to the story behind the poem: Jen sees her mother as a very bitter person who has had a lot of things go wrong in her life. She feels that her mother had conditioned or "designed" her to be someone who does not get close to people as a protective move so that she would not go through what her mother had experienced in her life. Jen was never clear to me about what those experiences were. Jen had two abusive relationships because that was the type of man who reflected her experience with her mother. She chose men who reinforced the belief that she was stupid, ugly, and could never be loved. Then she decided to date really good men, but when there was a conflict, she blamed herself, to re-create those personal doubts. The poem evokes the moment when she told her mother that she was dating a really good man and that she was not going to follow what her mother had conditioned her to expect anymore. Her mother reacted angrily and told her that he would probably not care about her, even though she had never met him.

To My Mother *(Jen)*
I won't be your *Frankenstein* any longer
After all the years, all the lies and *propaganda*
Your greatest creation has an independent mind
I've shattered the empty cup of life you gave me, and I'm stronger
I will no longer live my life alone always looking behind
The self-loathing and destructive ways you taught me
Are far behind me now, I have found my free will
I know who I am and what I passionately refuse to be
I am a person with intelligence and a big heart, I am real
The path you designed for me is not the one I will follow
All those years of beating me into your reflection
Have left me *craving desperately for a life less shallow*
I'm all grown up now and I've got my own protection
The *frigidity of my childhood* will no longer *haunt* me
Someday I will be able to trust a man, maybe today
The scars you composed inside and out will no longer be
the reason I can't let anyone close enough just so I run away
I will no longer live in fear of someone finding out
I have a *soft heart that breaks as easily as others'*
Today is the day I tell you what I am all about
I'm going to have a life that's my own not my mother's
I will not be afraid of losing control and loving a man
And allow him the opportunity to love me in return
Maybe I will start today—*today is the day I take a stand*
I know that I still have so much about life to learn
I think that this is a good start for the rest of my life

I will reveal myself to the person who is supposed to know me best
I know that I may be throwing myself onto a double-bladed knife
But isn't that what life and love is all about—taking a risk?
If I get hurt, so what—life is about hurting and loving and being better
   for the pain
If I never take the risk I will be deprived of what life has to propose
I want to learn and love and *if hurting is part of that then come on*
   let it rain
I'm tired of protecting myself from feelings and who really knows
Maybe I will be able to prove all that my mom said was wrong . . .
Maybe someone will love me and maybe I am not such a bad daughter
Maybe I will find my own special place in the world to belong
As painful as it may be for you mother, *I won't be your personal martyr*
Maybe I was supposed to be your *vessel for retaliation*
Because *life dealt you a really bad hand*
But you will have to find your saving grace in another occupation
Because the *revenge vocation has no merit where I stand*
Your savage words no longer strike me as volcanic as before
I am resigned for my steps on this path to be lighter
I will not try to bear it like a scarlet letter any more
Because I am a never-give-up prize fighter
And I have a lot more rounds left for me in this world

Use the following questions to organize your interpretation of the language and meaning of the poem into the following interpretive steps.

Step 1: Description
   Identify and describe the important language expressions that express Jen's conflicted relationship with her mother. What underlying relational issues and problems do these expressions connect together to express?

Step 2: Reduction to Central Themes
   In what ways do Jen's conflict with her mother and the way she expresses it both enable and limit the dynamics and outcomes of their conflict in important ways? How does their talk to and about each other both enable and limit their communication?

Step 3: Interpretation of Meaning
   In what ways does the language of Jen's conflict enable and limit the *meaning* of her conflicts with herself, her mother, and with men? How can they, as mother and grown-up daughter, question and possibly change the language of their conflict together?

How does the language of Jen's conflict function as a symbolic fabric that can be rewoven to look more like dialogic negotiation? What are the relational barriers to this goal?

Discussion Questions for Analyzing Jen's Poem

- How do each of the images and metaphors enable her to capture the depth and intensity of her conflict experience?
- How important are each of these images? Are there other ways she could communicate the same experiences and feelings?
- In what specific ways do you think that her choices to represent the conflict through these images might limit her understanding and experience of the conflict?
- In what ways do you think that how she represents the conflict hints at why her conflict with her mother is an ongoing and difficult cyclical pattern?
- Where do you think these habits of representation and the ways of doing conflict that they evoke come from, in her family background and in our culture?
- How can the enabling and limiting function of language as shown in Jen's story be something that you can learn from in terms of your practices and their cultural and contextual (even ideological) backgrounds?
- What patterns and habits of Jen and her mother do you think that she is still unaware of or that remain invisible to her because they are part of the taken-for-granted-ness that language embodies?
- How does the poem seem to provide a good way for Jen to examine the impact of her family background, culture, and experience on her conflict practices and ways of representing those practices?
- How might the language of her conflict story be a good starting point for her and her mother to dialogue about their relationship?
- What are the key images, issues, and questions that the poem generates for you, that you would use to facilitate dialogic negotiation between them?
- What images, issues, or questions do you think would enable Jen and her mother to talk about commonalities (first), and what would enable them to talk about differences between them?
- How might Jen and her mother use language images or metaphors to evoke a new or alternative archetype that moves their conflict forward or that enables them to vividly and clearly share their sense of division, if that is where the dialogue ends up?

- What are the images already in Jen's narrative that might prove to be the seeds of change as you facilitate their talk?
- If Jen was more or less unconscious of the language practices of her conflict with her mother before the poem exercise, what lessons or *aha* moments do you think the poem might lead to for her?
- How did her poem and the analysis of language used in the poem enable you to think about the creative and limiting effects of your own conflict language practices and how you might learn from them and possibly change your habits and representational choices?

Having discussed the important role of language imagery in making vivid and real the experiences of our conflicts and how we might use language as the symbolic vehicle for guiding dialogic negotiation and change, we move on to discuss the equally important role of the relationship between speech and silence in conflict language.

❖ SPEECH, SILENCE, AND THE POSSIBILITY FOR DIALOGUE

It might seem unusual to talk about silence in a chapter about language use. However, as you will hopefully see, silence—*what is not said*—is intimately tied to the meaning of *what is said*. Both speech and silence are also intimately tied to *what could be said* (Lanigan, 1988). Hence the idea, also Merleau-Ponty's (1962/1979), that silence is pregnant with possibilities. Silence intersects with language in some important ways for us. First, we rarely have all the language at hand to capture how we feel in something as often personally and emotionally charged as a conflict. Second, sometimes we know that any language we do choose is charged with relational and even cultural politics. So, much of the time we use what is at hand for us. Third, sometimes all we have is silence because we do not know how to talk about something that is out of our realm of experience but that may be central to someone else's existence. We may also be afraid of how we might be interpreted and where the conflict might go from there. Fourth, sometimes we do not know what to say because we do not know exactly how we feel. We recognize that choosing something to say may actually shape how we feel and will certainly shape the interpretations that others make about how we feel and hence will affect the direction of the conflict. Fifth, sometimes we do not know exactly how we feel because we do not know how to use language to express what it is we do feel. We may have never had such a conversation before. In everyday life, we feel comfortable most of the time because we know what to say. Conflicts often throw us into unusual, highly charged, and very important conversations. And yet, because of issues and stakes similar to the ones listed earlier, we are effectively paralyzed into silence. The conflict gets mismanaged and lingers and often does damage for extended periods of time, sometimes to aspects of the relationship that have nothing much to do with the specific conflict. Such is the case with Jamie's story that follows, captured in poetic form. Silence, we shall see, is a crucial part of language use. Silence is richly informative in that at once it reveals the constraints of language, the limitations of the people in the conflict, and the underlying or hidden possibilities for alternative forms of talk that might be more productive between them.

I want you to reflect on the crucial role of the relationship between speech and silence in the meaning of conflicts and in revealing possibilities for dialogic negotiation that are held in that pregnant silence but that might be born through speech. First, carefully consider the spoken words and actions that are described, evoked, and hinted at in the conflict story. Describe the characteristics of the communication in the family over the specific issue of Jamie being a lesbian daughter. Describe how each of the family members reacted to her news and how those reactions affected the flow of the relationship between the family members on the issue. Try to understand the things that have been said and done and that have come together to create the broken ties that are felt as very real relational effects of the conflict. As I have said, sometimes what is said in conflicts is both crucial in affecting the ebb and flow or escalation and possible integration of the conflict. Similarly, it is important to understand the meaning of what is said and done communicatively. As you describe the reactions, counterreactions, and evolution of the conflict (and devolution of the relationships), try to imagine why people said and did what they did. How much of what was said and done is related to the limitations of what people are familiar with and comfortable with? How much of it is based on the inability of Jamie's parents to relate to her experiences and her sense of self? How much of it is based on judgmentalism or other darker motives, if any? As you dig beneath what is said and done, consider what is not said and done, because in the relationship between the two is a deeper interpretive opportunity for you to understand their conflict and suggest ways to move it forward.

Second, I want you to carefully consider the silence in the story. Look beneath what is said and done and read between the lines and in the white space around the story, and you will uncover clues in the relationship between that silence and what actually manifests in communication. Silence is never neutral but rather is pregnant with possibilities, as I have discussed. In the silence are the choices not made and clues to the reasons why. What conversations never happened between these people that could have and perhaps should have? Why has so much possibility for closeness and love been closed off into silence for so many years? Go back to the moments surrounding the actual conflict. In Jamie's mother's sobs and cries and her father's run from the issue, there are clues in these communicative actions to choices not made that could have been made. Of course the people in the conflict may not be aware of those choices not made. They may not have the skill to express themselves any other way. What they do say may also be exactly representative and expressive of how they feel. At the same time, however, closing off possibilities and relegating them to silence may involve conscious decisions. It may also involve specific cultural and contextual factors surrounding the place and time of the conflict that feed into its form and content. This is a crucial aspect of silence—the things surrounding the conflict that are not so much in it but which might nonetheless have a strong influence on choices made. The first thing Jamie's father thought might have been, "How do I get out of this discussion as quickly as possible?" Such decisions that lie behind the talk are quite revealing—if you can tap into them. This is particularly useful to consider when you are interviewing people for their stories. They reveal contextual and personal constraints, motives, limitations, and so on if you can uncover them. This is a big "if" because people are often not fully conscious of what decisions they did not make and why they did not make them, and they rarely remember the minutiae of their thoughts and strategies behind how they acted in the conflict. Yet it is crucial to try to reach into the silences for clues to what did happen and therefore for clues to what might happen differently in the future. Explicating silence and its relationship to speech as it reveals the meaning of a conflict will stretch your interpretive skills and your ability to piece together the picture that is the meaning of the conflict *for the participants.*

Finally, it is important to examine the story for hope and to think about ways that it can be encoded into their communication as they might talk at this point, 12 years after the initial conflict erupted. My hope would be that they could talk before someone dies. I think there is enough hope in what has and has not been said so far and how Jamie talks about her family that this conflict could move in a productive direction. Your task is to think about shifting the potential energy that has been subordinated beneath the surface for 12 years into kinetic form with a content that connects that energy into dialogic negotiation. It is possible to see how any conversation between them might end up taking them back to the same old judgments and hurts. This is the volatile character of their conflict.

To develop productive dialogue, go back through the characteristics of what is said and done in the conflict, how this speech is connected to the possibilities that did not happen, and the reasons you think those things did not happen (constraints, limitations, hidden possibilities). From the relationship between the speech and the silence, develop some possibilities for how they might move forward from here. For example, if the reasons why Jamie's parents reacted as they did were related to their sense of disappointment that their daughter did not follow their values and beliefs in building a good life for herself, perhaps they can work to recognize what is good about her life nonetheless. At the same time, perhaps Jamie can work to understand that her parents' reactions were connected to their cultural context and worldview and that their disappointment can be understood in that way and not so much as a weapon used to attack her. In this way, the relationship between speech and silence reveals new communication opportunities. Spend time bringing to the surface all of the possibilities that you discover and develop them into a list of possible topics and new ways of seeing what has become an old and entrenched, but definitely not hopeless, conflict.

As you do your initial read-through of the poem, imagine how these otherwise caring and close family members might talk when there is no script that they know of to engage the topic. How might they create a dialogic negotiation in the form of a conversation to help them as they fumble for the right language to meet on the topic? How might they do the conflict effectively when it is so loaded with meaning? Why does it end up in silence, accusations, heated argument, personal attacks, and, most of all, long numbing distance in which no one makes the first move to reconcile? How can they find the language to heal from a break that seems as deep as this one and is so tied to parental expectations and disappointment on all sides? Perhaps in the interconnections of speech and silence—the spaces between what is said and what is not said—you have discovered some of the clues to what *could* be said. Engage the questions below to help you explicate this relationship between speech and silence and the connection between this relationship and possibilities for communication.

"Broken Ties" (Jamie)

(Background)

I was raised in a very small town in Northern Indiana. It is the kind of town where everybody knows everybody, and everybody knows everybody else's business. I am the middle of three girls. Staci, my older sister, was considered the "premadonna" of the family. Megan, my younger sister, was considered the bookworm.

I was really neither. I was the tomboy of the family. My sisters and I were very much loved and cared for. My family believed very strongly in having close relationships with one another. My family was very passionate as well as compassionate—the kind of family who would walk to the ends of the earth for one another.

I carried a heavy weight on my shoulders, though, in that I bore the ambitions and dreams of my parents. I was to finish high school, which I did! Go to college on a basketball scholarship, which I did! I was to be a leader, which I was! And I was supposed to marry my high school sweetheart, which I did not! And this is where my poetic narrative begins.

Broken Ties
All families fight and fuss and argue and disagree,
But when I was 17 a conflict arose to a much higher degree.
My mom had found some letters, and there it did not end.
She read on to find out that the girl was more than just a friend.
Though I was not ready, out of the closet I came.
Scared to death of what I'd face, I had disrespected our family name.
But what the hell, there I was, with the world all my stage.
Yet never did I consider what my parents felt . . . unadulterated rage.
My mother questioned why and wondered where she went wrong.
Her sobbing tears and heartbreak revealed like an old country song.
Dad simply acted like it was just a bad dream,
But it was obvious to all that he wanted to break down and scream.
They called in reinforcements, my sister and my grandma,
But much to my surprise they said, "Don't worry, honey,
there's nothing wrong with you at all!"
My parents were like lost children trying to find their way.
Confused, disappointed, and angry, because their daughter was gay.
Through hindsight I tried to explain this is how I'd always been,
But mom and dad couldn't take it, for I was living in sin.
So, out of the house I went to find a brand new life.
No friends, no parents . . . I had been stabbed by a friendly knife.
I couldn't believe how all of this happened, but I was praying for it to end.
I needed my family and I prayed, "Dear Lord, help me . . . an answer you
    must send!"
Days became weeks, then months, and then years.
I had to face my challenges and wipe away my hidden tears.
I stood strong in my values and my beliefs.
Never really realizing my parents experienced grief.
So it was on that day that I broke the ties that bind.
I searched for myself and the answers I only hoped to find.
Things have calmed down but they will never be the same,
And though I have dealt with some of it, I still carry the blame.
It has been 12 years ago since this ugly conflict reared its ugly head.
We will probably never speak of it, at least not until after one of us is dead.

Use the following interpretive steps to organize and interpret the answers to the following discussion questions that are in addition to the ones integrated into the foregoing discussion. The steps and related questions should enable you to explicate the relationship between speech and silence in Jamie's family conflict and to explore the possibilities for new or different conversations between these people based on that relationship between speech and silence.

Step 1: Description of Speech and Silence

Describe the speech between these family members. What is talked about and with what impact on the conflict and the people in it? Describe the silence between the family members that the speech points to. What is not talked about and with what impact on the conflict and the people in it?

Step 2: Reduction to Relationship of Speech and Silence

Explicate the constraints, the limitations of the people, and the possibilities revealed to you between the speech and the silence. What are the central oppositions between what happens in the conflict and what does not happen?

Step 3: Interpretation of the Meaning

Interpret the meaning of the conflict in terms of what could be but is not yet talked about. What possibilities in the silence show you what meaning is lived by the participants and what some alternative approaches might be for them in dealing with their conflict so that it might move toward taking on a new meaning for them?

Discussion Questions for Interpreting "Broken Ties"

- What are the characteristics of how these family members talked to each other before this particular conflict?
- How did each of them react to the news of Jamie being gay through their verbal and nonverbal communication about the issue?
- How did these reactions and patterns of communicating in the conflict create what appears to be a deep and unresolved conflict?
- What details of the story and of their relationships might lead you to have the hope that this conflict might be productively addressed, even this many years later?
- What ways of reacting and ways of talking were negated— never happened—because of the choices that were made?

- Why did certain possibilities for handling the conflict differently remain in the realm of silence? How were these silences related to constraints, skill limitations, and possibilities that remained hidden?
- How is the meaning of the conflict as the expression of several factors coming together, revealed by the way the conflict was handled and the things that remained silent and avoided?
- How does this meaning suggest possible, realistic ways of approaching the conflict that might take it from this point of distance and strained relationships through dialogic negotiation to something more fulfilling and reminiscent of their preconflict relationships?

Having examined language practices for clues to the possibilities that are embodied in the silence of a story—the stories not told and all of the language practices that might have been and that could be—we move on to examine what those dialogic forms of language might look like, as personified by Jamie's communication with her father. By contrast we will also examine what communication looks like when it is definitely not dialogic negotiation, as personified by Dana's grandmother in the poem that follows. In the next section, we link the ideas of presence (father), absence (grandmother), and possibility (her grandmother becoming more like her father) to our goal of searching for opportunities for dialogic negotiation, by showing what such alternative language actually looks like, as represented and personified in her poetic account.

❖ DIALOGIC NEGOTIATION AS CONVERSATIONAL SCRIPTS

The following poem shows the power of language to create differences that matter and the power of dialogue to explore and negotiate those differences. As you engage with the strongly evocative imagery and the powerfully emotional conflict that this poem evokes, I want you to compare and contrast the ways of talking that are practiced by Dana's grandma and by her father. I want you to explore what it is about her father's communication style and the content of his talk that led their relationship to where it is today. I also want you to explore the differences between the father-daughter communication and the grandmother-granddaughter communication as a paradigm exemplar of much of the dialogue and negotiation principles we have discussed so far in Part I of this book (see also Goodall & Kellett, 2004; Kellett & Dalton, 2001).

In your first reading of the poem, notice how Dana's grandmother's words make the differences between Dana and the others real and how they create the value judgment that makes a difference to the lived-reality of their relationships. The narrator is biracial, and her grandmother appears to dislike her for it. Why would her grandmother be so seemingly hateful about an issue such as this? What symbolic value does it have for her? Does it perhaps represent a shame or a lowering of the family's social status in some way? Dana is insulted in front of others while the other grandchildren are favored. Notice how Dana refuses to communicate with her for 7 years. The rift between them has to be connected in some ways to their communication relationship together.

Also as you read the poem, examine Dana's father's relationship with her and try to document the clues in the poem that indicate that he values her experience, understands her feelings, and is trying to develop a solution to their family conflict that engages her perspective and his own. Her father's forgiving manner and acceptance of his mother's attitudes do seem to lead to more positive patterns of talk between them. Her grandma's actions had caused her inner conflict and caused her to question herself, and yet her father seems to be more accepting. Her color will not wash out—hence the laundry image. Her dad is white and her mother is black, and yet, through the image of the matching sock, she visualizes and perfectly captures the experience of matching with her dad. She says that she used the metaphor of mismatching socks to describe how she felt. She felt like the sock that came out of the laundry with no mate. She looked for someone biracial who could relate to her but never found anyone who knew exactly how she felt. Her dad let her know that even though he did not know how she felt, he gave her the support and love she needed. She also recognizes that her grandma—an elderly Southern white woman—was probably reflecting the era when the mixing of races was more taboo, and she probably felt she somehow failed as a mother when her son defied her and Dana was born. Perhaps her grandmother wanted her to absorb the shame that she felt. Her grandma was the matriarch of the family and was able to define who Dana was and how she was viewed. Dana seems to have been made to feel that because she did not match, she did not belong, and therefore she ended up feeling like an outcast. Notice how she had little to no contact with that (white) side of the family. Use the questions that follow the story to explicate a comparison of conflict communication styles between that of the grandmother and that of her father. This comparison should lead to some useful insights into the characteristics and qualities of dialogic negotiation as a style of doing conflict. It should also lead to insight into the way that such differences are often represented by differences in key language practices that then find their way into our conflict stories.

Looking for My Matching Sock in the Laundry (*Dana*)
I never knew that I did not MaTcH
Never saw differences between them and me.
It took my grandmother's words in order for me to see.
But from the day she spoke those words
So full of hate, disgust
The difference became so clear,
My five year old heart began to bust.
Grandma would explain to others
That my tan was year round.
I had never noticed that compared to hers
Mine was extremely brown.
And Christmas after Christmas she had gifts for my brothers
And never any for me.
Daddy always sent them all back
And refused to let it be.
See, I never knew I did not MaTcH.
That sense of belonging I had was rocked.
And for many years afterwards
All communication with her was blocked.
She had made me feel like that sock.
Searching for the missing mate.
And all the while her echoing words
Would be filled with so much hate.
Daddy wrapped his arms around me
And soothed away the pain.
He described how his love for me
was anything but shame.
So even if I thought my mate would match
On the outside a little more
Daddy and I are close as can be,
Mated and tucked away In the drawer.

Use the following interpretive steps to organize the answers to the discussion questions. This will enable you to clearly articulate the relationship between the presence and absence of particular style and content elements of conflict language that contribute to the experience and outcomes of Dana's conflict.

Step 1: Description of Communication Styles
    Describe the characteristics of her grandma's communication with Dana. Describe, also, the characteristics of her father's communication with her as it is pointed to and highlighted by that of her grandma.

Step 2: Reduction to Thematic Differences
    Explicate the essential thematic differences between the two forms of conflict communication evoked in the poem. Specifically, try to point out how Dana's grandma's communication as the absence of dialogic negotiation differs from her father's communication as the presence of dialogic negotiation. What makes the two styles important as differences?

Step 3: Interpretation of Communication Styles
    Interpret how different styles of doing conflict impact its process and outcomes. How does the presence and absence of dialogic negotiation account for the differing quality of communication and outcomes of Dana's conflicts and to the enduring experience and quality of her relationships?

Discussion Questions for Explicating Dana's Poem

- In going through the poem carefully, how would you describe the characteristics of how Dana's grandmother talks to and about her?
- What particular language is used by her grandma to express her thoughts and feelings toward Dana?
- How does each of these characteristics of communication and language use practiced by her grandma affect Dana's thoughts and feelings?
- How do these effects in turn affect the communication between Dana and her grandma?
- How are all of these practices and their effects brought together and represented in the central imagery and metaphor of the poem?
- What do these images and central metaphor tell you about the family and their main dysfunctions relationally?
- Might the central images also be used as a way of opening up dialogic space between Dana and her grandmother or between conflicting parts of the family, thus allowing an exchange of concessions and demands in negotiation?
- How would you encourage such dialogic negotiation scripts to be developed, and how would you use the poetics of her

account as a starting point for examining the origins, affects, and possibilities for change in the family relationships?

- How would you describe each of the characteristics of how her father relates to her?
- How do these characteristics of communication affect her relationship with her father and her sense of self?
- What lessons might her grandmother be able to learn from her own son in terms of the language that can be used to approach conflicts more closely to our ideal of dialogic negotiation?
- How does her father model the characteristics of dialogic negotiation and an approach to the conflict through the meaning of the conflict for Dana?
- What lessons might you learn about your own language characteristics and practices conflict engagement? In what ways are you like Dana's grandma, and in what ways are you like her dad? In what ways or in what particular conflict would you like to be more like her dad if you could be?
- Imagine that you were helping this family to reconcile and rebuild their damaged relationships. How would you develop the conversation so that you would use the characteristics of her father's communication as the presence of dialogic negotiation and her grandma's communication as the absence of dialogic negotiation, to guide and to be guidelines for those conversations? Develop these characteristics into script form. For example, you should talk in the following ways: _____, and you should not talk in the following ways: _____.

Having examined some of the important ways that language, as the symbol system we all use to engage in and represent our conflicts, interconnects with the expression and structuring of the issues, themes, and experiences of conflicts, we move on to enable you to examine these issues through several exercises. These exercises push you to use the ideas of this chapter to learn from your own field of practice as a communicator.

❖ LESSONS FROM THE FIELD OF PRACTICE: EXERCISES
   FOR EXPLORING THE LANGUAGE OF CONFLICT

Work through the following exercises that will challenge you to apply the principles from this chapter into your everyday life in which you practice conflict. The exercises are designed to get you to work closely with and look closely at the language through which you engage in conflicts and through which you construct your stories. You will also be challenged to think about the representational issues associated with the language of your conflicts.

Exercise 1: Personal Poetic Account

Adapt a conflict that you have experienced into a poetic account as three of the stories in this chapter illustrate. This could take the form of a poem, sonnet, song, or any other form that gets you to think carefully about how to capture and represent experience through the poetic form of language. As you develop your poetic account, carefully bear in mind the following five guidelines.

a. Use evocative language. Poetic language is different from every-day forms of talk that tend to be more descriptive in style. Focus on using wording and phrasing that capture and communicate the essence or core meaning of the conflict.

b. Use precise language. The wording of your poetic account should be precise and efficient, with everything designed carefully around communicating the central meaning of the conflict experience.

c. Use poetic devices. Metaphors, similes, and vivid and emotional imagery that appeal to the senses often characterize poetic representations. Use these where they help you to communicate the meaning of the conflict.

d. Carefully compose the structure of the poem to parallel and evoke the meaning. Develop repetitions, parallelisms, alliteration, antithesis, or rhyming patterns and organize the language around particular rhythms if these help you to evoke the meaning of the conflict in important ways. The musical structure of the poem should help to evoke the meaning of the conflict.

e. Communicate a central thematic idea. You are trying to evoke the meaning of a conflict so that someone reading the poem might understand at least some of that meaning that you are coding into language form. The account is a piece of communication, so decide what it is you are trying to communicate and organize the poem around this central theme or set of themes.

After composing the poetic account, use the following discussion questions to explore your experience with the language of conflict.

Discussion Questions

- What language devices and structures did you choose to communicate the core meaning of the poem?
- What imagery did you consciously avoid as you were composing the poem because it did not accurately represent the conflict experience?
- How did the poetic structure and language devices open up your ability to communicate the essential meaning of the conflict?
- In what ways did the poetic structure and language devices constrain and limit your choices of representation? How did these constraints specifically impact how you represented the conflict?
- How does language both help you to create and also constrain the expression and representation of conflicts more broadly?
- What are the implications of these creative and constraining functions of language for how we do dialogic negotiation?

Exercise 2: Exploring Your Conflict Language Habits

Language practices form the symbolic fabric of how we do conflicts when they become habits. The habitual form and content of our conflicts is connected to the cultural and historical context of our lives—where we are in the world and how conflict talk typically gets spoken there. Our habits are reflections of our own biographical characteristics and personalities and family backgrounds, as well as the dynamics of the particular relationships in which the conflict has meaning. This exercise is designed to get you to tap into these contextual features of conflict language and critically examine how they combine for you as habits of language practices that can be questioned, affirmed, or possibly changed.

- How do you typically approach verbal and nonverbal communication in a conflict with a close friend or loved one with whom you desire to maintain the relationship and resolve the conflict effectively?
- What typical things would you say or do to create an environment of collaboration with them?
- What kinds of things do you typically or consciously avoid saying or doing that might jeopardize the relationship or the feelings of the other person?
- If someone else were to describe your conflict style, including the typical phrases, tactics, and so on that characterize you, what things do you think would be listed?

- What do you typically say when you are angry in a conflict, when you know that you are wrong, or when you want to escalate the conflict by shifting the blame?
- How do you typically talk in a conflict that has an intensity of meaning that makes it very personal and difficult?
- What typical imagery and metaphors do you draw on in conflicts or when talking about them afterwards?
- How does silence figure into your conflicts? Do you use silence effectively (cooling-off periods, pauses to allow the other to think, and so on) or abuse it as a way of avoiding conflict or as a passive-aggressive tactic (the silent treatment)?
- In what ways do you use dialogic negotiation effectively?
- Where do these habits and practices come from, and in what ways are those habits strengths or weaknesses for you?
- Which of your habits are cultural, in that this is just how things are done where you are from for someone like you (age, sex, race, class, etc.)?
- Which of your habits of language are based on your family background and are inherited habits?
- Which of your habits are based on you personality type, worldview, and particular mood at the time of any particular conflict?
- How do you typically approach talking and behaving in a conflict in which someone is angry with you or being very difficult, aggressive, argumentative, and competitive? What are the ways of talking and behaving that allow you to compete with that person?
- How does the style of the talk affect the process and outcome of the conflict?
- When is the last time you tried a new tactic or a new approach to talking in a conflict and what opportunities for dialogic negotiation did that experiment lead to?

Exercise 3: Language Role Play—Planning the Wedding, Planning a Life Together

It is a truism that couples often focus so much on planning their wedding that they do not always effectively prepare themselves for the life together that the wedding ceremony represents. The young man and woman who are depicted in the following poem are planning their wedding. Their conflict shows that they have some interesting differences in how they express themselves and their love for each other, as well as some interesting dynamics of jealousy, insecurity, and power. They also seem to be settling into a pattern of how they deal with this difference. She gets jealous about something because she is not sure of how he feels sometimes, he tells her that her questioning is ridiculous, and then she thinks it through to where she agrees with him. She blames herself for the little conflicts that pop up around this pattern. With a discussion partner, try to imagine how these patterns might come to a head in the complex and often difficult time of planning a wedding. What is likely to be a trigger for their conflict cycle as they plan the ceremony and choose the pretty platters? Role-play their inter- action around this conflict and allow the conversation to evolve around the conflict pattern outlined earlier. As you get into the conflict, take note of the language that comes out of you as those feelings of jealousy are pushed aside with the denial strategy of calling those feelings ridiculous. As you get into the characters, note the nonverbal and ver- bal characteristic of the language that marks it as conflict communica- tion. Try to work the conflict through beyond the specific wedding planning to address the deeper issue of communicating love and deal- ing with feelings of jealousy and insecurity. Use a dialogic negotiation style and strategy where you can. Note how the language of the con- flict changes over the course of the interaction.

Carefully read the following poem and develop the characters you will role-play based on the personal and relational clues you are given. Then answer the questions that follow the poem to explicate the importance of language in conflict.

Ridiculous *(Jen)*
Ridiculous,
That is what you always say
When I am upset or not feeling the right way
I don't know what is so hard to understand
I say what I feel, and you don't lend a helping hand
I want you to understand me
But, you just will not let yourself see
I am the one who thinks about us all the time
And you say all I do is fuss and whine
I know you love me to no end
Yet sometimes I still will not bend
We have fun together every day
The two of us in our own way
Sometimes when we fuss and fight
I can see the both of us wanting to see the light
Happiness is our goal
Overlooking its existence with our souls
I love the way you look at me

Like no other could even see
You kiss my forehead every night
At this moment we know it's alright
Ridiculous,
That is what you love to say
It makes me wonder if I am ok
Sometimes I argue about crazy things
The truth is I just want you to see my wings
I feel like a toddler jumping up and down, screaming "look at me!"
Everyone around you, you always see
I'm just wondering about little ol' me
Ridiculous,
I am tired of hearing it
Damn, where is the relationship kit?!
You say concentrate on what really matters
Land, house, ceremony, registering for pretty platters
We know exactly what this fight is all about
So let's just fix it, so I don't have to pout
I am looking and I can see, you are ready to give up
This time it will be different you'll see
I will not act like a sad little pup
Today I will leave it be
I am going to get over all this jealousy
Ridiculous, you say,
You are right today

Discussion Questions for Explicating Language in the Role Play

- For those actually doing the role play, how did the language you chose as you engaged in the conflict connect to the communication goals and outcome needs you were thinking about, as well as to the character you were playing, as you talked?
- How did your language make the conflict real? What was it about the way you talked to each other that was different from ordinary conversation? What specific words, phrases, tactics, tone, energy, intensity, and interaction processes made it feel like a conflict?
- If the conflict was divisive and difficult, how did the language used reflect and help create the divisive process and unequal outcomes? For example, how were threats, accusations, lies, denials, belittling statements, finger-pointing statements, face attacks, expletives and foul language, and so on used to express and create the conflict? How were these tactics connected to both the

specific conflict over planning the wedding and the deeper relational issues of love, communication, jealousy, and insecurity?

- How effectively did the specific and deeper symbolic issues get
  expressed and negotiated through the conflict? How was this effectiveness linked to the language in the conflict? What did the players express effectively, and what did they not express effectively?
- How were dialogic negotiation tactics, such as trying to see and
  acknowledge the perspective of the other, allowing each other to
  express themselves fully, and allowing the interaction to emerge
  and evolve toward mutually beneficial solutions, acknowledg-
  ing and working from the foundation of commonalities and
  shared interests, and so on, that are evident in the language of
  the conflict? Was the fabric of the conflict woven from dialogic
  language? If not, why not? If so, what could the role players
  have done differently with language?
- As the conflict moved through to the deeper issues, how did the
  verbal and nonverbal language of the conflict change? How do
  these changes help create positive or negative direction in the
  conflict?

❖ CONCLUSION

This chapter has probably pushed you to become much more self-
conscious about language. It did me in developing the ideas and
writing them into this chapter. The self-consciousness should not be
something that makes us shy about expressing ourselves in conflict or
so critical of the discourse we create as we do our everyday conflicts
that it silences us. Rather, I hope that you have become more aware of
the habits of your language practices as you engage in conflicts and as
you represent their meaning. If you tend to use the language of war to
structure how you think about, act, and make sense of your conflicts
with others (or with very specific people), then perhaps you can step
back from that and ask some good questions about why this is the case.
I hope that you have also become more aware of the origins of how you
use language in your conflicts in the personal, relational, familial, and
cultural contexts from which your language practices come. Another
really important set of critical questions has to do with examining the
language not used that could have been. As you have discovered, the
way that we use language in conflicts necessarily means that certain
choices are not made. These choices to leave out possible ways of talking are also related to your personal, familial, and cultural context.

Perhaps in the relationship between the language used and the language not used, there are possibilities for rethinking our language practices and impacting the process of how we do conflict as a result. This is the true value of becoming self-conscious about language. It makes you sensitive to and skillful at using symbols as possibilities for connecting with yourself and with others in ways that achieve your goals.

I encourage you to express yourself as fully as possible in your conflicts, invite others to do the same, and at the same time, explore and play with the creative opportunities that language embodies for all of us. This ideal is at the heart of our goal—that you use meaning and an understanding of how meaning systems, such as language, are used and can be used for managing conflicts more effectively, perhaps in ways that surprise everyone involved.

Part II

Conflict Stories and the Negotiation of Relationship Dynamics

4

We Belong Together but We Still Have Conflict

Negotiating Synchronicity in Relationships

❖　　❖　　❖

[Synchronicity is] a kind of simultaneity . . . a meaningful coincidence of two or more events, where something other than the probability of chance is involved.

—Main (1997, p. 93)

A story that a student of mine—Annie—told me recently really made me laugh. She was telling me about how deeply she feels for her fiancé and how they just know they are meant to be together. At the same time, they have a conflict we might be able to relate to. He is a farmer and wants to revive the family farm when he gets out of college. She is comfortable with the idea of being a farmer's wife and looks forward to their life together. He is currently trying to teach her to drive a stick-shift truck on his family property. He feels that she should be able to do as many of the things that he can when they are farming, and she understands the need for teamwork. However, she cannot get the hang of the mechanics of clutch and gas, and they are having fights during her lessons. She is wondering why learning this task is so difficult and is starting to question her ability to learn and his ability to teach her. She feels very close to him, but this specific context is sparking some fiery conflicts. The conflict does not threaten their relationship, but it does put a strain on things that might create difficulties for a couple less convinced of their belonging together. Should she give up on the idea of being a farmer's wife, or simply learn to drive from someone else, or take the truck out herself and learn? If she did either of the last two, they might find a healthier balance between their sense of shared destiny and their management of the everyday conflicts that inevitably exist in dialectical tension to that sense of closeness.

Naturally, like Annie, we often feel deeply connected to the people with whom we share the close relationships of our lives. We often experience such close relationships as synchronicity—which has to do with the belief that people are brought together with us into relationships by forces or circumstances that are unexplainably beyond chance and therefore meant to be. Archetypal stories, such as love at first sight, meeting through perfect timing, "We just knew," "I knew she (or he) was the one," or "God brought us together" are quite common and are usually tapping into this belief in synchronicity. However, the sense of wonder or beauty that comes with this belief can also exist in dialectical tension with the everyday reality of working through conflicts. "If it was meant to be, why is it so hard?" is quite a common question that I hear and that illustrates this dialectical tension of perfection and flawed or difficult reality. Maintaining the everyday balance between these tensions is a goal that will keep people busy for that lifetime together as friends, lovers, or family members. Let's face it: Even experiences like "true love," where synchronicity seems to connect people in perfect timing and balance, are not immune from conflict or from the work of maintaining and consciously evolving that relationship through communication.

In this chapter, we will explore the constraints and opportunities that the archetype of relational synchronicity seems to be related to. Specifically, we will explore the role of conflict in expressing and possibly negotiating the balance that is necessary between the idealized—even spiritual—belief in perfect timing and true love and the everyday reality that relationships are also conflicted and require the work of effective dialogic negotiation to survive and flourish.

Main topics and learning goals in this chapter:

- Relational synchronicity and conflict
- Understanding and negotiating conflict as clues to nightmare relationships

- Understanding and negotiating true love
- Graveside dialogues
- Lessons from the field of practice

❖ RELATIONAL SYNCHRONICITY AND CONFLICT

In this chapter, I would like us to focus on and explore the implications of synchronicity and its connection to relational conflicts that can provide ways to begin dialogue and negotiation to bring about change in relationships. The Jungian approach to synchronicity, as the opening quote suggests, maintains that synchronicity occurs when there is a perceived connection between events and people in relationships that cannot be explained by chance (Bilsker, 2002; Davis, 2003; Hauk, 2000). These tangible moments of synchronicity in the lives of people are not simply bland happenings. Rather, they are also deeply symbolic in that they are connections between the often unconscious desires of people and events in the outside world. Moments of synchronicity are not simply events, they are *momentous*, like meeting one's soul mate as if by chance (Aziz, 1990; Mansfield, 1995; Stein, 1998).

I would like us to engage with the idea that conflict provides ways of pointing to—and possibly working on—the tensions that are set up in relationships when the people believe they came together through fate, chance, or God's work as a perfect and unproblematic union. Of course there is nothing wrong with such mythology—it is richly rewarding to believe you are with the person you were meant to be with. For many of us, relying on this archetype is more blessing than problem, especially if we work to balance the ideal of synchronicity with the work of achieving symmetry in everyday life. However, this myth can and frequently does set in motion the conditions for conflicts of various types. These conflicts can be difficult, and they can also be opportunities for growth and learning. Conflicts enable us to negotiate and renegotiate agreements on goals, expectations, priorities, and lifestyle issues in the same way that Annie and her fiancé's conflict did for them. In this chapter we will examine some of the most common forms of conflict that express and negotiate balance between synchronicity and symmetry.

When Nightmares Come True: There's Nothing I Can Do

A book on relational conflict would not be complete without a good mother-in-law story. This one has a slight twist in that it is the wife and her mother-in-law who are locked in an unfortunate and quite antagonistic double-bind conflict. Sara's story illustrates the very diffi-cult and conflicted relationships that can emerge when there is a sense of synchronicity and yet a deep sense of dread about a connected relation-ship (Ehrlich, 2001; Gallin, 1998). Sara told me privately that she feels completely committed to her husband, and at the same time, her mother-in-law is her worst nightmare come true. Perhaps our worst night-mares do come true *because* they are our nightmares—thereby creating synchronicity between our internal fears and external reality. As night-mares, they hold a powerfully evocative, perhaps archetypal, place in our unconscious, and when we meet that nightmare in life, a syn-chronicity between the internal nightmare and external reality can occur. The specific conflicts that these women find themselves in are clues that point to or symbolize *deeper thematic conflict issues.* These con-flict issues reflect a lack of balance in the relational dynamics of the two women and an inability to negotiate an effective balance of *boundaries, expectations, and appropriate role behavior*—common sources of relational conflict. These deeper themes connect to Sara's feelings of living in a nightmare, which seems to paralyze her in a difficult conflict with her mother-in-law, and a vicious cycle continues. The conflict may also provide metacommunication by pointing to and talking about those deeper issues and the tensions that result as they manifest in the par-ticipants' daily lives together. As you study the following story, which is written in poetic form, note how Sara openly says everything she would like to say to her mother-in-law but probably never does in real life. As you think about the poem, consider the ways that her con-struction of the relationship as a nightmare immobilize her and set in motion an inability for them to negotiate these underlying themes at the heart of the meaning of their conflict.

Family Ties *(Sara)*
Have you ever had someone make you crazy?
I have.
A family member.
One related only by law who lives to make my life miserable.
have you ever known a person who waves their hands in your face
    and repeatedly squeals, "I'm not touching you, I'm not touching you!"?
that person is my mother-in-law.
she whines, giggles, and jokingly tries to tae bo kick her sons as a form of
    flirting.
Is it just me, or is it normal to flirt with your sons like
    a teenage girl?
She acts like a retarded, hyperactive child.
so why does she treat *me* like one?

it shoots over the phone line and burns in my brain.

"Are you taking care of my little baby boy?"

She says it so sweetly so that I can't prove she's being a pain in my ass on
purpose.

"Why miss Sarry, one day I might could Southernize you"

I'll die first.

I'd rather be dead than be like you.

"For a yankee, you seem to be unusually domestic"

That's smart coming from someone who has never traveled north of the
Mason-Dixon line in their life.

She can ruin my day in an instant.

She comes to all of my husband's soccer games.

He's almost 27 and she shows up to every game he coaches and plays in.

she calls every Saturday night to see which church service we're going to
so she can follow and sit right next to us.

He's not 12, quit following him like he needs you.

Joel is 20 and lives at home.

Bother him a little longer, John's done his time.

You make me insane.

how can you act so aggressive and strong at work, and then refuse to
pump your own gas?

your husband is whipped.

No one but a downtrodden, crushed man would drive 20 miles from
home to come pump your gas because you think the smell on your
hands is "Not lady like."

Why can't you just act like a normal human being?!?!?!?!

It's not that hard.

You treat others with respect and don't act like a moronic child
with ADD.

Most of all, quit treating me like a dependant lost child so that you can
still feel like you're the mama.

Don't tell people that you're my mother now.

Just because you never had a daughter doesn't mean you can start
claiming me.

You're not my mother.

My mother has class.

She's smart, beautiful and has no psychological problems.

just because she's 500 miles away doesn't mean you have the right to
claim me.

I told my mother you said that, too.

She was angry.

she dislikes you already and you're making it worse.

most of all get off my ass about graduation.

Don't sulk and yell at me because I am not going to the
big ceremony.

it's my choice and I don't want to go.

I don't care if your sister and niece who I've only met once feel offended.
they're not my family.

I'm not even inviting my own aunts, uncles and cousins.

What makes you think yours deserve to go?

They can come to my graduation party like everyone else. Don't ask me
for two more tickets to the department graduation for your son and
father.

They don't care if they're there.

How dare you say you've earned these things after "nursing" me through
school?

You didn't do shit for me except give me a hard time and make my life
miserable.

Not one dime went to my education, nor did you help me with my
school work.

Grow up, learn some respect and leave me alone!

❖ UNDERSTANDING AND NEGOTIATING CONFLICT AS CLUES TO NIGHTMARE RELATIONSHIPS

The following interpretive steps and related questions will help you
to explicate some of the difficult conflicts associated with relationships
that are characterized by synchronicity and asymmetry.

Step 1: Describe the specific conflicts that are a part of the everyday relationship of the women.

Step 2: Reduce these conflicts to the more symbolic or thematic issues that these surface conflicts point to.

Cluster the deeper issues together according to their thematic interconnections. Recognize that the behaviors explicated in Step 1 have
meanings as those behaviors *and* as symbolic expressions of deeper
thematic issues.

Step 3: Interpret how these surface conflicts are interconnected around a core set of meanings that divide them and show them to be in opposition.

Interpret how the surface conflicts provide an opportunity for Sara
and her mother-in-law to access and talk about the deeper issues that
seem to show a lack of balance between synchronicity and symmetry.
To get you started, I have developed a chart of some key ideas that will
help you work with their conflict.

Meaning Analysis for "Family Ties"

Step 1: Description of Their Tangible, Everyday Communication as Signs of Conflict

Mother-in-law squealing and waving her hands in Sara's face

Mother-in-law tae-bo kick-boxing and giggling as flirtatious behavior with sons

Mother-in-law acting like a hyperactive child and treating Sara like one

Mother-in-law's comments to wife about taking care of her baby and about becoming "Southern"

Mother-in-law's overinvolvement with the soccer game attendance and the church-going coordination

Mother-in-law treating the husband (the mother-in-law's son) like a 12-year-old

Mother-in-law trying to claim wife as a daughter although she is radically different from her real mother

Mother-in-law pushing Sara to go to the graduation ceremony and claiming that various family are disappointed that she isn't going

Contrary to the mother-in-law's belief that she nursed and helped Sara through school, she made her life miserable, gave her a hard time, and was no help

Step 2: Reduction of Signs of Conflict to Their Thematic Issues

Mother-in-law's behavior is inappropriate for a mother-in-law and for a mother (and for a human being).

Mother-in-law's babying her son to preserve her hold on him is a way of competing for him, which is one aspect of their power struggle.

Mother-in-law's pushing her daughter-in-law to fit in with her culture and family and personal expectations is another aspect of their power struggle.

Step 3: Interpretation of the Core Meaning of These Thematic Issues as Their Family Conflict

Sara's meaning: You're not the mother or mother-in-law figure or even the person you think you are or that I want you to be.

Mother-in-law's meaning: You're not the Southern wife and daughter-in-law I wanted for my baby boy.

Interconnections of their meanings as their family conflict: The son-husband is the context of the conflicted power struggle between the two women. There will likely always be a manifestation of this power struggle on the more tangible and everyday surface of their communication if the conflicted power relationship is not resolved. Looking at the conflict from outside, it seems that the core meaning that all of the surface conflict symbolizes is that *neither one of them is living up to the other's expectations, and each feels it is up to the other person to change.* As metacommunication, each of their little battles along the way center on telling the other person this truth without explicitly stating it in those terms. They may get to this point, but at the moment, they are stuck in an angry mode of saying it symbolically through metacommunication but not really *saying it.* They remain paralyzed in their relationship, yet there are opportunities to renegotiate expectations and boundaries.

Discussion Questions for Further Reflection

- Why do you think the participants do or do not dig deeper into those relational issues and the tensions they produce in their relationship?
- How is this communication paralysis connected to Sara's living-nightmare frame for the experience?
- How would you guide them toward negotiating a more productive and hopefully more symmetrical relationship together, given the analysis that we have provided? What would they have to exchange (give and take) to make real progress on their relationship?
- In what ways are they quite similar in their positions in the conflict (see the preceding interpretation in particular) despite their opposition?
- How does the meaning of the conflict express their nightmarish views of each other?
- Is there a sort of synchronicity to their relationship in that they both appear to be the one thing they did not want in each other? What are the chances of their worst nightmares about each other being true?
- In what ways would your expectations in guiding them be affected by the depth and intensity and specific details of their conflict as explicated above?

- What did this story and the discussion of it bring to mind about your own family or relational conflicts and their symbolic as well as tangible meanings?

Having discussed conflicts as clues to nightmare or difficult relationships, we move on to examine and learn from the role of conflict in a relationship in which both parties seem to have achieved the perfect balance of true love.

❖ UNDERSTANDING AND NEGOTIATING
    TRUE LOVE: WHEN DREAMS COME TRUE

The following story illustrates the centrality of conflict to the communicative work necessary to find a realistic balance of true love and realism (Gaylin & Person, 1998; Goldhill, 2004; Rubin, 2004; Sternberg & Barnes, 1988). You will see both sides of a "happy" love story in which both people experience the same synchronous coming together as equal partners through the same conflicted experience and the same mysterious and seemingly inevitable chain of events. Bear in mind that a significant part of the synchronicity involves the faithful construction of the synchrony through their narratives, and a significant part of the equality and sense of being at the same place at the same point involves working on the details. Just because a relationship seems meant to be, this does not mean it is a given or that it does not require relational work to achieve and maintain the symmetry that the people assume will follow from the synchronicity. We will examine their story and then use discussion questions to learn from their relationship journey.

"Jason's Story" (Jason)
    When I met a beautiful blonde named Alex, I already had a girlfriend from high school who I had been seeing for 3 years. I proceeded to cheat on my girlfriend Tyra with Alex. I did not recognize the consequences, nor did I tell her that I had a girlfriend. When I started seeing Alex, I was messing around with three other girls. I needed attention and felt lonely all the time. In high school, my girlfriend cheated on me and so I thought why did I have to be? Cheating was like therapy for me, and boy did I need a lot of therapy!
    "Whoa! What a nice piece of ass!" We all agreed. I had just spotted my next victim in the Rec center. I wanted to get to know her. Already engaged to Alex at this point, my cheating hadn't slowed down—in fact it was in overdrive. You're probably thinking "this guy's an asshole," but stay with me to the end before you judge me. We exchanged numbers and Katherine and I began a relationship. I thought this was going to be another insecurity-based relationship but little did I know what God had in store. At first it was going to be a short-term rendezvous

but as we got to know each other, I realized how much we had in common. We were two pieces of a puzzle that belonged side by side. And then things got deep. We connected on such a high level of energy, emotion and truth that I could not let her go—all the while, I had a fiancé.

My fiancé and I never really got along. It was more a chemical connection than anything else. This made it easy to leave emotion out when I cheated on her. She was in nursing school so it was easy to see Katherine. Neither had any idea I was being a selfish, misled asshole. As I got to know Katherine more and more, I realized that our two pieces of the puzzle had become one. After 5 months, our year in school had ended, and we both cried when she had to leave for the summer. We talked during the summer, but I was back with my fiancé out of obligation. When school started again, I thought it would be easy for us just to be friends since she had probably met someone.

When I laid eyes on her again, all the old feelings came back to me. I tried to ignore them and play it off as though we were just friends. But cupid had found his victim, and it was me. I couldn't believe how my heart dropped when I saw her again for the first time. Now fellas, I tried to play it off, but I couldn't cheat love this time. I dated Katherine and Alex at the same time for about 7 months, but this time Katherine knew I had someone, but Alex didn't. To make a long story short, I was being a yeast infection for not stepping up to the plate by breaking up with Alex. I never promised Katherine anything, we were living for the moment, and she knew it.

Around the 5-month mark, all my friends were telling me to break up with Alex as well as my family because they had caught on to the situation. But I was scared because Alex was my future. I felt obligated to her for many reasons. We were engaged, and she was buying a town house for the two of us, and we had been through so much at this point.

About a month before we were supposed to move in together, I decided at the last second to take a trip to Jamaica for spring break with some friends. Katherine was supposed to go to the Bahamas, but as fate would have it, she ended up not even 2 miles from me in Jamaica. All I could think about was Katherine. There were tons of beautiful women around me and cheating was everywhere. But for once in my life, it hit me—it was time for me to grow up and kick my insecurities in the ass.

"Katherine, I need you in my life. You are all I have thought about since I've been here. I love you with all of my heart. Can you ever forgive me for what I have done?" I pledged my love for her and, for the first time, promised her that I would do the right thing and follow my heart. We had long intimate moments in Jamaica that were like unwritten poetry. When I got home, for the first time, I really knew what I had to do. I had to sack up and be a real man. This was something I hadn't done since being cheated on in high school.

I promptly broke up with Alex and got the ring back from her. It was one of the hardest things I have ever had to do. But I faced my fears and realities and did something that turned my life around. Not only was it better for me, but it was also best for all of us. Now I am with Katherine, and I am very much in love. We have a complete understanding and honesty between us, and we trust each other completely. I have changed my life around so that I could be a better man for her and myself. My cheating days are over. And last time I checked, Alex was doing fine, too. She doesn't talk to me, which I understand, but all the same I am glad that she is happy. I realized that cheating came from all of my insecurities, and it was wrong. This old dog was willing to learn a new trick.

Katherine's Story

Almost 3 years ago, I met Jason. Everything about him was different from any other person I had ever dated or even been around. There was a sincerity and humbleness that I couldn't find in anyone else. And believe me, I had been looking for my one true love, someone just like Jason, since I was 15 years old. After a week of seeing each other, I found myself crashing down around him—falling intensely in love. And I wasn't afraid. Through every step of our relationship, he told me how he felt about me. He told me how special I was and what a wonderful and beautiful person I was. No man had ever given me the attention that I needed and the expression of their feelings like this before. I thought love like this only existed in the movies—until now.

We dated for 5 months my sophomore year in college when it was time for me to go home for the summer. Tears swelled up in my eyes. Saying goodbye had never hurt so much in my life. My father waited patiently in the moving van for me to pry myself from his arms.

Jason and I spoke every day that summer, most of the time for hours on end. We talked about family, friends, feelings, ex's, and so on. Then about half way through the summer, I didn't hear from him. I had called him earlier that day, but he didn't return my call which was very unusual. I was worried but decided not to call and to wait for him to call. He finally did the next evening. That was the first day I had told anyone I was in love with them. Jason reciprocated the feelings but in the next sentence he broke up with me.

"You're just too young," he exclaimed, "I want to settle down soon." But I knew in my heart that was bullshit. How could anyone deny a love like this? He made me want him even more, and I could feel anger and vulnerability stirring inside of me. When I realized that my tears would not win him back, I knew that I had to fight. I knew that when I went back to school that August, he would be with me once again. He had to. It had to be this way.

In the pit of my stomach I felt that there was someone else—even though he claimed there wasn't. I continued calling him every day, but he didn't answer his phone or return my calls. I was desperate and was calling more than ever, not caring if I pushed him further away. I tried more than ever to rid my mind of him, but it was like he was living inside of me. I couldn't even look at other men and feel an attraction. I did speak with him one last time before I came to Greensboro. He told me to call him when I got back in town, so I did.

"I don't know what's going on, guys," I sputtered. We were sitting in Casey and Lacey's dorm room, and I had just gotten off the phone with Jason.

"He's going to be here in like 15 minutes!"

As it turned out, Jason was back together with his ex-fiancé. It wouldn't be until later that year that I would find out they were never really "ex's." When he did finally arrive at the dorm room, I was on air, not knowing what to expect. But as soon as I saw him again, all of the familiar feelings started rushing through my system. As I watched him from a distance, all I could think was "This can't happen."

After about a week of Jason and I seeing each other every day and speaking several times a day, we went to the library to study together. We spent over an hour laughing, flirting, and reminiscing about the past. The other girl didn't exist to me. I didn't know who she was, and I had never heard her voice. She was just an object in the way of our happiness. As we left the library, our hands brushed against each other. I felt the pit of my core deepen, and I grasped on for a split second.

"You want to hold my hand?" he asked. Of course I did. And I didn't let go until we got to his car. He drove me to my house where I tried to coax him in to actually study this time. I sat and read out loud as he lay softly on my bed—eyes closed. He looked so peaceful and beautiful, and I wanted him to stay there forever. I nuzzled my head in between his arm and his body and just listened to him breathe. He looked down at me with love in his eyes.

Jason and I continued our relationship as if his fiancé didn't exist for the next 8 months. Sure, there were minor interruptions and inconveniences here and there, and my friends gave me a lot of shit for it, but I knew what we were doing. I was going to give him my everything for as long as I could, and if I ever had to give up, then I would.

When spring break rolled around in March, Jason was going to Jamaica with some of his brothers and I was going to the Bahamas with some of my friends. I couldn't wait. At this point in time, I was growing exhausted of all the emotions that I couldn't fully express to Jason, and I was tired of being the other girl. I needed a break. It was dawning on me that I might never have him all to myself. Then the news came from Casey . . .

"Katherine, our travel agent didn't get us plane tickets, and there's no room on the airplane. They're trying to work something out, but I don't know what's going to happen yet. They might send us to Jamaica."

I was going to the exact same town as Jason. When I got there, I decided not to pursue him. I had to get over him and not see him.

My second day there, I was swimming in the water with some of Casey's sorority sisters when I looked up and saw him. He had found me. I waded out of the water and said hello. I gently gave him the cold shoulder. I was flirty but short—not really knowing what I was doing. But boy did I play my cards right. The next day Jason found me again.

"Can we walk down the beach?" he asked warily. After we were out of sight of the others, he pulled me close.

"Katherine, all I can think of is you. I've been in Jamaica 3 days now, and Alex has called me every day. I feel bad, but I don't even want to talk to her. All I've wanted is to be with you. I left you a message at the front desk of your hotel. Me and some of the others went looking for you at your hotel the night before, but I couldn't find you! Katherine, I want to be with you. I am tired of being with someone who I am not in love with. If I leave her, can you ever find it in your heart to forgive me and be with me?" He rambled on more, but I couldn't hear a thing. Tears of joy flooded my lashes and spilled onto my cheeks. I embraced him and pulled him tighter than I ever had. I kissed him—I truly kissed him passionately and, for the first time, with complete conviction.

From that day on, Jason and I have been together. I have been so blessed to find my true love and to actually be with him. I think that's something that many people take for granted, but I never will. I will always know the feeling of not being able to have someone completely.

Negotiating True Love

Use the following interpretive steps and related discussion questions to explicate the role of conflict in the relationship of Jason and Katherine.

Step 1: Description of the Conflict
Using the following questions, describe the details of the story that show that the couple has a conflict, the details that show they believe they are meant to be together, and the details by which they seem to be equally in love and equally powerful in the relationship.

- What are the details of the story that suggest that they have had a meaningful conflict?
- What is the basis of that conflict and why is it inevitable and necessary to move their story forward?
- What are all the details of their story by which they construct the sense that their relationship is both meant to be (synchronicity) and by which they experience it as equal and balanced (symmetrical) and realistic?
- How do you know that this seems to be "the real thing," true love that finds its way through a tough conflict? Are you convinced that their story is equally true for both of them? I am, but I have the benefit of knowing them as real people. What makes you think they have everything aligned effectively?

Step 2: Reduction to Themes in the Balance of Synchronicity and Symmetry
Explicate the various thematic relationships between the conflict and their experience of synchronicity as a story (dramatic tension, the inevitability of their relationship, the near loss of each, etc.).

- What thematic roles does the conflict play in foreshadowing, highlighting, and making vivid and dramatic their seemingly inevitable fusion?

- What common themes seem to exist between the two stories that tell you that they are in love and yet have worked through similar issues through their conflict?

Step 3: Interpretation of Meaning of Their Relational Conflict

Develop a statement that you think captures the meaning of their conflict as something that points to, and makes real, the experience of synchronicity as true love. What does this suggest about probable strengths and possible weaknesses in their relationship for the future?

- What is the meaning of the conflict in terms of how it symbolically points to their synchronous and equal relationship? How would you sum up or title this story as a conflict that points to true love?
- What will this couple need to continue to work on to maintain their relationship?
- What might be some issues that could challenge or prove difficult to their relationship in their future or even their belief in the synchronicity of their relationship?
- What will they have to continue to believe to maintain their sense of synchronicity in their lives together?
- How might they maintain a healthy dialogue about their relationship so that they maintain the perfect balance that they believe they have found by negotiating effectively?
- Can you think of examples from your life of this perfect balance that they seem to have found? How did you arrive at such a relationship, and how did conflicts figure into the meaning of that relationship as perfect balance?

Having explored a case where conflict played a symbolic and tangible role in creating the experience of relational fusion—the coming together into a well-balanced relationship—we will explore the role of conflict in relationships where such timing is not so perfect. Conflict can arise as a symbolic expression of that mistiming.

❖ GRAVESIDE DIALOGUES: CONVERSATIONS
   I SHOULD HAVE HAD BUT DIDN'T

Sometimes in loving relationships there are absent, mistimed, or misplaced expressions of love because the people in it either never get to the point where they can express that love fully or conflicts keep them from working on the relationship. Family relationships often have this form of constraint because people rarely say everything they wish they could say. Unresolved conflict can manifest in many forms of difficulty in relationships (Levi, 1986). Sometimes feelings of unfairness or injustice or mistreatment hold a relationship suspended in conflict. Sometimes we just assume family will always be there and expressing love is not necessary because everyone just knows they are family and that they are loved. This misalignment, whatever its cause may be, generates conflict when conversations that need to happen and conflicts that need to be expressed remain hidden or muted. The presence of conflict is often symbolically expressive of a lack of something more connective and fulfilling that might have happened at a given moment but did not. Conflicts are often ways of symbolically working with things you would have done differently—sometimes called "the woulda-coulda-shoulda experience." Within the conflict is expressed a deeper sense of loss and a desire to have done something in a different way. Typically, these are often internal (intrapersonal) conflicted experiences rather than external (interpersonal) ones, and they focus on themes of regret, loss, and unmet wishes. The presence of regret stands in place of—symbolizes—the absence of something; in the next example, it's an appropriate ending to an important relationship.

The following poem reflects the desire to have had particular conversations that would have represented the author working on a conflicted relationship before her mother died. This phenomenon, which I call graveside dialogue, occurs because people have the conversations sitting at the gravesides that they did not have when the persons were alive. Such conflicted experiences are one-sided conflicts (monologues) and are attempts to express and resolve them after the conflict partners are gone. Of course, the other person does not necessarily have to be dead, but this is a more common phenomenon than you might think. Writing a letter to someone that you never send but that is used to express all of your thoughts and feelings on an issue is another form used with people who are alive but not in your life anymore. Typically, if the conversations do not happen while the conflict partner is alive or available, the survivor often feels compelled to continue the conflict management process after the person is gone. Such is the power of conflict as a dynamic in our personal relationships and as an expression of absence. In our personal discussions about the content of the poem, the author, Lyndsey, revealed that her mother had not acted quickly in getting treatment for her cancer. Lyndsey also revealed to me a need to forgive her mother and herself for not finishing their time together harmoniously and for not dealing with the conflict when there was a chance to do so.

The first moral of the story is this: If you can, have the conversations you need to have before people are gone. It may seem difficult to go there, but it will be much more difficult when you are the only one talking. The other moral of the story for us, as students of human conflict, is that conflicts do not go away just because the people involved do.

I Wish (*Lyndsey*)
I wish I had been there from the beginning to the end.
I wish I'd have known I wouldn't get another chance again.
You had your reasons for not being honest right away
But I want you to know I would have loved you anyway
After such a long time it seems we just got it right
The cancer was too strong, you couldn't win the fight
Your eyes were scared, your body weak
You and I didn't get our last chance to speak
If I had have known that you were leaving today
There are so many things I needed to say
You are my inspiration, my guardian angel
You always put us first, and I will be eternally thankful
You fought so hard for the rewards to be so few
You gave it your all we knew this to be true
Now that you're gone I cry every night
Who will be there to replace your bright light?
So I ask you God to help me now
It's very hard in every way
To live my life without my mom—
Each and every day

Analyzing and Working With Graveside Dialogues

Use your answers to the following questions to develop a meaning chart of the relationship between the presence of regret and conflict and the desire for what is absent—effective conflict communication. Begin by (1) describing the emotions and images of Lyndsey's mother and their relationship that are present and tangible. (2) Then, from the presence of these things, imagine what absence is under the surface of her experience. What is the relationship between the absence of specific conversations in their communication and the presence of deeper relational themes that show their underlying, deep love? What are these underlying themes? For example, is there a symbolic relationship between the apparent fact that her mother fought so hard against the cancer yet Lyndsey could not seem to make the effort to fight for peace with her mother? Does this, and other things you find under the surface, hint also at guilt as well as regret? (3) In relating the presence (description) to the absence (reduction), what do you interpret to be the meaning of Lyndsey's regret and the basis of the conflict? What does she wish she would have done differently? How does the conflict have meaning as an asynchronous love? What could have been done differently, and why wasn't it done differently because of assumptions arising from their deeper relationship of synchronicity? How did the nature of their relationship hold back these conversations from happening? Reflect on how Lyndsey's conflict symbolizes a desire for something different.

- What does Lyndsey wish that she woulda-coulda-shoulda said and done differently in this specific conflict?
- How do you think this conflict over not ending their relationship well is connected to the broader context of their relationship as mother and daughter over the years? Do you think they had a close relationship except for this event or a more distant one symbolized by this conflict about the ending?
- Why would doing this conversational script differently have made a difference to how their relationship ended, and why is this difference important in her life?
- What does her desire for ending their relationship differently tell you about the importance of conflict and conflict management in close personal and family relationships—especially in the processes of saying goodbye and grieving?
- What conversation would Lyndsey most like to have had with her mother before she died? What might she have said, and what might her mother have said? Act this conversation out with someone and see how it progresses and how it feels. Record your experiences as a journal entry if you are keeping a conflict journal.
- What conflicted conversations do *you* need to have with people before they die or become completely estranged?
- What role might such a conversation have for you in resolving or managing a conflict with that person?
- What happens to the energy and the meaning of your conflict if you do not have this conversation? Might you end up having a graveside dialogue as Lyndsey does?

Having examined conflicts as symbolic expressions of absence, loss, and regret, we move on to examine their valuable role in providing relational motifs that people can draw on as they remember and compare and contrast past, present, and sometimes future events (temporal distance) through story motifs. You will see that relationships can and often should be renegotiated from the moments of synchronicity that appear through conflict. As our feelings of connectedness to another person and the myths that we hold dear change, conflicts can help people to renegotiate and redefine relationships and may even allow them to terminate relationships that seemed destined to be through profound moments of synchronicity. The following story analysis illustrates the relationship between synchronicity, conflict, and change.

Negotiating the Meaning of Differences: Best Friends Now and Forever

Relationships that seem to be born of perfect moments of synchronicity often leave little room for the necessary discussion of differences and asymmetries than can grow and threaten them. The following story represents an archetypal best friend story that I hear over and over again. It is one that helps us understand the role of conflict in changing relationships and the myths that we bring to them that set up the conditions for often difficult conflicts to occur. In the story, notice how the two meet in what seems like a moment of perfect synchronicity—they became instant best friends. Perhaps this experience of synchronicity covered over some of the main asymmetrical aspects of their relationship. They are very different people despite the magic of finding each other. The conflict illustrates the complex relationship of synchronicity and symmetry and especially the need to constantly negotiate change in relationships as the lives of the people evolve. One of the classic myths of friendships is that they are static— what we *mean by* "best friend" stays the same for us over time because the meeting occurred in a flash of synchronicity. Another is that you can assume that relationships stay the same even though the lives, identities, and experiences of the participants change—we will be best friends forever just because we are best friends now. In reality, relationships and their meaning for us are organic and ever-evolving things in which changes are often achieved and expressed through conflicts—especially if handled through dialogic negotiation. Conflict often serves the creative functions of (1) forcing the partners into a different relational definition and understanding. We often initiate conflicts as a way to introduce change and to express differences between the persons we were and who we now want to be viewed as in the relationship. Conflicts in relationships also serve the creative function of (2) allowing relational partners to express built-up tension and resentments that show that things have changed. Conflicts create a rupture in one or more partner's ongoing set of assumptions and, if the conflict is managed effectively, allow a new set of shared assumptions about the relationship to be negotiated.

As you will see in the following story, conflict often becomes a concrete way of expressing differences and forcing change in the meaning of a relationship and the ways in which the two relate to each other from that point on. There are two main phases that I want you to analyze in terms of the role of the conflict. First, there is the opening up of the conflict—the escalation—in which specific, tangible behaviors and actions symbolically show that things have drastically changed. I take this phase to extend right up to the moment when Sara tells her old best friend that she is acting like a spoiled brat; this is probably an important moment in expressing a turning point in their relationship. Second, there is the phase from this volatile moment on, when the conflict starts to redefine their relationship through Sara's wedding and into her married life, as she bonds with her husband as her new best friend.

The changes that you will uncover in how the friends behave become a way to symbolically redefine meaning and definition of the relationship itself. The symbolic dimension has to do with the underlying aspects of the meaning of the relationship as they move from best friends to more distanced childhood friends with less in common. Use the discussion questions that follow the story to examine how they move from unquestioned best friends, through a volatile conflict in which their relationship is questioned, to a new relationship in which they rebalance the dialectical tensions and meaningful themes that define their new relationship. As you read the story, consider how Sara's mythology of friendship is based on its origins in synchronicity and how this results in the death of the relationship.

"Is a Friend a Friend Forever?" (Sara)

Mary was mad at me. For the first time in 6 years, we were not seeing eye-to-eye, and it was driving us both crazy. Since that first day of 6th grade when I started at a new school and she asked me to eat lunch with her, we had been inseparable. However, at the beginning of our senior year of high school, we started planning very different paths for our lives. I knew I didn't want to spend my whole life in Ohio and that I wanted to see what was out there. Mary, on the other hand, was a homebody. She had never spent a night away from her parents until she was 14, and the possibility of living in anyplace but home was out of the question. When I told her that I had been accepted to Elon College in NC, she cried. She had decided on Ohio State so that she could make a daily commute and still live at home. She claimed that I was abandoning her and demanded to know why I couldn't just stay in Ohio like most of our friends. I felt awful, almost like I was abandoning a needy child who needed my guidance and support. After a lot of thinking, I realized that Mary was an adult now and that I wasn't responsible for her care. I still loved her dearly, but I couldn't alter my life just to suit her.

In August, I left for North Carolina amid tears and promises that things would never change between us. Little did I know how much things would change. Soon after I began at Elon, my relationship with my new boyfriend in NC changed. Things became much more serious, and I began spending more time with him. I also made a lot of new friends, especially my new roommate and best friend in North Carolina, Emily. Mary and I would call back and forth, and she would tell me that she wished I would come back home. We were a little less close than we had been, but things were still OK. When I announced my engagement the following year, Mary did her best to be happy for my fiancé and me. I asked her to be one of my bridesmaids, and things were going well.

Mary, timid as she may sound, has an angry side which explodes sometimes without warning. It was one of these episodes that caused our big break. The Christmas before my wedding, my fiancé, his 19-year-old brother, and I drove back to Ohio to visit my family. While there, we attended a Barenaked Ladies concert with my sister and Mary. There had been some mounting tension between Mary and me because she was telling me I was too young to get married and my fiancé was controlling, but we tried to keep things calm. On the ride to the show, Mary and my future brother-in-law demanded that we put in CD after CD of hip hop and rap music, which they know I dislike immensely. After the concert, we went out to grab some fast food. My fiancé and his brother had been bickering in the car, as siblings sometimes do. He was telling his brother that demanding we change the CDs all night and acting like he had, was rude.

All seemed well, when all of a sudden out of the back seat, I heard Mary scream at my fiancé, "Stop acting like you're our father and trying to tell us what to do!"

I was so surprised I turned around and said, "What did you say?"

She just looked at me with fury in her eyes and said,

"You heard me; he walks around all day with this 'be mature' attitude like he is better than us, and it makes me sick. He treats us like we're all children!"

I was so enraged I yelled back, "He only treats you like a child because you act like a spoiled brat!"

Just at that moment, we arrived at my parents' house. Mary jumped into her Mustang and sped off. I ran up to my room crying. Although we eventually smoothed things over, our friendship was never quite the same. She took every opportunity to talk about how much she hated Emily—my freshman roommate—right in front of me. Even though she had only met her once, she had a bitter hatred for her. This was especially problematical since Emily was one of my other bridesmaids. My poor little sister had to keep Mary under control so she wouldn't say anything rude to Emily.

Although Mary was still in my wedding and we see each other from time to time when I am in Ohio, we've never been close since that night when she lost her temper and started saying unkind things about the other people that I love.

Negotiating Change and Synchronicity

The story confronts the participants with the fact that their relationship had changed as indeed they had as individuals—particularly Sara. Somehow through time and through their conflict, they moved from being united *despite* their differences to being divided *by* their differences. Conflict in friendships can often confront us with lessons about our assumptions about friendship (Mauthner, 2002; Meyer, 1998). The question we have to consider is what stays the same—what do we still share if anything and ultimately is it worth the work of keeping it going?

Step 1: Description of the Conflict

Describe the evolution of the conflict between Sara and Mary in terms of important behaviors and changes in their relationship. In what ways is this conflict an important symbolic turning point for them both and a powerful, tangible catalyst for changing their relationship? As the conflict evolves, how does their relationship devolve?

Step 2: Reduction to Fundamental Thematic Oppositions

What are the central thematic oppositions between Sara and Mary in their definitions of what it means to be a best friend, as they emerge through the conflict? How do these deep differences symbolize irreconcilable distance—asymmetry—between them when compared to their early experiences of being inseparable best friends?

Step 3: Interpretation of the Meaning as Symbolizing Permanent Change

What is the meaning of the conflict as it symbolizes devolving symmetry and almost forgotten synchronicity? How is the experience of synchronicity made fragile by the quality of their relational communication? What could Sara and Mary have done differently along the way to maintain the relationship?

Discussion Questions for Analyzing and Negotiating "Is a Friend a Friend Forever?"

Questions for the first phase of the conflict:

- What were the things that symbolized their inseparability early in their best-friend relationship?
- What are the things that symbolize that this inseparableness is in question?

- Why is the moment when Sara is accepted to Elon an emotional one and one that suggests future conflict between them might be imminent?
- Why does Sara's moving to North Carolina mean abandonment for her friend and progress to Sara? How is this particular thematic difference significant to their conflicted relationship, and why had they never explored their real differences before?
- How is "being responsible" for the other person an important theme?
- How do these specific, tangible differences become symbolic of changes in the relationship as Sara and Mary confront these relational themes?
- Sara and Mary promised that things will never change. Why is this unrealistic for their relationship? What would be a more realistic promise as Sara gets ready to leave Ohio?
- How does Sara getting engaged and making new friends become symbolic of change in their relationship?
- How are the themes of staying the same versus changing important underlying differences and tensions in their relationship? Who and what has changed and who and what has stayed the same?
- How are Mary's comments on Sara's upcoming marriage, her behavior toward music, and her apparent hatred of Emily all symbolically important amidst their plans to enjoy a concert together? What is she really saying here?
- The volatile moment of conflict between Sara and her fiancé and Mary is the point when this conflict comes to a head. Why are the themes of "maturity," "control," and "acting like a spoiled brat" under attack here? How do the issues in this moment of conflict have broader significance to Sara and Mary's conflicted relationship?
- How does the moment when they scream at each other, a very volatile and emotional point in their conflict, represent the fact that they have not worked on their relationship? Why are they screaming now, when all of their differences could have been talked about and become clearer as they evolved as people?

Questions for the second phase of the conflict:

- After their screaming match, what changes in their relational communication mark changes in their relationship?
- How do the changes in their relationship and changes in them as people symbolize their newly defined, distanced relationship with each other?

- How would you define their relationship now, compared with it starting out as "instant best friends"?
- Do you think this conflict is both inevitable and necessary in their lives?
- What advice would you have given them at the moment when they promised that nothing would change? How would your advice have helped them manage their conflicted relationship? Base your advice on the archetype of synchronicity.
- What best-friend conflicts does this one bring to mind for you, and how effectively did you negotiate a similarly changing relationship?

Having examined some of the more common conflict scripts that manifest from the constraints of the synchronicity archetype, we move on to examine crossroads moments as opportunities for conflict dialogue that emerge from synchronicity.

❖ LESSONS FROM THE FIELD OF PRACTICE: EXPLORING SYNCHRONICITY AND SYMMETRY IN YOUR CONFLICTS

Exercise 1: It's About the Principle of the Thing

Think back to a close relational conflict where the principle behind your position was at least as important as the thing or things being fought over. Why was the principle or the symbolic value as important, if not more important, than the tangible object or focus of the conflict? What was the relationship between the symbolic and tangible aspects of the conflict—how did they interact and give meaning to each other? How did the symbolic value affect your emotional experience and your actions in the conflict? How were these experiences connected to your relational synchronicity and the myths that arise from that archetype? How might you have communicated more effectively about the symbolic as well as the tangible aspects of the conflict, remembering that it is often much easier to be aware of and able to talk about the tangible aspects?

Exercise 2: Understanding Archetypes and Myths in Relational Conflicts

Think about a conflict that you have successfully worked through in an intimate relationship in which you experienced synchronicity. Which story script from the chapter was your experience most similar to, or did it serve a different function or functions? What was it in how you communicated that meant the conflict was successfully managed or that the myth became problematical in your relationship? What did you learn from that particular conflict, and how have you adapted that lesson for subsequent conflicts?

❖ CONCLUSION

Conflict ought to be a perfectly normal part of the ongoing and ever-changing work of trying to discover and maintain balance or symmetry in relationships. Partners are faced with real choices and opportunities to move toward more effective balance as they negotiate their conflicts effectively. Conflicts also sometimes confront partners with the fact that their experience of synchronicity in coming together needs to be met with the work of achieving ongoing happiness. This chapter shows that conflict provides valuable clues or windows into relationships in a variety of ways that can be useful in understanding deeper themes or issues and as good starting points for dialogue and negotiation. We have explored several of the functions of conflict in constraining, balancing, questioning, and rebalancing the dynamics of relationship.

I hope that you will use the energy that conflicts embody to negotiate more effective and peaceful relationships, if that is what you desire. I also hope that you will consider carefully the archetype of synchronicity, as it provides a powerful foundation for many of the myths and related conflicts that characterize our close relationships. At least, you should be more sensitive to recognizing what a particular conflict tells you about a relationship and about how you might use conflict to say things to the people with whom you have ongoing relationships. You can say and do many things with a conflict, and your conflicts will say many things about you to other people. Reading these clues and lessons is the basis of healthy relationships in terms of managing conflict in them, challenging some of the myths that we often bring to relationships, and doing the work that helps you move and evolve with ever-moving relationships. In the next chapter, we dig deeper into how conflicts represent crossroad moments in relationships and how to navigate through those moments effectively through dialogic negotiation.

5

Where Do We Go From Here?

Negotiating Through—and Learning From—Crossroads Moments in Relationships

❖ ❖ ❖

We can learn to view conflict as a positive force necessary for the development and maintenance of a worthwhile and fulfilling relationship.

—Kellett and Dalton (2001, p. 182)

Almost all relationships move through stages and phases of evolution toward closeness and sometimes of devolution toward breaking apart. Central to those moves forward, closer together, or further apart are conflicts. These are often big conflicts that we might refer to as *crossroads moments, moments of truth,* or *turning points* that force relational partners to question the quality of their communication, the meaning and strength of their relationship, and the balance of their commonalities and differences as they talk into reality their future path forward—or apart (Baxter & Bullis, 1986; Baxter & Pittman, 2001). Turning points are conflicts associated with major changes or transitions in the meaning and quality of a relationship (Beebe, Beebe, & Redmond, 2005; Conville, 1991). Though there are many categories and types of turning points (Vaughan, 1986), for our purposes, these crossroads moments often take the form of conflicts that challenge the participants in a relationship to decide where to go from here or to shift their definition or perspective on the relationship in an important and lasting way (Conville, 1998). How partners negotiate these moments together has enormous implications for the shift in the relationship that does occur, whether the relationship progresses or ends, and the quality of negotiation through such moments can have a lasting impact on the happiness and health of the relationship.

Crossroads moments can be negotiated and navigated effectively and become emblems or motifs of a relational success in memories of past encounters with conflict (Knapp & Vangelisti, 2005, p. 57). There are times when a crossroads moment is felt by only one person or is ignored or repressed in the relationship. Sometimes we fear such moments, particularly if they are difficult or conflicted in nature, and will simply end relationships rather than do the work of negotiating through them collaboratively. Sometimes the lack of effective negotiation of these turning-point moments can result in tensions, accumulated grievances, and problems that surface in other places in the relationship.

Let us begin with a quick example to illustrate what we mean by a crossroads moment. We will come back to this particular story later in the chapter when we listen to the other side of the story.

Imagine being a 20-something new mom who has been married for 4 years to the man you know you are meant to be with for life. You and your husband have full-time jobs outside the home. When you get home in the evening, your husband Bill settles down to watch television while you prepare dinner, take care of the baby, wash dishes, do laundry, and clean the house. You usually fall into bed exhausted. Then the baby wakes you up, and your husband does not even seem to hear the noise. You start the day early and go off to work already tired. This, you might think, is a situation ripe for conflict to happen. Then one evening about 10 p.m., you are standing in the kitchen drying dishes when Bill calls you into the den and says, "While you're up, how about changing the channel. This program really stinks." You are at a crossroads moment. Exhausted and angry, you do not want to live like this anymore. You start packing a bag, threatening to leave, and you tell Bill that you do not want to take care of two babies alone anymore—the 1-month-old and him. Bill says he is sorry, and asks, "What can I do?" He adds, "I didn't know you were unhappy, and I thought you liked doing all of the jobs . . ."

Conflicts such as Janet and Bill's provide a richly symbolic way of talking about and working on relationships, even when the people in them believe they are meant to be together for life and that things should fall naturally into place because of that. Their assumption that everything was fine because they loved each other limited their ability to see that they needed to have healthy dialogue about themselves and their life together and negotiate everyday agreements that made up their real life together. It also caused them to repress grievances and other important topics. Their lack of communication ultimately led to a conflicted moment in time where they both stood together to question their relationship and decide how to move beyond that turning point. They took the opportunity for open dialogue, navigated and negotiated the moment effectively, and the conflict became a valuable symbolic motif story or relational legend for them. That conflict allowed so much to come out and so much to be said about their experiences of married life thus far. How she felt, why they were conflicted in their marriage, why he did not help, and that he was willing if she would just ask were all productive conversational opportunities that were expressed and made into possibilities for their negotiation of their relational rules, goals, and expectations by this conflict. As our opening quote suggests, this negotiation, in turn, helped them achieve a healthier and more fulfilling relationship. From the stark moment when they confronted their conflict, they could negotiate to rebuild a lifestyle that was fairer and more equitable and symmetrical or even end the relationship.

In this chapter we will explore a few of the more common crossroads moments, such as that of Janet and Bill, and discuss how to negotiate them effectively, given the importance of such moments to relationships. There are many forms of crossroads moments, and I am sure you have lived through some that we will not explore, but the general lessons are perhaps the same.

Main topics and learning goals in this chapter:

- Understanding the meaning of crossroads moments
- Relational motifs: Look how far we have come
- Understanding and negotiating patterns of light and dark
- Understanding and negotiating the meaning of differences
- Lessons from the field of practice

❖ UNDERSTANDING THE MEANING OF CROSSROADS MOMENTS

Crossroads moments occur when a relational event, such as a conflict, makes one or more relational partners ask really profound questions about the relationship such as, "Is it worth staying with this relationship or are we breaking up?" Such moments can arise when one or more partners has serious doubts (Is this "the one" for me?), when external forces threaten the integrity of the relationship (cheating, for example), or when the balance of rewards and costs are not working well (Is this relationship worth the work?). Crossroads moments can occur in intimate, family, friendship, and even work relationships. They sometimes serve the function of bringing mutual doubt, frustration, restlessness, questions about differences in relationship goals, values, and expectations, and questions about the very purpose and existence of the relationship to the surface. This surfacing function means that crossroads moments can be transformative.

Besides being potentially transformative, these moments often trigger difficult conversations. "We need to talk!" is a statement that many of us have some fear of hearing. Although often difficult, conflicts at these pivotal moments can also provide for the expression of desires for change in relationships—for redefinition, renewal, revision, and even healthy ending. If we listen closely in these conflicted moments, we can often hear the constructive suggestions in the middle of the conflicted, divisive, and often destructive argument—again, the story behind the story. We often shy away from these powerful moments. We may even ignore the obvious fact that we are both standing at the crossroads, because such conflicts can bring to the surface the so-called darker side of a relationship and the fact that it is ever-changing and requires work. But if we are willing to listen carefully, conflicts can provide clues to deeper relational dynamics that need to be addressed. As I've mentioned, such conflicts can be used as ways of opening up communicative possibilities for changing relationships and negotiating life beyond the crossroads. We will begin with a success story, one that illustrates how a couple used a crossroads moment to renegotiate their relationship and move closer.

❖ RELATIONAL MOTIFS: LOOK HOW FAR WE HAVE COME

When we go to family reunions, we not only get to relive some of the old memories and adventures that are central to the history of the people in the family, we also get to hear the stories that people hold near and dear *about us*. Sometimes the stories people remember and retell about us surprise us because we do not necessarily remember the incident being retold or find it strange that the other person remembers us in that way through that particular story. It can be a strange experience to hear these stories because we get to meet—perhaps confront—who we *are* and who we *were* to other people. Even a short story told on such an occasion can be highly symbolic in that it captures a great deal of family history and relational identity and so on. Such stories are symbolic motifs—they stand in place of, symbolically represent, and evoke a much bigger set of experiences than the one incident being relayed. Conflict stories can become motifs when they are used at a later time to illustrate how people moved through crossroads moments.

As motifs, conflict stories in relationships can come to take on a symbolic function as pointing to progress, changes, even transformation and how people have become closer through negotiating the crossroads moment. In fact, motif stories are important for recognizing and accepting differences between people and differences and evolutions over time as they capture the meaning of those differences for us (Feeney, 2003). Such turning-point moments are often called *reflective turning points* because they retrospectively symbolize that something has changed (Beebe, Beebe, & Redmond, 2005). There may be conflict episodes that you are able to talk about, even perhaps joke about in your close relationships, now that they have taken on a symbolic function, as a motif of how things were and how they are now. The archetypal morals of such stories can be, "Remember that time when . . ." or "I can't believe we fought over that . . ." or "Look how far we've come together." These markers of change in story form provide relational partners with ready-made and easily revivable stories about themselves that trace the impact of how they dealt with crossroads moments. The moral of the story can be about remembering the early, conflicted days; how things have changed between us; how we learned a valuable lesson; and what we needed to change so that this type of conflict does not now happen, to name a few. Such stories also reflect conflict experiences and make them accessible as topics of discussion, sources of humor, and reaffirmations of the bonds of the long-term relationship.

Motifs can also be used to help manage the tension and difficulty of a current conflict. For example, how many of us have used the archetypal tension-relieving statement, "Well, one day we might look back on this and laugh"? Couples often use this motif to diffuse the volatility of a current crossroads conflict and reaffirm the long-term nature of the relationship. It symbolizes a desire to move beyond the conflict and maintain the relationship into the future.

Motifs can also be dark in nature. There are conflict stories that are carried in families for generations that still revive old feelings of hatred and betrayal and maintain the symbolic barriers that are at the heart of the conflict being retold. You can probably think of archetypal stories in your family that have a darker, more divisive, purpose.

As you explicate the story that follows, try to bring to the surface the role that this conflict plays as an emblem of how they successfully negotiated change in their relationship. Consider the following questions as you read the story and step into their relationship for a few moments: What function or purpose does the story fulfill within their marriage? And what motifs does it bring to mind for you from your own intimate, friendship, and family relationships?

"Tired of It—or Just Tired?" (Bill)

It was an ordinary evening, and Janet had seemed like she was in a pretty good mood at dinner. After dinner, I was watching some TV while she finished up in the kitchen. It seemed like she had been in there for a long time, so I called her into the den where I was sitting. She came out of the kitchen still holding a drying towel. She looked tired and out of sorts. I thought I would tease her a little, to get her out of her mood.

"Hey honey, would you do something for me?"

"Sure. What?"

"How about changing the channel for me while you are up?"

I thought she would hit me with the towel or something, but instead she kept walking toward the bedroom—and she was crying.

"Honey, what is it?" I said.

"I just can't take it anymore! I can't keep doing everything by myself. If I don't get more help from you, I may as well go home to my parents in North Carolina."

As she said these words, she was actually beginning to pack some stuff. As she packed, I was unpacking. I knew she was probably just really tired, and tomorrow, after she'd gotten some sleep, she would be fine. I knew Janet loved being a mother and that she usually liked cooking and taking care of the house. As a matter of fact, it was a goal for both of us to be financially able for her to stay home all the time and let child care and housekeeping be her only job.

But she was really going on and on about how hard things have been for her and about how I didn't carry my load around the house. I knew there was some truth to what she was saying, but I swear, I had no idea she felt so burdened. She could have told me before, and I would have been happy to have helped out more. But she never told me how she felt.

So I promised her I would do whatever it would take to make things fairer and to do more to help. It was no big deal—I've helped more ever since. I would have been happy to help all along if she had just said. But anyway, things are great now. We've made it through almost 24 years together, and we're both very happy. We had a few things to work out at first, but everything turned out fine, and now we can look back and joke about that TV incident.

Use the following interpretive steps and related questions to dig into this motif story and the lessons about conflict that it illustrates.

Step 1: Description

Describe the specific communication practices that show that Bill and Janet had a deeper conflict about issues of imbalance, unfairness, power, and role expectations. Describe also the main distinctions between communication practices then and now in their relationship.

Step 2: Reduction

Reduce your description to the essence of their negotiation effectiveness by explicating the specific ways that their changes in communication connect to changes in how they negotiated their underlying issues and challenges. What demands on her part were expressed? What concessions were made on both sides? How did these exchanges create valuable changes?

Step 3: Interpretation

Interpret the lessons learned by them and by us in terms of how to effectively negotiate through a difficult crossroads moment. What did they do effectively? What might they have done differently in the first place? What did you learn from their experience? Why is this something that now has a positive meaning in their relationship?

Some additional discussion and reflection questions:

- What is the main moral of this story that each of these lessons and changes constitute and that makes it symbolize so much for this couple looking back from years later?
- Why is this story still so evocative and meaningful to them 24 years later? What other crossroads stories might they have?
- What details of the story tell you that this couple might have lived together quite happily for 24 years? That is, what habits of communication do you see forming or being reformed in this conflict that you think will have been good habits for their long-term relational health and satisfaction?
- What are some conflict stories in your relationships or in your family that function as positive or unifying motifs that represent how you have negotiated dialogically through difficult crossroads moments?
- What is it about those conflicts and the moral of their stories that make them good motifs in your relationship?
- Under what circumstances do these stories come up in talk, and what do you get from them?

- What are some crossroads stories that others might include you in, in ways that you find surprising or revealing of your identity as seen by others? What is it about the image of you in the stories or in the incident remembered by others that you find surprising?

Having discussed the constructive and creative character of cross-roads conflicts moments, we explore a relationship in which the depth and difficulty of the conflict are due to the apparent fact that the people in the conflict are deeply in trouble. The couple, at the end of the story, reach a crossroads moment in which they (more him that her perhaps) have to decide and hopefully negotiate what patterns will be repeated and what might need to be addressed and changed. The crossroads moment is a sort of disruption or rupture in their ongoing, everyday reality that opens up questions that might change their relationship forever, or they might simply retreat into repeating unhappy and dys-functional cycles. The crossroads is the place where these existential decisions are made and have their impact on their relationship. See what you can learn about how to negotiate through a crossroads moment by more effectively balancing patterns or relational dimen-sions that night be termed light and dark in character.

❖ UNDERSTANDING AND NEGOTIATING PATTERNS OF LIGHT AND DARK

Conflicts can remind people that they are in the wrong place and wrong time although they might be with the right person. Crossroads moments are often quite difficult conflicts that require a lot of dialogic work to bring into harmony because such patterns are often ingrained and repetitive in family cultures (Watt & VanLear, 1996). The characters and their motives and actions in the following story represent the rela-tional expression of light and dark sides of relationships, both of which are quite common in the patterns and cycles of families over genera-tions (LePoire, Hallett, & Giles, 1998; Messman & Canary, 1998).

The light side can be defined as communication that constitutes healthy or effective relationships (symmetrical, nurturing, equal, and constructive), and the dark represents negative or unhealthy qualities (asymmetrical, abusive, manipulative, addictive, and toxic). The turn-ing point here has to do with recognizing the deeper connection to, and struggle between, forces that have affected the family for generations and changing those deeper systemic patterns. This might be termed a *causal turning point* (Beebe et al., 2005, p. 288), in that deeper systemic issues in the family cause this particular one to bubble up again. Of course, it is unlikely that people believe they truly represent darker elements in family conflicts. We probably all believe we represent more light than dark, and this is at the heart of the conflict between these forces. We get *the narrator's* representations of the characters and their relationships, and yet everyone in the family probably has a justification as to why their actions are right. This oppositional sense of rightness is at the heart of the conflict; the struggle is between people who believe they represent light and are working against darkness. This sheds some light on the rigidity of the characters in their positions and also can help explain the volatility of the conflicts that sometimes characterize close relationships in families. As much as we love the other people in our stories, we are likely to believe strongly that we are more right than they are.

This story of "wanting it all" moves through several relational twists and turns, each of which represents the conflicted struggle between the forces of light and the forces of darkness—particularly as these forces focus on issues of closeness, control, love, and trust. Jeff, the narrator, does not spiritualize these forces necessarily, but note his insistence that God—the ultimate force of light for him—resolves the conflict. As a reflection of these struggles between light and dark, there are repeating patterns set in motion within the family and then within his marriage. The conflict between light and dark thus has repercussions for everyone in the family over generations. Each new generation provides an opportunity to renegotiate reality and bring new light. At the same time, inevitably some of the same old dark remains, remanifests, morphs into the particulars and specifics of the new generation, and sets the struggle between light and dark in motion again. As you go through this story, pay particular attention to who is represented as working for light and dark in the family. Also pay close attention to the pattern of behavior in the family and how this sets in motion a ripple effect into Jeff's relatively new marriage that suggests imbalance. Imagine, also, how this couple's long-term struggles between light and dark might play out over time in their future together as they hopefully try to move beyond this crossroads together.

"Wanting It All" (Jeff)

I always had a very close relationship with my Grandma. I spent the first 8 years of my life living with her and grandpa in Florida, while my parents finished their college education in Texas. In a way, I felt more like my grandparents were my actual parents, and my parents were just some friends that I saw from time to time. At the age of 8 I moved to North Carolina with my parents. From then on, I visited Grandma each summer, playing golf, swimming, fishing, and so on. She provided the love and tenderness of a mother that my own mother was unable to give due to emotional problems, including obsessive-compulsive disorder (OCD) and bipolar disorder (BPD).

Grandma instilled in me that while you will have friends and other people in your life as you go down the road, the only people who will stick by you through thick and thin are your family. She was very good at handling finances and did her best to teach me how to handle money. Even when I was in the Air Force I would fly to Florida to see her as often as possible. My parents and sister would drive down from North Carolina (NC) and we would all stay at Grandma's for several days, doing the things we enjoyed.

After my enlistment in the Air Force, I decided to move back to NC to finish college. I also missed my family and was lonely in California. I had been in two serious relationships while out west, neither one ending well, and not having a girlfriend also played a large role in my decision to move back east.

I met my wife, Karisa, during my first evening class at Rockingham Community College. Obviously, when we met, I had no idea we would eventually unite our lives in marriage. We began dating and became exclusive immediately. Also around this time, Grandma moved to NC, and she and I were both living with my parents and teenage sister. While I maintained a close relationship with Grandma, it was becoming increasingly difficult because I was spending a lot of time with Karisa.

While I saw Grandma as the nurturing, caring, mother figure she had been to me as a child, Karisa never saw this side of her. By this time, Grandma was in her late 80s and had faced many health problems. She was depressed, bitter, controlling, and very demanding of my time and attention. She became increasingly jealous of the relationship I had with Karisa and was constantly rude to her—sometimes ignoring her completely when she visited the house. On one occasion, Grandma and my mother cornered Karisa and verbally attacked her, telling her that she was no good for me and was only looking for someone to give her a free ride in life. Needless to say, Karisa was not happy with the nature of the relationship I had with Grandma. To make matters worse, I felt it was disrespectful to approach Grandma about her behavior and therefore never defended or protected Karisa from Grandma. This left Karisa feeling helpless and vulnerable. I almost lost the best thing that ever happened to me over my relationship with Grandma.

Not long before Karisa and I got married, Grandma moved back to Florida because of increasing conflict between her and my mother. I loaded her belongings into a U-Haul and drove her home. She refused to attend the wedding and told my family she did not approve of the marriage.

Unfortunately, a few months into our marriage, Grandma—who never seemed to learn her lessons with Mom—announced she was moving back into mom's house. I knew that my mom's only interest in Grandma was financial. She wanted to get her hands on whatever money Grandma had left. Over the years, she had helped my parents with large financial gifts to purchase homes, cars, furniture, and so on. For some reason, mom always thought that Grandma owed her whatever she wanted. I looked at Grandma as some one who had provided me with a home to escape my mom's madness, and I felt obligated to offer her a home where nothing would be expected in return.

I discussed with Karisa my desire to ask Grandma to move in with us. Karisa felt that Grandma's controlling behavior would overtake our home and marriage and did not want her to move in. I promised Karisa that I would not pursue the issue. In spite of my promise, I later extended an invitation to my Grandma. She thanked me for the offer but moved in with my mom. When Karisa found out that I had gone behind her back on it, she was hurt and angry and felt that I chose Grandma over her.

That summer, after having promised Karisa for the previous 6 months that I would not help Grandma move back in with my mom, I left her in our new house with our belongings still in boxes, a wrecked car, and another broken promise. Needless to say, this only exacerbated the situation, leaving Karisa feeling even less important. When I returned with Grandma, Karisa and I argued about the situation for months. Adding fuel to the fire, I visited Grandma daily, took her out to eat, and tried to spend quality time with her that mom was incapable of giving.

This conflict was eventually resolved by God. Grandma died the following spring at the age of 88. The last time I spoke to her was only hours before her death. Two months later, Karisa and I moved to Greensboro (I refused to leave as long as Grandma was alive), allowing us the opportunity to get out from under my family's influence. Unfortunately, the wounds inflicted by my choices during this time still cause conflict and pain for us to this day.

Interpreting and Learning From Patterns of Light and Darkness

Follow the three interpretive steps listed here as you reach to understand how the everyday conflicted reality of this family represents the struggle between the oppositional forces of light and dark, the problems in how they have negotiated their conflicts so far, and the challenges of negotiation they face in order to move forward. It would also be useful to understand how these struggles set in motion patterns of conflict across generations and across time that represent their habits of negotiation as a family. From this, you may be able to reflect on and understand the patterns of relationship between light and dark in your own family relationships.

Step 1: Description

Describe all of the characteristics of communication as light and dark issues. Describe how these light and dark aspects are expressing a specific set of conflict themes in the family that are clues to imbalance and other dysfunctional habits and patterns.

Step 2: Reduction

Explicate how these light and dark conflicts are expressing deeper family patterns and cycles that show ineffective conflict patterns. What are the dark patterns that recycle, and how do they show deep issues of the family that lead to this crossroads moment?

Step 3: Interpretation

Interpret the meaning of the light and dark as conflicted manifestations of family and relational patterns and cycles. How is this moment of clarity and questioning also an opportunity? What do they need to discuss and decide in order to move beyond the crossroads? What exchange of specific concessions might be a healthy one for the couple to engage in so that their relationship might move toward more light-oriented patterns?

More Detailed Questions That Might Help Your Analysis

Use some or all of the following questions as you carefully read through the story. You do not necessarily need to use all of the questions, but select a few that you think might help you get at the meaning of the crossroads moment.

Questions for the Description of the Light and Dark Aspects of the Conflict

- Early in the story, what positive qualities and experiences are associated with Jeff's grandmother, and how are these light qualities contrasted with his mother?
- How did Karisa represent the light side, and why did his grandmother switch from the light side to the dark side in her actions and motives?
- How is the dark side that the grandmother later manifested related to Jeff's mother's dark side? Are there parallels?
- Do you think that Jeff's seemingly polar experience of women as either very light or very dark gives you a clue to his relationship with, and representation of, Karisa?
- How is his up-and-down relationship with Karisa connected to his representation of his mother and grandmother?
- How do his broken promises, half truths, and preoccupation with his grandmother show his dark side and his attempt to show light qualities, and what impact do these have on his relationship to his wife?
- How are Jeff's problematic behaviors connected to deeper dysfunctions within the family? Where does he get these habits from?

Questions for the Reduction to the Forces of Light and Dark

- What are the specific qualities and characteristics that are depicted as being on the dark and light sides of the family relationships?
- How do the light and the dark specifically manifest in each of the characters as they move through the conflict? How does the dark side of one person symbolize or point to the light side of another, and how does the dark side of one also connect to the dark side of the others?
- How does this manifestation of both light and dark underlie the family patterns and cycles of how its members negotiate their conflicts?

Questions for the Interpretation of the Meaning of the Conflict

- How would you summarize, in a sentence or two, the fundamental relationship of light and dark in Jeff's family, particularly at this crossroads moment? Base your interpretation on a careful description and reduction of the story. I would summarize the conflict, for example, by saying that the family has a dysfunctional sense of what it means to be a close and responsible member of the family. I would also say that this dysfunctional balance makes the dark side of motives and actions manifest and continue across generations as controlling, deceptive, and overdemanding expectations, among other things. These behaviors then create feelings of hurt, anger, and unimportance for others. These feelings bring out the dark side of others and maintain relationships that seem out of time and out of balance, and so the patterns continue or change at this point in the story. To change would take an enormous amount of dialogic energy. You may come up with a different interpretation. If so, compare it to my quick summary to see how you arrived at your interpretation. Perhaps you see a certain symmetry in their asymmetrical patterns worth further discussion.
- How do you think that Jeff's choices still cause pain today, as he asserts at the end of his story? How do you think the pattern of darkness and light is continuing through their marriage as conflicts?

Additional Discussion Questions for
Your Personal Reflection on Light and Dark

- In your family, what are some of the issues of balance or imbalance between the forces of light and dark?

- How do the light and dark sides help to shape the kinds of conflicts that emerge and reemerge in your family?
- How do these struggles between light and dark shape you as a communicator and, in particular, your patterns of negotiation and conflict behavior?
- How would you like to renegotiate the balanced or imbalanced relationship of light and dark in your family if you could?

Besides expressing things such as the light and dark aspects of relationships, conflict can actually be crucial in the negotiation and renegotiation of important relational dynamics. These dynamics might include reaching agreements on important relational issues, such as how to live together, lifestyle, priorities, and values. Crossroads moments can be profound opportunities to really get to know the other person and discover the meaning of differences as things that can either enrich or challenge a relationship. We next discuss this creative role of crossroads conflict in moving an otherwise healthy relationship forward and deeper.

❖ UNDERSTANDING AND NEGOTIATING
     THE MEANING OF DIFFERENCES

One of the effects of falling in love is that it partially blinds us to the work that lies ahead if the relationship ends up being long term. Possibly this is nature's way of helping us to jump in and not worry too much about the consequences. People often say that relationships such as marriage are a lot of work, once the blinders start to come off. Most of us pride ourselves in doing a good job in our work lives. So it is logical to assume that we would naturally want to know how to do the work of intimate relationships well, for the sense of accomplishment and satisfaction that a successful relationship brings. Rarely, however, do we receive the training necessary to do this work, and as my students often tell me, effective role models are not always readily available to them. Most of us end up figuring it out as we go along. This process is often punctuated by conflicts of various magnitudes as couples are forced to confront the meaning of differences that emerge between them and make sense of those differences within a bigger picture of their commonalities. The crossroads experience offers an opportunity to explore such meanings and their implications as well as hopefully negotiate a mutually beneficial path beyond it (Booth, Crouter, & Clements, 2001; Harris, 1996; Scanzoni, 1979). As such, this might be termed a *sense-making turning point*, where a couple is trying to figure out what their differences really mean within the marriage context.

Figuring it out as you go is one of the things that can be both fun and challenging about relationships. This ongoing figuring out is also what tends to generate friction between couples, as they are often figuring out answers to fundamental questions, such as the following:

- How will we fuse ourselves and our ways of life to live together—what stays and what gets left behind as we develop shared traditions, goals, and values?
- What are our assumptions about communication—what will we and what will we not talk about, and how do we talk to each other?
- What are the issues that we hold dear, what priorities do we have, and how will we negotiate our similarities and differences on them?
- What are our mutual lines and borders of acceptability and unacceptability, and what space for negotiation or division do these lines create?
- What are the levels of trust, disclosure, independence, accountability, satisfaction, and so on that we have together?
- How will we balance the key couple conflict areas of power, intimacy and sex, and resources and money so that we negotiate our future together?

These are some of the important aspects that need to be negotiated in relationships. Conflicts emerge when there are oppositions on how these things get negotiated and particularly when oppositions start to mean that there are real differences between the couple. Often the most volatile conflicts in relationships can be traced to the fact that the symbolic meaning is at least as important, if not more so, than the tangible thing being fought over. How often have we fought about something that looks so trivial to an outsider but so crucial from within the context of the relationship?

As you read the story that follows, consider how the couple works out the symbols that will mean that they are progressing or not in their negotiation of the early stage of their marriage. There are key behaviors that are taken as clues by Kit and Jen—they symbolize their sense of where they are on these and other key relational dimensions. Identify the symbols that point to the health of their relationship *for them*. Recognize, also, that key behaviors may well represent different things for each of them, and it is often these symbolic differences that are at the root of a conflict. The second key question is to consider how the conflict itself represents—symbolizes—this couple's figuring out of these more specific and concrete relational dimensions. How well does the conflict work as a way of negotiating their differences? What does the tip of the iceberg seem to point to: a big impending crash or a small obstacle on their journey that they may easily sail around?

"Is Trigger the Tip of the Iceberg?" (Kit)

About 3 weeks ago, I had owned my new dream car—a 25-year-old Ford Bronco—for about a week when a conflict happened. The person I bought it from did not hide the fact that it leaked when it rained because the weather stripping on parts of the truck was old and worn out. So I knew it was a drawback going into the deal. It was about a week before it rained and I was able to see where, and how badly, it leaked. It just so happened that my wife was in the truck with me when it was raining and leaking through the seal between the removable top and frame. Even I admitted that seeing water dripping off the rearview mirror was a bit annoying. This is the dialogue at this moment as best as I can remember it:

"Where's the water coming from?" (an expected and not unreasonable reaction).

"Jay didn't replace the seal between the top and the frame after he took the top off last summer. And I haven't had time to get to it yet." (Why try to ignore it, honesty is supposed to work!)

"You knew it leaked and you paid all that money for it!" she said confidently and a little sarcastically.

"You have to expect glitches in a 25-year-old truck, and besides, it's not that hard to remedy. Don't you feel how much your cool factor has been raised just by being seen in a truck like this?" (I figured, try to be positive.)

"It just seems like a money trap" (my wife is always honest and direct).

"Aw, Trigger runs like a champ, he just leaks a little, which I can fix for about 10 bucks and an hour's worth of time."

She was quiet, and so was I until we got to where we were going. We didn't talk about it any more at that time.

This doesn't seem like a big conflict, but if it keeps bothering me, it may be bigger than it appears. There are certain times in my marriage that I remember some of the best advice I was given on my wedding day, surprisingly by boss and good friend. He said his uncle on his wedding day told him to pick his fights and not to fight for or about something unless it is important—whatever it may be. The key is to figure out what is important and what to let bounce off you. In this case, I figured that my wife talking junk about my car was her prerogative and that I know, no matter what she says, Trigger is a good truck. I told myself, "Just wait until she needs you to haul off yard waste, then she'll appreciate the practicality of my buying Trigger." This time I let it bounce off me, but my worry is, when will it be too much and I'll react defensively?

I thought back to my discussions with my wife about buying the truck, and she would always say it was *my* decision. What I really wanted to hear from her is that she either did or did not want me to buy the truck. As with almost every other couple in America, one of our main areas of conflict is money. She is much more logical and future oriented. I am much more in the moment and the present. I wouldn't say that my wife is a control freak, but she does not like to roll with the punches. She would rather be alert and in control enough to block them. My wife will be going for her PhD next semester and is extremely worried about money. To me, this is why she said the "money trap" thing. I feel like I gave her the chance to speak up and say whether or not she wanted me to buy the truck. I consistently asked her what she thought because I know she is much more logical and sensible than I am. I feel that now she is very nervous about my having bought Trigger. It seems like any time I mention anything about the truck, she mentions bills we have to pay.

It seems that my buying the truck is a financial thorn in her side, and she probably felt that if she told me she didn't want me to buy the truck that I would resent her.

We are both avoiding the conflict, which isn't very healthy. I just feel that even though I was able to blow it off this time, this same conflict will resurface and perhaps be worse on the next go-round. I don't know if the smart thing to do is play the waiting game or to bring it up and try and get it over with. I really wonder when the problem is money if it truly can be solved. To me, I got such an early model truck because I can do all the repairs on it, which will save money. To my wife, I feel like the first time something basic goes wrong with it, my wife will give me the old "I told you so." I hope I am over reacting but we have been married a year and a half and money is always what she worries about—whether it is me wasting money on nonessentials like beer or us eating out too much. Her reluctance to give her opinion on the Bronco even when openly invited is what worries me the most and is why I think this is just the tip of the iceberg of the conflict.

Analyzing and Working With Dialogues About Difference

Use as many of the following questions that can help you to explicate the quality of the negotiation of Kit and his wife. Your analysis should provide an interpretive account of the meaning of the tip of the iceberg and its relationship to their deeper relationship yet to be negotiated and developed. As part of your interpretation, explain whether you think the tip to the underwater iceberg is problematic or just natural. Are they floating along on it together or heading right for it? A clear picture from a third party is often an excellent starting point.

Organize your analysis around the following interpretive steps:

Step 1: Description
Describe the specific issues and behaviors that they are in conflict about over Trigger. What do the specific conflicts seem to be about on the surface and more generally in their evolving relationship?

Step 2: Reduction
The Trigger conflict illustrates certain important differences and oppositions in worldview, priorities, and personalities that are in

tension in their relationship. How have these tensions brought them to a crossroads moment? How do these tensions point to a need for more effective communication in their relationship?

Step 3: Interpretation

Interpret the meaning of the Trigger conflict as either a small issue (tip) that they can evolve beyond or a large issue (large hidden iceberg) that will sink them.

They have to decide on the meaning based on the depth of differences relative to their sense of synchronicity. What does the conflict suggest about where they go from here? How might they share concessions based on each other's differences that would help them to effectively negotiate the conflict and therefore their relationship? When my students discuss this story, they frequently say that Jen should be fine with Kit having Trigger as that makes him happy and allows her to negotiate something that is important to her. Do you agree?

Discussion Questions for Analyzing
"Is Trigger the Tip of the Iceberg?"

- What does the behavior of buying the truck represent or symbolize for Kit and for Jen? How are they similar or different on these meanings (e.g., living in the moment versus planning for the future), and how is that important to the conflict?
- What might "the coolness factor," "money trap," "leaking seals," "eating out," and "a thorn in the side" represent or symbolize in their relationship?
- What do the wedding advice and Kit's uneasiness about the true size of the conflict (tip or iceberg) represent in terms of what they are working on relationally? Is his concern a healthy or unhealthy clue?
- What does this silent game playing ("Just wait until . . .," "I will be able to say "I told you so," etc.) tell you about the key issues and possible differences in their relationship and how well they are negotiating those differences?
- How do you think this conflict represents their habits and differences in how to communicate about conflicts?
- How effective do they seem to be at negotiating important relational dimensions and differences?
- Develop some good discussion questions and issues for them to think about to help them to have conflicts in the future that use effective communication about and negotiation of differences.

Having explored the various interconnections of the symbolic and tangible aspect of conflicts, with myths arising from synchronicity, we move on to some discussion and reflection exercises that connect these concepts to your own experience in your own fields of practice and in your everyday lives.

❖ LESSONS FROM THE FIELD OF PRACTICE: WORKING FROM CROSSROADS MOMENTS TO WHERE YOU WANT TO GO

Exercise 1: Negotiating Crossroads Moments—Personal Reflection

Recall a crossroads moment in a close relationship that you and the other person or people negotiated through effectively. If you cannot recall one that resulted in an agreement that you were both or all happy with, recollect one in which there was no resolution or in which only one party was happy with the result. Reconstruct as many of the details as you can about your thoughts, actions, and communication in that conflict episode. Also recollect as much about the other person or people as you can in terms of their actions and communication.

- What are the factors that brought you to a crossroads moment with that person or those people?
- What were your common goals, interest, and motives in the crossroads moment?
- What concessions did you both show willingness to exchange?
- How did you consider and work with the goals and interests of the other person or people?
- What was the final agreement that you came to, and how was effective communication and your willingness to negotiate central to the quality of that final agreement?

Exercise 2: Negotiating "Miller Time"

The following poem is a lighthearted look at the conflict of a young couple who are cohabitating. To give you some background, the boyfriend, Tim, bought his girlfriend, Rachel, a Jack Russell terrier puppy for Christmas: Miller. Their relationship as a couple is healthy and loving. They also both love the dog, and when Miller behaves well, there are not really any problems. However, when Miller is chewing things and tearing things up, it causes conflicts between Tim and Rachel. They do not see eye to eye on how the dog should be disciplined and punished. Tim gets angry when the dog misbehaves and sometimes takes it out on Rachel by blaming her. Sometimes the conflicts carry over into other aspects of their relationship. Rachel acknowledges that Miller has brought additional happiness into their relationship, but she and Tim struggle to find the right balance of patience and discipline on which they can agree. They both want to avoid the dangers of letting the dog issue separate them in frustration. Read the poem carefully, and then discuss the questions that follow, as a way to figuring how you might help them to negotiate this relatively small but important relational conflict.

Miller Time *(Rachel)*
On Christmas morning a big surprise
I held out my hands and closed my eyes
I didn't know just what it could be
I opened my eyes to see the cutest puppy
White with little spots and squinty dark eyes
This little dog was the best Christmas surprise
Who would have known that this gift, so sentimental
Would turn our apartment upside down into drama central
We thought to call her Miller and she would be the best dog
Slowly but surely I found Tim would not think this for long
First she didn't know when she was in or out
So she'd just use the bathroom whenever the feeling came about
Then she started chewing things, of his mostly, not mine
Tim would yell, "No mam, this is not yours its mine!"
She never really listened to him but for me should would do just right
Whenever she would pee or poop it was sure to start a fight
Tim says that I don't punish her and she's never going to learn
Every time she does something wrong he thinks I am not concerned
I wanted her to listen so to doggy school we went
She learned new tricks and I really felt this was money well spent
But she still jumps and bites and chews and daddy spanks her behind
But then at night she cuddles up tight, and it's daddy and Miller time

Discussion Questions

- What factors do you think are limiting Rachel and Tim's ability to negotiate this conflict, given that their relationship seems very happy and healthy?
- Could their conflict about the dog have broader implications or meaning in their relationship, such as being a metaphor for how they might differ on child-rearing perspectives?

- Why is it important for them to negotiate this conflict effectively? What other areas of their everyday life might this carry over into?
- What are their common goals and perspectives, what are their significant differences and misunderstandings, and how might they negotiate more effectively if they talked about these commonalities and differences?
- What concessions might be most effective for each of them to trade that might move this conflict forward?
- What might they do that would make their conflict worse than it is now?
- How does their story remind you of similar crossroads moments in your life and how you negotiated your way through them?

❖ CONCLUSION

There are many moments in all types of relationships when things come to a standstill or when issues come up to the surface and force the people in those relationships to confront where they really stand and what that means for their relationship. Sometimes the crossroads moment means that the people part directions and take different paths. Sometimes they have been on different paths and finally recognize the need to be moving in the same direction. In either case, the quality of negotiation—how they negotiate to maximize the desired outcomes for each partner—is crucial in predicting which direction they move toward beyond the crossroads moment. This chapter has challenged us to consider the choices we make that lead us up to and through difficult or big conflicts. Of course, we cannot always decide how life goes because we cannot always collaborate with the other person in the conflict, but if we approach a crossroads moment with a spirit of dialogue and negotiation skills to match, then the chances are good that desired outcomes will follow.

Part III

Stories and the Psychodynamics of Conflict

6

What Is This Really About?

Working With Displacement
in Conflict Communication

❖ ❖ ❖

The kernel of all jealousy is lack of love.

—Carl Jung (as quoted in Main, 1997)

Much of what we assume about achieving collaborative negotiation within a rational framework of conflict management has to do with people arguing or dialoging about the *actual issue* that divides them. To negotiate a resolution to a conflict presupposes that the to-and-fro exchange of communication is focused on an actual, tangible issue on which the participants disagree (e.g., Fisher & Ury, 1981). In the everyday reality of conflict, however, this is not always how people behave. Communication often has less to do with participants following rational techniques of resolving specific and clear disputes or incompatibilities and more to do with creating a conflict that is tangential or only symbolically related to the divisive issues. It is often the meanings in and behind a conflict that divide people more than the tangibles that are closer to the surface—the issue of love behind the jealousy, for example. The result is that people often argue about one thing, and it is really about something else that they may not be aware of. The results displaced and shadowy conflicts can cause lasting damage to relationships (e.g., Spitzberg & Cupach, 1998), and yet it may be possible to improve negotiations by understanding displacement as a common habit of conflict communication and learning to negotiate on both levels of surface and displaced meanings.

For example, imagine what it would be like to be involved in the following true story. Recognize that the couple may not have jealousy issues, but think about how this conflict illustrates Jung's idea that many surface conflicts may be displaced manifestations of deeper issues of the meaning and day-to-day expression of love in our relationships. In this story, a newlywed couple find themselves arguing about where the milk should be positioned in the fridge. They know it is a relatively unimportant dispute in terms of the tangible aspects of the conflict, and yet they find themselves digging in against each other on the issue. If we look a little more closely, we find that the conflict means different things to the two participants, based on their historical association with milk placement. When we delve deeper, we find that for the husband, the top-shelf placement of the milk symbolizes the point in his life when his family regarded him as a grown-up young man who was able to reach the top shelf. For the wife, her family traditions hold that the milk should be placed inside the door. The participants in this typical newlywed conflict are ostensibly arguing about the same thing in terms of tangibles; however, the energy of the dispute indicates that it is a *symbolic displacement* of their differences in long-held assumptions about where things should go in the house and what that placement means to them personally as "being grown up" versus "maintaining tradition." In this way, people often create elaborate and often unconscious symbolic barriers to addressing the more systemic issue generating conflict between them—in this case, their differing assumptions about organizing the home. In many conflicts, that deeper issue is often much more emotionally charged, which makes it all the more difficult to handle.

"Just have two milk cartons," might be your suggestion. This compromise might be fine for this particular case, but because the conflict is connected to a broader historical meaning for both of them, the conflict might get further displaced and pop up somewhere else. "Just talk about what's really going on," might be another suggestion you would have. So many times, people will not or cannot do this because they have not thought about the relationship of the surface conflict to its deeper meaning or they do not know how to have such a conversation. It's useful to negotiate this conflict from the context of its meaning at this point in their marriage, and it's very useful to know *how* to do that.

This curiously pervasive habit of creating conflicts that are meaningfully and even unconsciously connected to the actual basis of the conflict, yet not necessarily the conflict itself, is the topic of this chapter explicating the phenomenon of symbolic displacement. Again: Symbolic displacement occurs (1) when people engage in one conflict through, or in place of, another symbolically related one or (2) when a participant's behavior is an expression of displaced or unconscious meaning of which either or both may be unaware.

The trick to managing displaced conflicts effectively is to figure out how the surface conflict points to a more fundamental but less tangible one and to address that deeper issue. This can be a complex challenge, especially considering that the various participants may be operating on different deeper meanings or be unaware of or unwilling to address the deeper conflict. Ignoring this interpretive challenge can be the basis of creating misunderstandings that can escalate a conflict; addressing it can improve conflict communication based on negotiating from the various levels of meaning.

The main foci for this chapter have to do with why people engage in symbolic displacement in conflict, the symbolic processes at work, the meaningful relationships between the symbolic and the displaced conflicts and what the displacement symbolizes, how explicating the process of symbolic displacement can help us deepen our understanding of the norms of how people manage conflict in their everyday lives, and how a deeper understanding of displacement processes can help us be more effective in communicating about conflict.

Main topics and learning goals in this chapter:

- Symbolic displacement and the meaning of conflict
- Dangers and opportunities of displacement and conflict dynamics
- Forms and functions of symbolic displacement in conflict
- Symbolic displacement as a more or less conscious stratagem
- Symbolic displacement as conflicted desire
- Lessons from the field of practice

❖ SYMBOLIC DISPLACEMENT AND
   THE MEANING OF CONFLICT

Conflict can be displaced or misdirected when the participants are working on different assumptions of what the conflict is about (Cupach & Canary, 1997, p. 15) or when the target of conflict energy needs to be changed from the actual source to a more publicly acceptable or weaker target (Folger et al., 2005). It can come about through inaccurate perception, misattribution, lack of coordinated meaning, or selfish strategy, and the conflict is displaced, or *misplaced* or *misdirected*, from the issue of dispute or the other person in the conflict. One classic example of the dangers of displacement is in scapegoating (Gemmill, 1990). Building on this insight, we should recognize the importance of coordination in the meaning of a conflict for the participants. Sometimes a displaced conflict offers the participants a way of engaging in a strategic avoidance of the real conflict or the source of the conflict, which they may feel a need to do for various reasons. Conflicts become complex and often dysfunctional when the participants are not expressing the systemic or real conflict or not in conflict about the same issue as the other. Displacement can have a profound effect on the goals, demands, and concessions that make up the talk of the conflict. At the same time, the process of displacement is itself an important part of understanding conflict energy and negotiation behavior. There is something about how and why displacement occurs that is not so much about mistaken assumptions and attributions or rational strategy but, rather, it is a clue to the symbolic nature of the ways people create and maintain conflict as they do. *Displacement is different from misplacement.*

The process of displacement has been partially explored in the field of conflict or dispute resolution (e.g., Coser, 1956; Smith & Berg, 1987). Symbolic displacement as a concept also has a rich tradition of being explored within psychiatric and psychotherapeutic contexts (Abramsky, 1996; Clarke, 1998; Schmukler & Garcia, 1990). Such displacement is seen as an interpretive clue to the *deeper meaning* of behaviors such as phobias and stress disorders or displacements of psychosexual concerns. Most of us can accept the valuable notion of displacement as an interpretive clue, but I also want to stress that symbolic displacement is a habit of many forms of conflict behavior not necessarily of a clinical nature: *Symbolic displacement is a normal part of how people express, manage, or avoid everyday conflicts.* There are valuable clues to how people manage conflict to be found in exploring the symbolic activity of displacement. A discussion follows of how to analyze conflict stories for evidence of symbolic displacement; then we explore how to build effective negotiations on this understanding.

Analyzing Conflict Narratives for Symbolic Displacement

In the next sections, I first discuss the concepts as they apply to the main interpretive steps as they apply to analyzing and understanding displacement in conflict. Next, using the simple example mentioned in the beginning of this chapter, I illustrate the process. Then you get to search much deeper into each of the subsequent stories presented in the chapter.

Key to the Meaning of Displaced Conflict

As usual, there are three phases in how to interpret the milk story. First, we begin by describing the conflict and what it seems to be about on the surface. Then, the second step involves looking for the clues in the story that point to displaced meanings. The third step is to figure out how the relationship between the displaced and more surface conflicts might help the people in the conflict to negotiate more effectively.

Step 1: Description of the Conflict

It is important to begin analysis with a careful description of the communication and the basis of the dispute that drives that communication. The key analytic questions and tasks for completing Step 1 are as follows:

- What is happening in talk and action that shows you there is a conflict between these people about something specific and tangible?
- Describe everything in the talk and action that shows there is a dispute here. Identify specific words and phrases as well as any nonverbal clues.
- What specific tangible and current behavior is the conflict about?
- What are the things that are dividing these people and keeping them divided on this issue?
- Does the issue match with the talk and action? Does the conflict seem to be only about what's being discussed?

Step 2: Reduction to the Relationship of the Dispute to Displaced Conflict

The clues to help you figure out the displaced conflict lie in the relationship between the surface dispute and deeper meaning. Reducing the conflict to its essence means examining the communication described in Step 1 with the following key analytic questions:

- Are there clues and hints that the issues identified in Step 1 point to something deeper going on between the people?
- What details in the story point to something beyond the tangible, manifest dispute?

- How do the details of the story hint and point, veil and unveil, reveal and shadow at the same time?
- Are there clues in the energy level and level of competitiveness that indicate that some deeper meaning is involved? How do the clues bridge the manifest, expressed present issue and the shadowed absent one? How do those clues express something deeper? You may find that the story contains dramatic hints and portents to something beyond the present. For example, there seems to be too much energy for the issue at hand—there is an energy-significance imbalance; there must be more going on than appears; something doesn't add up; the narrator is actively disguising another meaning; the narrator is showing you almost directly that there's another issue; there appears to be a vested connection to an older pattern or cycle—something is working as a generative substructure, a symbolic or parallel expression of the dispute.
- What additional questions arise for you that suggest a deeper, more symbolic interpretation is reasonable?

The key issue to remember here is that communication and action work at *both* a local *and* a deeper symbolic level. The analogue (both-and) nature of communication allows the meaning to function simultaneously on two symbolically connected levels.

Step 3: Interpretation of the Meaning and Implications of the Conflict

The meaning of the conflict can be discovered through careful reflection on the relationship between the surface communication and the symbolic clues discovered in the reduction. It may be that the best you can uncover are possible meanings, if they are still hidden even after careful analysis. You may find yourself guessing at them. When working with examples from your own experience, if possible, go back to the participants in the conflict and ask them if your analysis makes sense. If you cannot do that, at least be guarded in your assumptions about what is true. People often create labyrinths of displaced meanings that are hidden beneath and beyond what you see.

The key analytic questions and tasks for completing this step are as follows:

- In looking at the relationship of what you discovered in Steps 1 and 2, what do you interpret to be the deeper, more enduring dispute or division that makes this conflict make sense as a meaningful whole?

- Why are deeper issue(s) displaced and not addressed by the participants?
- How do these deeper issues structure the surface of the conflict?
- As an exercise in critical reflection, consider what specific insights the participants could learn from your analysis that might help them communicate more effectively about their conflict.
- What are the conversations that the milk-divided couple ought to be having but are not?
- What specific things could they do to negotiate their relationship development more effectively in terms of understanding the demands of the other, making meaningful concessions, talking about the meaning of their demands, and determining how they might better coordinate such exchanges as they negotiate?

The Illustration

Step 1: Description of the Conflict

The couple is arguing about where the milk should go in the fridge. They each have arguments as to why their perspective is correct and the other one is wrong. There is sabotage of the others' actions: The milk gets moved when the other one is not around. The issue flares up and is obviously annoying to both of them. They snap at each other occasionally when they are tired. There is some angry talk, but mostly the talk focuses on how unreasonable the other is being and how silly the conflict might look to other people if they knew. (Note that we would include specific words, phrases, and repeated arguments here, if we had access to that.)

The couple cannot agree on where the milk should be placed in the fridge. They have different assumptions about where milk should go *and* why it shouldn't go where the other person thinks it should. Hence, there is a dispute important enough that it is structuring their communication as a conflict.

Step 2: Connecting the Surface to the Displaced Conflict

The fact that the couple are locked into an oppositional stance on the simple issue of milk placements hints that it is about something more, or something different, than the specific issue. The conflict contains hints about family tradition for her and about being treated as a grown-up or as a child for him. These comments may be displaced onto other examples, such as how she talks to him like a child in other contexts and how he talks about or relates to her family in other contexts.

The conflict could be a turning-point issue in their relational develop-ment as a married couple. It seems to be significant as an issue and also as some sort of minor power struggle. Fortunately, they resist taking a quick compromise as a solution to this particular conflict. Also, they look back on it a year later and laugh about the silliness of it.

Step 3: Understanding the Conflict Meaning and Implications
     The milk conflict is a displacement of a deeper, but not relationally threatening, conflict—a clash of personal and historical associations with milk placement. This deeper conflict is not necessarily debilitating or bad. Rather it seems to be part of the couple's ongoing negotiation to create a shared set of home organizational practices that integrate respect both of their interests and needs. The seemingly silly conflict probably emerges because they are not consciously communicating about that deeper nego-tiation process effectively enough. What follows is a description of how analyzing displaced meaning in conflicts follows the process of how people actually create displaced meaning. This is a key to research that actually gets into the lived meaning of the experience for the participants.

❖   DANGERS AND OPPORTUNITIES OF
     DISPLACEMENT AND CONFLICT DYNAMICS

The following list represents some of the important dangers and opportunities associated with working with displacement issues.

- *Increased volatility and sensitive hot buttons*

Meaningfulness makes a conflict volatile, but when a conflict is dis-placed, then that volatile energy is expressed in connection with a related issue. *Hot buttons* may form and heat up when the parties develop a *hypersensitive shortcut* between the manifest and deeper meaning of the conflict ("You make me feel like a powerless child again"—"You make me feel that my family traditions don't matter"). Hot buttons are clues to displaced energy that point to the presence of a displaced conflict.

- *More competitiveness and defensiveness*

The more something means personally to someone, the more energy gets channeled into competing for and defending the chosen position on that issue. If the deeper conflict is meaningful but not addressed, then competitiveness and defensiveness about the surface issue may increase because it represents the deeper issue symbolically.

The person may not even know why he or she is getting competitive and defensive and why negotiations break down.

- *Ongoing cycles of dysfunction and avoidance*

When the energy associated with the deeper meaning of a conflict gets displaced, it is likely to come out somewhere else. People may find themselves aggressively in conflict about seemingly trivial or inane issues—like where the milk goes in the fridge. This energy is a clue that displacement is occurring. Typically, if a displaced conflict gets further displaced, then the distance of the surface conflict gets farther and farther (more symbolic) from the original root conflict. The reasons for a conflict may become more and more shadowy, more and more displaced from the deeper issue that may need to be addressed. This is how conflicts can get stranger and stranger, dealing with displacements of displacements, and so on. It may be that in some cases, the relationship between the surface and deeper conflicts remains inaccessible. Layers of meaning can build up through repeated avoidance and displacements into other areas of relationships. Knowing that there might be a deeper structure may provide some opportunities for opening up dialogue, but if the deeper meaning is obscure, be careful not to fill in the last step of interpretation with further displacements.

The main opportunities are as follows:

- *Getting to the real conflict*

Instead of fighting about milk, sabotaging each other, and spreading the conflict to other aspects of the relationship, if you are able to examine the displacement in the conflict, you may also be able to address and negotiate the deeper conflict that is at the heart of the division. Also, you will be much less likely to redirect the emotional energy and possibly anger at a target other than their source—thereby avoiding a series of additional conflicts.

- *Becoming better at reading the clues, signs, and symbols*

Reading signs and clues effectively takes practice. A good place to start is in taking the time to carefully describe the communication in a conflict and learning to discern what those details tell you. It is as important to know when not to overanalyze things as it is to not overlook the clues that are there. Sometime it really is just about the milk jug! Sometimes it is about a lot more. As a participant in your own conflicts, you can get better at reading the clues and signs to deeper symbolizations that are pertinent and personal.

- *Empowerment through the use of symbols*

Displacement may give you an acceptable level of safe distance from the deeper issue, and this may actually be valuable in keeping negotiations flowing. Deeper issues may be too volatile, too dangerous to the relationship, too interconnected with power issues, and so on. Working through the displaced issue may get you to the same end point: mutual respect for each other's perspectives and relative differences. Using something like the milk dispute as a parallel or symbolic way to tell another that you have a more substantial conflict, or as a safe way into or around a deeper conflict without opening it up fully, is a symbol-using skill that can be very useful in keeping negotiations reasonable and civil.

- *Seeing ruptures as opportunities*

It is very interesting to me that the thing that seems most tangible in a conflict—what people are fighting about here and now—is often the most richly symbolic. Looking at it through the symbolic-tangible relationship, the tangible issue in the here and now is the *rupture point* through which the broader or deeper issue is accessible or over which the symbolic issue is most deeply and actively covered with the layers of meaning: The thing that is fought over most protectively may be the place where the displaced conflict is the most deeply buried. Often, the most fought-over tangible is thus most closely connected to the main problem being symbolically displaced. This most tangible issue may also be both the biggest clue and the biggest diversion from the deeper meaning of the conflict. This may be the best place to dig. As you learn to delve effectively, you will become more sensitive in everyday life to the "white space" between the lines—the things not expressed that are pointed to between those things that are expressed.

❖ FORMS AND FUNCTIONS OF SYMBOLIC DISPLACEMENT IN CONFLICT

Many types of displacement have been explored, particularly in the psychotherapeutic context referred to earlier. Three main functions or types of displacement have a particular bearing on more everyday forms of conflict communication, ways that displacement serves a specific—sometimes strategic—purpose in how people manage and negotiate conflicts. Describing the functions allows us to get at some of the typical meanings of displacement in everyday life conflicts.

The Unspeakable and the Unutterable: Symbolic Displacement as an Expression of Unconscious or Dangerous Conflict

The following narrative excerpt illustrates how conflict surrounding a family secret often gets displaced into a symbolically related though distanced set of conflicts. As you read the story, look in particular for how the conflicts surrounding rule enforcement are a displacement of family conflict surrounding rule breaking. Look closely at the curious reversal of rule breaking and rule enforcement whereby the father turns the children into the rule breakers and necessitates his overactive enforcement. Look for the dynamics in the story whereby the related conflicts surrounding the children's rule breaking make sense as a displacement of the father's guilt only when they realize the connection between the original and the displaced conflicts *as a symbolic relationship*.

Look carefully also at the possibility of the father displacing his own frustrations over not having the family he wanted into the over-dominant rule enforcement. How is this displacing the sense of loss onto his children's behavior? Or perhaps he's saying, "If only you'd follow the rules, I would have followed them, also." Think about how his children have to show their worth through labor as a way of displacing his own penance. It also cuts off their ability to ask questions— perhaps *the* question that he fears being asked. Perhaps his cutting off of any questioning of his authority blocks the possibility that he will be judged by his children. Think about how his fear gets displaced into authoritarianism and monologue. How does his guilt get displaced into not asking for help effectively, and how does this create communication problems? These are just initial ideas to guide your reading. Note any other clues to displacement that you notice along the way.

"A Father and Son" (MB)

My parents have been together for 25 years. They dated through the majority of high school and got married shortly after graduating. I was their first bundle of joy, and my sister followed 3 years after. We grew up with our parents being present and active in our lives and have always been there for us. However, our father has always been someone with a temper and easy to catch a very quick attitude. He always wanted things done when and how he wanted them. If they weren't, the attitude level would increase, and you might get scolded, slapped, or spanked. If the bed wasn't made before going to school, you got a spanking. If the trash wasn't taken out before he got home from work, you got scolded. He felt that we were always there to do whatever needed to be done, and when it wasn't done at his discretion, then you faced the consequences. At times, we would spend hours doing lawn work or cleaning house without anyone's assistance or supervision.

I can remember one incident, when I was very young, in which he came home and was very upset about something. I asked him a question and he cursed at me. I fled to my room and cried because there was nothing else I could do. We weren't allowed to voice our opinions about anything. We were supposed to take the blows and keep on moving. My sister and I always felt like we were mistreated. Sometimes we dreaded to go home in fear that he would be there to enforce something.

Even when he asked my mother to do something, she would get upset because of the way he asked her. He tends to yell when he asks for favors from his family. We don't understand why there is a need to holler and get upset when he asks us to do something for him. Its not that we don't want to assist him; it's the fact that he chews us out in the process of asking. . . . I try hard to alleviate the hollering and bickering between us, and in the process I start something new.

When my sister started high school, she must have decided that she wouldn't take any more of the negative treatment. While she was young, she just took the verbal abuse that he spit out at her. When she got to high school, she began to take up for herself until one day she couldn't take it anymore. He came into her room and demanded that she clean it up. Out of nowhere, she turns around and punches him in the eye with her fist. She couldn't believe it, he couldn't believe it, and my mother couldn't believe it. The punch started a whole new array of conflicts and caused a lot of negative silence and tension throughout the family.

A couple of years later, my father's past takes a visit to the present and informs us of what's been going on all along. My sister worked at a retail store in the mall. On her way to work one day, she is approached by a girl who appears to be younger than her. The girl approached her with the shocking news that our father was also her father. My sister was amazed by what was said and confronted my mother with the information. My mother confirmed that it was true. My sister was furious about the situation and my mother was afraid. She did know that my sister would try to contact me with the news; therefore, my mother called me before my sister could. She told me about the incident and her reasons for staying with my father and asked me if I wanted to talk with him. I agreed to, and she put him on the phone; however, when he started talking, I didn't want to hear any explanations. I told him that we would talk about it later—unfortunately we haven't.

The Meaning of Displacement and the Unconscious Conflict

Complete the interpretive steps illustrated earlier. Some clues are provided to guide you, but you need to develop the analytic skills of working with often hidden meanings. A good question to get you started might be, "If you could find out one thing that would help reveal the meaning of the conflict, what would that piece of the puzzle be?"

Step 1: Description of the Conflicted Relationship

- What is happening in talk and action that shows you there is a conflict between these people about something specific and tangible?

- Describe everything in the talk and action that means there is a dispute here, especially about asking for help. Identify specific words and phrases as well as any nonverbal clues that signify that there is a conflict. How do these people talk to each other, and why do they follow those patterns?
- What particular issue or tangible and current behavior is the conflict about? Look for what everyday issue is triggering their conflict.
- What are the things that are dividing these people and keeping them divided?
- Does the issue match with the talk and action? Does the conflict seem to be about what's being discussed? If yes, then work with that issue or behavior.

Step 2: Reduction to the Relationship of Surface Conflict to Deeper Issues

- Are there clues and hints that the issues identified in the description point to something deeper?
- What details in the story point to something beyond the manifest dispute?
- How do you think discipline and punishment patterns in the family are clues? Consider the father's insistence on the perfection of others; the relationship between actions and consequences for his children; his style of enforcement of rules; the relationship between asking and shouting; and the pattern of moving between the stages of silence, build up of tension, and violence. These are all clues that a deeper conflict besides the one surrounding his style of asking for help is at work here.

Step 3: Interpretation of the Meaning of the Displaced Conflict

- In looking at the relationship of the surface to deeper meaning, what do you interpret to be the deeper, more enduring dispute or division that makes this conflict make sense as a meaningful whole?
- What are the implications for understanding the relationship that these people have negotiated with each other, and what they might consider in terms of what it would take and how they might renegotiate their relationships?

To discover the deeper meaning, look closely at the relationship between the father's secret sin and the children's public punishment; between his authoritarian style, his secret sin, and their inability to challenge or question him; and between his imperfection and his treatment of them when they are imperfect in his eyes. Much of the family culture revolves around preventing his secret from becoming public. Herein lies the deeper set of displaced issues that fuels their smaller and more everyday conflicts.

Consider the following additional questions as you explore the meaning of this family conflict:

- Why are deeper issues displaced and not addressed by the participants? Consider the real difficulty of exploring this secret as a family. Consider how it seems understandable how this conflicted family culture developed, now that you know the meaning of the deeper conflict surrounding his secret. Consider how family secrets affect your family.
- How do these deeper, more enduring issues structure the surface of the conflict? Consider how the small, everyday fights that pop up make sense given the meaning of the deeper conflict.
- How does reflecting on the meaning of the conflict help you understand how this these people are expressing and managing conflict through communication?
- In what ways is their approach effective or ineffective? Why or why not? Consider how fragile the father's hold on the family is and how so much energy is poured into covering the secret. Consider how effective the covering strategies are and what the cost to the family may be. Consider how you would act if you were the father or MB in the story and how your interpretations as that person also help form and shape the meaning of the story.

Guidelines for Improving Communication
About the Unconscious and Displacement

Here are some guidelines for improving communication about unconscious or unutterable issues:

- Recognize that surface conflicts in your family or other relationships are often about something that cannot be talked about. Recognize also that it probably cannot be talked about for good reasons to those in the conflict. There may be pain associated with the deeper truth or background context. There may also be a lot of work that has been done to cover over and create distance from it.
- Recognize that not every surface conflict has a deeper displaced meaning—there is not always a dark shadow beneath every

story. This recognition can release you from the fear associated with raising a small conflict into talk because it might open up a Pandora's box of related issues. It may not.

- Understand the deeper meaning of the conflict by stepping back and analyzing the surface and deeper structure, but also understand that your interpretation might be deeply personal. If you are involved in the conflict, this can impact your interpretations substantially.

- Work to improve the deeper-level talk where you think it will improve the health and well-being of the family, but recognize that it is being displaced for a reason. People may resist your communication, and you may release conflicted energy that has built up around the deeper issue. The art of conflict management involves considering carefully what is ideal and realistic, constructive and destructive, and what will give you or your family the best return for your efforts.

❖ SYMBOLIC DISPLACEMENT AS A MORE OR LESS CONSCIOUS STRATAGEM

Besides displacement being the result of mistaken assumptions or unconscious issues, it can be a strategic, conscious choice that makes sense within the broader context of a relationship. Rather than addressing the basis of a dispute, participants may choose to displace the conflict into other related, but often quite tangential, disputes. These choices indicate a negotiation *stratagem*—the combination of *strategies* and *tactics*—that displaces the conflict and allows the participants to avoid dialogue or negotiation of the root issues in their conflict.

The following narrative excerpt illustrates an archetypal breakdown of relationships within a friend-roommate context and the ways that the deeper conflict is lived out, maintained, and even escalated through strategic displacement. As you read the story, look for ways that this conflict walks a line of ambiguity between engagement and avoidance. Also consider how the strategy of passive-aggressiveness is achieved through the tactics of the spiteful games that they play. Think about how the participants displace the deeper conflict into a series of smaller, more immediately dramatic and episodic conflicts. As you study the story, consider what deeper displaced messages these games are communicating between these roommates as they *unite* together in their *division*. Consider also the simple things they might have done to more effectively negotiate their space and lifestyle.

"Break the Door Down" (Jeannie)

Excitement overwhelmed us as we moved into our apartment. All four of us were anticipating nothing but the best when we arrived together that August. Life was great for Christy and me. We were living on our own in a new city, new apartment, with new roommates, at a new school, and we were oblivious to the fact that this perfect living arrangement would not be perfect for long.

Jennifer and Kathy began aggravating us near the middle of November, and we had the same affect on them. Before long, the rivalry became too much for everyone to handle. Christy and I would mix their sauces together (example: Texas Pete and chocolate syrup); they would leave us nasty notes all over the apartment and hide our best food from us if they did not go ahead and eat it first. Christy and I were usually better at playing these little games. One day, I rewired their ugly Christmas tree so it would no longer light up and spin around while Christy stood guard at the door. The winning had to come to an end at some point, and that day finally arrived.

Maintenance had put a chain lock on our door shortly after we moved in because someone had attempted to break in. I arrived back at the apartment with my boyfriend, after being gone for the weekend, at around 11:30 pm. Unfortunately, the chain lock was on the door, and the roommates pretended to be asleep and not hear me banging on the door to come open it. My hands were full with luggage, and I could not find my phone to call one of the roommates to open the door. It was cold outside, and I was tired and ready to get to bed.

I became so upset my body was trembling, and I yelled at Jim to break the door down, and he did just that. The molding broke off all the way around the door, but it still closed tightly. Neither of the roommates came out to check on the commotion.

Suddenly I hear a man knocking at my door and saying for me to open it. The man was quite persistent, so I asked who it was. "Officer somebody," he replied. When he came in, I told him my account of the event and he was thoroughly pissed because when the roommates called, they said it was a peeping Tom.

Luckily, the apartment manager sided with me, in that the roommates knew I was back in town that night. The manager informed them that they would be responsible for anything like this in [the] future. Neither of the roommates said a word to me concerning this situation. The rest of our time lived in that apartment was definitely a struggle and quite vindictive on a daily basis. Christy and I prayed for the day when our lease would run out, and we have not had any contact with them since they moved out.

The Meaning of Displacement as a More or Less Conscious Strategy

Use the three interpretive steps and related questions to analyze the conflict. Again, I provide some clues to guide you, but you need to develop the analytic skills of working with often hidden meanings. Again, begin with the following question to get you started: "If you could find out one thing that would help reveal the meaning of the conflict, what would that piece of the puzzle be?"

Step 1: Description of the Surface Conflict

- What is happening in talk and action that shows you there is a conflict between these people about something specific and tangible? Describe everything in the talk and action that means there is a dispute here. Identify specific words and phrases as well as any non-verbal clues that signify there is a conflict. For example, one pair putting the chain lock on the door from inside and pretending to be asleep and one of the other roommates having the door broken down as a way of handling their passive-aggressive actions are among the behaviors that signify a conflict manifesting as the door incident.

- What specific issue or tangible and current behavior is the specific conflict about? Consider, for example, how the door incident seems to be about being inconsiderate and sabotaging each other as roommates.

- What are the things dividing these people and keeping them divided? Does the issue match with the talk and action? Does the conflict seem to be about what's being discussed? If yes, then work with that specific issue or behavior. Consider, for example, how the conflict is about the door incident. Being thoughtless and inconsiderate as roommates seems to connect to a deeper set of relational themes for these people. It is about being thoughtless and inconsiderate, but it seems to be about a lot more than the door or thoughtlessness and inconsiderateness. These roommates are saying something more profound about their relationships with each other. Next, examine the clues as to what this deeper message might be.

Step 2: Reduction to the Strategy of the Displacement

- Are there clues and hints that the issues you have identified point to something deeper going on between the people?

- What details in the story point to something beyond the surface dispute? Consider how the door incident seems to be connected to ongoing themes of rivalry, aggravation, spiteful sabotage of food and personal belongings, nasty notes that stand in place of communication, and all-around *spiteful games*. These themes are clues that more is going on here. The fact that a simple locking-out incident generated so much hateful energy is a real clue that the trouble is about much more than the door. The "closed door" is a specific incident that serves as a displacement of all the underlying and only partially communicated dislike between these people. Perhaps the door—often an image of open communication—is metaphoric of their relationship, also. They are closing each other off and locking each other out. What do you think?

Consider, also, the ambiguity of the conflict as a clue. It is about the door *and* the deeper issue of disliking each other and changing the relationship to one of spiteful but unspoken meanness. They know it is about both, but they seem to choose to avoid the deeper issue by staying in the cycle of revenge, passive-aggressiveness, competitiveness, and avoidance around surface and petty conflicts. The everyday conflict of their relationship is maintained, and yet the basis of the conflict is not stated; perhaps it is too incendiary and escalatory. The passive-aggressive tactics point to a deeper conflict and yet strategically this keeps the energy focused on the negative and competitive sabotage they seem to thrive on.

Notice how these little conflicts are energizing for them—even fun—as they seek revenge and fuel the deeper message of dislike. Consider how their strategy—perhaps only partially conscious—is to maintain the conditions that generate the surface conflicts. This constant conflict perpetuates the affirmation for each pair of the feeling of rightness and maintains the thrill of revenge as they attack the enemy. These are all clues that it is much more than a surface dispute about locking the door.

Step 3: Interpretation of the Strategic Displacement in the Context of Their Relationship

- In looking at the relationship of what you discovered in the foregoing two steps, what do you interpret to be the deeper, more enduring dispute or division that makes this conflict make sense as a meaningful whole?
- Why are deeper issues displaced and not addressed by the participants?
- How do these deeper, more enduring issues structure the surface of the conflict?
- How does reflecting on this meaning of the conflict help you understand how these people are expressing and managing conflict through communication? In what ways is their approach effective or ineffective? Why or why not?

The following scenario is an initial draft of my interpretation of the conflict. What would you add to or change, based on your analysis?

For these roommates, *ambiguity* is at the heart of the meaning of this conflict. Showing each other that they are in conflict but not addressing the root of it may be a response to the dangers of opening up a conflict in the confined and volatile space of a home. There may be a sense in which the displacement allows these people to have a *parallel* or metaphoric conflict rather than simply avoiding it. They know they're in conflict, and that's the message and meaning, but the actual tangible conflict is too volatile or risky to engage. This ambiguity also allows an easy *bridge* to the more volatile conflict. The conflict channel is open if anyone chooses to go to that topic, but no one has to. It is also a good way to experience *being right* at the expense of the others. The construction of the other as enemy allows the roommates to be right and even justified in their passive-aggression. So the conflict seems to serve *multiple strategic and tactical goals* for the participants. One can assume that the other roommates also are in the thrill of the contest, as they seem to be also caught in the cycle of sabotage and revenge. In essence, the *vindictive games* that they are locked into are a way of saying we are different, better, and in opposition to you. *We really don't like you.* Perhaps they're saying, "We're cool and attractive and you're not." Perhaps locking the one roommate out is a way of saying, "Hey, you don't look so cool now!"

Guidelines for Improving Communication About Strategic Displacement

Here are a few guidelines for thinking about strategic displacements and how you might work with them more effectively:

- Recognize how seemingly minor conflicts are often strategic ways of saying things that are difficult to say, not really openly saying them and not dealing with the energy they take to engage and that they release. Try to understand why that deeper issue—such as why and how much you dislike the people with whom you are in conflict—is so difficult to talk about.
- Recognize when you are being strategically ambiguous in engaging in a surface conflict at the same time as, or in place of, a deeper one, and ask questions about why you are using ambiguity to achieve your conflict goals.
- Try to understand why you are displacing the conflict into a specific incident or event, why you are in conflict about that event in particular, and how it is strategically connected to that deeper conflict that you are displacing.
- Try to approach the conflict with the skill level and maturity to openly engage and negotiate the deeper issue, if this is possible.

At the same time, recognize that at close quarters—such as when you are living with people—that openness comes in waves rather than all at once and that it comes with risks and dangers. Be able to talk about the effects of displacement on your experience of living or working at close quarters with people, and use the commonality of experiences you might discover through such talk as a starting point for more collaborative and honest dialogue.

- Recognize that the participants in a conflict—including yourself—may not necessarily have the skills to engage in the conflict in a reasonable and mature way.
- Carefully consider some examples of strategic displacement that you have engaged in with roommates and people in close proximity. How would you evaluate your skill level in dealing with them? How would you handle the displaced issue differently if you faced the same situation again?

❖ SYMBOLIC DISPLACEMENT AS CONFLICTED DESIRE

Now we turn to a more complex and often tangled form of displacement that occurs when we displace our conflicts into aspects of our experience that have to do with desire and particularly sexuality. Conflict is often closely connected to sexuality in several important ways. This is because sexuality is both explicitly tangible and is an area of human activity and experience that is deeply connected to symbolic issues. Sexuality is also an area of activity through which other issues and themes that may be conflicted are expressed; sexuality can be a sort of barometer of other health and dysfunctional issues in a relationship. Conflict can often be sexually energizing for people. It can be an area of relationship where other conflicts get expressed and have a deep impact on relational health and happiness. Such themes as danger, vulnerability, power, and desire can be displaced from one conflict area into the realm of sexuality, where these themes are often more vivid and identifiable for people than in another conflicted aspect of their lives. It is in this way that people often fight about sex and sexuality as a displacement from another conflict that people are either less aware of or do not want to explore. This fact often creates challenges as people negotiate their conflicts since the surface and deeper meanings can get tangled and connected to deep emotional and bodily experiences.

As you examine the following story, consider how the interwoven sexuality, danger, and vulnerability stand in place of a desire for better workplace communication. Consider how the woman represents the pejorative scapegoating of deeper organizational dysfunctions. The blame for organizational weaknesses is symbolically displaced onto her: She is the danger from within that must be expelled or transformed. You can imagine some people saying that things worked just fine until she came along. Part of this is displaced blame and part is a form of denial. In the conflict about her disruption of the culture is a deeper displaced message about the dysfunctional organizational culture. The issues are displaced into the realm of sexuality because the opportunity conveniently presents itself to do so and because this makes the dangers all the more vividly connected to desire and, at the same time, all the more distanced from internal organizational issues.

The conflict over sexual desire and the danger that this Jezebel represents is a displacement of a deeper desire, a tale of desire for a safer workplace culture. That this could happen carries with it a moral tale of the fragility of the workplace culture. We can read this web of desires as interrelated, and it can be read as such if we trace back through the displacement that she represents. The sexual inappropriateness and the havoc that this woman can wreak can be a useful lesson in their own lack of restraint, issues of professionalism, and cultural and communication vulnerability. She represents danger and vulnerability as a female sexual presence; she also represents the symbolic demonization and purging of that danger and vulnerability and fragility. At the same time, the storyteller's desire is to show the fragility of the organization through its dangerous vulnerability to being disrupted so easily. The choice that the workplace members face is to listen to the story as a systemic lesson about them all or to demonize the individual and construct the whole incident into an isolated aberration. The members have two main narrative options—to scapegoat an individual (a low-status female) or to learn collectively and renegotiate a way of working in a culture that is more resilient and less fragile and vulnerable. Let's see how displacement can help us unravel this tangled skein and explain the decisions that they do make.

"The Work-Place Jezebel" (Jen)

At the first interview, Jacky was everything we were looking for in a receptionist. She dressed professionally, she was articulate, and she was bilingual. The manager of the Customer Development Center (CDC) for PK Dodge (PKD) was excited for Jacky to start. The following week, she came in to start her training. She was picking up on everything so fast, and the CDC manager thought he had found his cure-all for the problems the CDC had been experiencing.

By Jacky's 3rd day, there were inconsistencies. She no longer dressed in a business casual manner; she came in looking like she had been dragged out of an all-night rave. She began to talk in an unprofessional manner and lie about her work. This was just the tip of the iceberg. I had only been at work for a few hours when the managers started rolling in to my office to "talk" about the new girl. Before I go into all that happened, I want to cover the atmosphere of PKD for those of us who worked there before Jacky rocked our culture.

At PK Dodge, we all, for the most part, get along. We will have our little tiffs here and there, but never anything that doesn't blow over in about 48 hours. We are a car dealership so we have all kinds of people working there . . . We have groups of people who go out after work, we have people who date other employees, but one thing that has always been understood is, whatever you do outside the dealership does not get brought into the dealership—leave all baggage at the door. This not only ensures that everyone keeps a healthy work environment but also that situations don't get out of hand.

Things aren't always so rosy, though. We have married men messing around on their wives, wives messing around on their husbands, all the things that are made for TV movies. But as I stated above, it was never allowed to interfere with work. And up until recently, it never had.

Jacky started off putting her foot on the wrong side of a very thin and fuzzy line. She had made it known that she had had a "foursome" with one of the managers (Sam) and a married salesman, along with one of her friends. She tells me in front of another manager that she intends to have a relationship with Sam. She then tells me in front of customers and a sales manager about going out with Sam and two salesmen to a strip club and performing oral sex on a female stripper while the guys watched.

Jacky has had at least one semiloud confrontation with Sam in the dealership showroom. My office has been bombarded with employees and managers complaining about the atmosphere she has created. Our manager has decided that it is somehow my job to control the issue, even though I am not in a manager position. He is passing the buck, and that infuriates me even more—he has never been a good manager, and I have always had to do the dirty work. I am tired, I am run down, I am burned out. I have been trying to remedy the situation with her work performance, but I have been unsuccessful because she has a bad attitude toward me. I continue to get static from my manager for not correcting the situation. . . . Jacky has divided the workplace. She did it in 3 weeks. To me this is amazing. However, when I look deeper into the situation, I feel that this fracture started way before she came to work at PK Dodge.

The Meaning of Conflicted Desire and Displacement

Can the systemic problem be a cry for help, an expression of desire that is tangled up with the specifics of the conflict? One set of tangled desires seem to be displaced onto a conflict about another set of tangled desires. The system has generated a conflict that shows the problem in the system, thereby providing feedback to itself that change is needed. How does the conflict displacement work as a systemic clue that something deeper is amiss in the organization? How are the desires tangled, and how does this displace a set of related tangled desires?

Complete the interpretive steps as we did for the previous examples so that we can perhaps shed light on these broader questions. Again, if you could find out one thing that would help reveal the meaning of the conflict, what would that piece of the puzzle be?

Step 1: Description of the Surface Conflict

- What is happening in talk and action that shows you there is a conflict between these people about something specific and tangible? Describe everything in the talk and action that indicates there is a dispute here. Identify specific words and phrases as well as any nonverbal clues that signify there is a conflict.
- What specific issue or tangible current behavior is the specific conflict about?
- What are the things that are dividing these people and keeping them divided on those issues? Does the issue match with the talk and action? Does the conflict seem to be about what's being discussed? If yes, then work with that specific issue or behavior.

Step 2: Reduction of Desire to the Surface Conflict

- Are there clues and hints that the issues you have identified point to something deeper going on between the people?
- What details in the story point to something beyond the manifest dispute?

To help you answer these questions, consider how the sexual danger Jacky represents is a clue to workplace vulnerability and the desire for workplace safety and a return to some sense of rational order. Consider how scapegoating is a clue that there is more energy associated with danger and vulnerability with a displaced issue than she alone really represents. Consider also how this scapegoating connects to denial of the systemic dysfunctions that her presence exposes. Consider also the energy that her controversial actions release and how quickly things break down around her. See if you can find other clues that indicate more is going on here than a promiscuous and difficult employee who has thrown things into disarray.

Perhaps the desire to combine elements such as work and play gets displaced into a conflict over why work and play combine badly in Jacky's choices. This conflict about work and play clashing perhaps reflects a desire to combine them more effectively. After all, that is how the narrator describes the culture before Jezebel came along. The lesson from the clues is that this organization is not what it could be and is not what the employees think it is in terms of effectiveness and their resilience in dealing with and recovering from crises.

Step 3: Interpretation of Displacement as Desire

- In looking at the relationship of your description and reduction, what do you interpret to be the deeper, more enduring dispute or division that makes this conflict make sense as a meaningful whole?
- Why are deeper issues displaced and not addressed by the participants?
- How do these deeper issues structure the surface of the conflict?
- How does reflecting on this meaning help you understand how these people express or manage conflict through communication? In what ways is their approach effective or ineffective as a negotiation of a solution? Why or why not? What might they do from here to renegotiate their workplace culture in terms of setting demands and managing the concessions necessary for the people remaining in the organization to move forward?

To help you get to the deeper meaning, consider how this conflict is a displacement of desire for an effective, strong, rationally operating workplace. The deeper issue has to do with making the systemic changes so that an external danger cannot tear the organization apart again. The displaced conflict is a moment that problematizes the organizational culture and shows the members that they have a problem. The meaning of this conflict, therefore, has to do with learning to become a better organization. Consider what would have to change for that to happen (management style, hiring and training procedures, a fragile culture, blurred lines between fun and work), and you have reached beyond the displaced conflict over sexuality to the tangled desires for systemic change that are at the heart of the meaning of this conflict.

Guidelines for Improving Communication About Conflicted Desire

Conflicts are multifaceted in the perspectives of the people involved, and they are also connected to several levels of tangled, mixed, and intertwined motives, desires, and so on. The following guidelines will help you to work with these conflicted desires more effectively.

- Recognize how desire in one conflicted issue often gets tangled up and symbolized by another one—often in the form of a conflict steeped in or focused around sexuality. If in your relationships you experience conflicts that are interconnected with or expressed through issues of sexuality, try to look beyond that to what is being symbolized. Learn to look for the real lesson about your desires that are being displaced into the surface conflict. Be able to talk about the effects of this kind of tangling of work issues with sexuality and the lessons about work that you learn from it. Use these lessons as the starting point for questioning and changing your workplace or relationship where it is possible and practical to do so.
- Recognize that tangled desires can often help you to learn deeper lessons about what you really want in other aspects of your life. You can start to see how sexuality connects to patterns of displacement for you, if this is the case.
- Recognize that when conflicts get tangled up with sexuality, they can be volatile and difficult to work with, as they often release a lot of energy into the conflict. Sexual energy can charge up a conflict and prime it for an intense experience.

Exploring and becoming more conscious of these various forms and functions of displacement can make us much wiser communicators when we face the inevitable conflicts of our lives.

❖ LESSONS FROM THE FIELD OF PRACTICE: EXERCISES FOR EXPLORING DISPLACEMENT

Complete the following exercises as a way to either prepare for or follow up on the discussion of this chapter.

Exercise 1: Exploring Your Displacements

You have spent time developing skills to explore other people's displacements and their functions. Here, I challenge you to explore and learn from *your* displacements in your conflicts. Answer the following questions and think about ways that these answers might lead to change or more effective communication in the pertinent relationships.

- Are you in a relationship in which you can see that you are or have been displacing an underlying conflict into another one?

- Why is the conflict being displaced, and why is it being displaced into the conflict that it is?
- What are the issues being displaced for each side of the conflict? (Each participant may be displacing different issues in the same dispute.)
- What does the more surface conflict do for you and your communication? What function does the displacement serve (avoidance, passive-aggression, etc.)?
- How would you begin a conversation with the other participant to explore the displaced conflict?
- What will happen to the conflict if you actually have this conversation?
- What will likely happen to your relationship if you get to the real conflict? What are the probable risks and the possible rewards?
- What are some important insights about displacement that will help you to negotiate that conflict more effectively in terms of understanding and managing the exchange of demands and concessions that are important to resolving that conflict?

Exercise 2: Collecting and Analyzing a Displaced Conflict

Step 1: Collect a conflict story from at least one of the participants in a conflict, and preferably from each. The story should be one in which the participants are displacing a deep conflict through a more surface or manifest one. You can collect such stories by using one of the following sample scripts:

Please describe a conflict in which you knew the thing being argued about wasn't the only or even the main thing that the conflict was really about. You may not have known that it was about something else or more at the time. You might have realized this later . . .

Please describe a conflict in which you consciously changed the issue being argued about to either avoid the real conflict or to use the conflict you initiated as a way of getting at the person or bringing out another issue . . .

Be careful to document and collect as many of the details of the story as you can, including actual talk where possible and any background thoughts and emotions that the narrator felt were important in the conflict. Or write the story of a conflict that you are or were involved in that you know involved some form of displacement by you.

Step 2: Using the three interpretive steps, analyze the story for the structure of how it works as displacement.

Step 3: Based on your careful interpretation, decide what main form of displacement is going on in the conflict.

Step 4: Discuss the following questions:

- Why did the participants displace the conflict?
- How do you know there were elements of displacement in the conflict—what are the clues in the story as told and perhaps in the story not told? Are there clues in key things that you think might be left out of the story?
- What strategic role does the displacement play in the communication about the conflict (unconscious, strategic, systemic clue)?
- What impact does the displacement have on the participants' communication and broader relationship?
- What advice about conflict and communication would you give the participants?
- What are some good questions that you would have the participants explore if you could help them to negotiate their conflict?

❖ CONCLUSION

We people can be very creative in our use of symbols, even to the point where we may be arguing about something other than the actual conflict that divides us, and we may not even fully realize it. We may also be fully aware of it but still prefer to displace our conflict into a different arena or onto a different target person. Sometimes this is for our own psychological protection, and sometimes it is a way to avoid the conflict. Sometimes it is a way of working out the energy of a conflict on an easy target. Whatever the underlying or more explicit communicative function, the phenomena of displacement has some interesting and important implications for how we engage in conflict and how we should question our assumption that conflict is a simple process of discovering differences and working toward common solutions. We cannot always assume that the people with whom we are in conflict share the same experiential and meaning frames for the conflict. We can only discover such similarities and differences through effective dialogue that is mindful of the relationship of symbolic and tangible issues that are configured in particular ways through displacement.

I hope that this chapter has made the point for you that it is important to be on the same page in terms of what the conflict means to the people involved. Hopefully it is also clear how conflicts can be about so much more than they appear to be. Displacements are worth examining because they reveal these depths and divergences of meaning and the patterns of habits in how we express our conflicts that are so crucial to understanding why people get into the conflicts that they do and why they use the displaced issues that they do to express those conflicts. The challenges of this chapter are to think carefully about what is and what might be being expressed in a conflict and to work toward a common understanding—even if that common understanding is that you are both arguing or fighting about completely different underlying issues.

Another implied challenge is for you to have the courage to be explicit and honest about the actual divisive issue in a conflict and not to retreat into a labyrinth of connected but displaced ones that only diffuse the conflict in the short term but spread the conflict into other aspects of your relationships in the long term. How many of us have damaged or ended relationships over one issue only to realize later that it was really about something else that you might have addressed more effectively? This is where the cost of displacement is high and the rewards for working with displacement are worthwhile.

7

What Do We Represent to Each Other?

*Understanding Projection
and Negotiating Conflict*

❖ ❖ ❖

*We need only to think of the people whom we judge or
dislike or against whom we hold secret prejudices to find
ourselves in the grip of our [own] darker nature.*

—Zweig and Abrams (2001, p. xvi)

The shadow [we see in others] is [often] the rest of who we are.

—Brewi and Brennan (2001, p. 261)

Recently I was explaining the ideas of this chapter to a former
student who happened to drop by my office as I was writing. As I
explained the concept of projection, he said that he had had a recent
experience that was a perfect example for me to use. He told me of a
friendship with a young woman in which she had actively pursued him

romantically for a while. Apparently she would not give up the chase (this is his side of the story, after all) and that this had created enough conflicted tension in their relationship that he was having a hard time even being friends. I asked him why. He explained that she told him that she saw him as a perfect catch because he was an African American male who is not only handsome but is in graduate school, working toward a professional career, has his act together, and so on. He represented those idealized qualities that she was apparently looking for. He did have an intimate relationship with her briefly, but told her that his long-term plans had to come first for now and that they should be just friends. She was confused because she had assumed that he was *the one* and that, in fact, she felt that God had affirmed this for her during prayer. How could he not see the same truth? She was angry because the intimate relationship did not continue but also because he did not live up to her idealized notion (and her probably idealized story of their relationship) of a "perfect catch," and this lead to conflict for them. You can see how the qualities she projected onto him led to pressure to live up to the ideal and how this led to withdrawal by him since he did not want to live up to that image. His withdrawal led to disappointment for her, as she was sure this relationship was meant to be ("God told me that you're the one, but now you're telling me that you're not . . . ?"), and then to conflicted tensions in their friendship. She apparently has not given up the chase for her ideal man and may end up in the same college for graduate school. Such is the power of faith in our projections; they can be so real to us, whether idealized or negative.

In conflicts such as the one just summarized, people often see motives, qualities, characteristics, and desires in another person that are really projections of something in themselves, and sometimes that something is related to an ideal that is not really part of the other person's true identity. Projections are often images of our own peculiarities and experiences that we think belong to the other in the conflict. This way, the other person can come to symbolize our own often dark motives or our own ideals. In terms of communication, it is a short step from negative projection to both blaming the other and to justifying competitive, aggressive, or even violent conflict behavior. It is also a short step from idealized projection to disappointment when the other person does not meet those ideals, and it's another short step to conflicted tension and blame that can lead to conflict when the other feels pressured to change in order to live up to the ideal.

This chapter provides a way of gaining insight into the how's and the why's of constructing negative and idealized projections in conflict. We will explore how people symbolically construct projections and what this means within the dynamics of conflict communication and as a source of learning. Key questions include the following: How do people create and integrate their projections into the process of conflict communication? How can we learn to recognize, and possibly confront, our projections as a way of improving our conflict communication skills? How can we use this understanding and learning to negotiate conflict more effectively?

Main topics and learning goals in this chapter:

- Learning to read between the projections
- Projection and the symbolic relationship of people in conflict
- Projection and conflict discourse patterns and dynamics
- The connection between projection and enemy making and blame
- The limiting effects of projection
- From projection to integration: Negotiating new meanings
- Lessons from the field of practice

There is a lot of truth to the adage that we should be careful how we talk about others, because much of the time we are talking about ourselves. This is particularly true when it comes to issues of guilt and blame—we often accuse others of the things that we feel guilty of ourselves deep down. Projection is also connected to the darker emotions, such as jealousy and possessiveness, that are at the core of many relational conflicts. How often is it that people who are possessive about where their relational partners are and who they are talking to end up being the ones who are at least thinking about cheating? In such cases, they are likely to be projecting their guilt onto the other. How often is jealousy fueled by the perception that someone else has the quality or characteristic that you most desire for yourself? As a personal preparation exercise, ask yourself the following questions to begin exploring projection in your conflicts so that you will be ready to explore those of others with care and sensitivity:

- What qualities and characteristics, and motives (positive or negative) do I most often see in the actions of others in everyday life and specifically when I am in conflict with them?
- What things do I tend to accuse others of without evidence? Are there any feelings of guilt on your part that these accusations are connected to?
- How have feelings of jealousy or possessiveness fueled conflicts that I have been part of, and how are they possibly connected to projections?

- How do these perceptions form a somewhat consistent pattern in how I view others?
- What do these judgments—negative or idealized—actually say about myself?
- How do these judgments impact my conflict practices and style and my typical experiences of conflict?
- How do my patterns of projection affect how I make sense of and explain what's happening in someone else's conflict as an outside observer (bear this question in mind as you examine the following story)?

Now that you have thought about your own experiences with projection, let's move on to examine a relationship at a crossroads moment and how understanding projection might be important in enabling the couple to negotiate their relationship past that moment to an ending or a new beginning.

❖ LEARNING TO READ BETWEEN THE PROJECTIONS

Taking a look at the following story is a way to become familiar with interpreting the dynamics of communication as they reflect habits and tactics of projection. This is a lot like reading between the lines for the way things connect together in the story. We will consider and apply more theoretical concepts as we move through the chapter. For now, familiarize yourself with as many as possible of the ways that projection works in this specific conflict. We do not always have the luxury of having access to both sides of a story. The following narrative (as told by Robyn, a researcher) outlines the perspective of one conflict participant for us. It is a long story, but it details a great deal of projected images by the narrator, Terry, and we can guess at the impact of the pressure that those images create in her relationship and communication with James. On your first read-through, (1) try to imagine James's perspective and the divisive impact that Terry's projections might have from his side. Then (2) go through the story carefully, paragraph by paragraph, as you follow the concepts of the chapter, and note or underline any signs of or clues to the various forms of projection that you think might be going on. (3) Note carefully how each of those examples of projection connects to the conflict and perhaps even stimulates the energy of the conflict. Try to piece together how the projections are part of why they now stand at an important crossroads in their relationship. After reading between the lines of the projections on both sides, we will develop some ways that the couple might negotiate a new meaning for their relationship. The new meaning is likely to be either an ending or a new beginning, but they are unlikely to be at their current crossroads for long given that it seems that an important conflict is brewing.

What's Love Got to Do With It? (Robyn)
> James and Terry sitting in a tree . . . K-I-S-S-I-N-G
> First comes the love
> Then comes the marriage
> Then comes James with the baby carriage

Terry's Side of the Conflict

I met James at the beach after I graduated from high school, during senior week. I was there with some of the girls I graduated with, and he was there with some of his friends. He was a soldier in the army, stationed at Ft. Bragg, so when we were home, we were only 30 minutes away from each other. I thought it was strange that it took us being at Myrtle Beach at the same time for us to meet, but I was glad we did. He told me at first that his name was Angel, and I thought he looked like one. He also reminded me so much of the good things in my father. It didn't matter that I was younger than him. I was 18 and he was 23.

My parents have been in a happy marriage for more than 20 years. I've always wanted a love like theirs—a faithful husband and wife who come together to raise children and build their lives together. My parents made it seem easy. While I watched so many of my friend's families deteriorate because of divorce, abuse, and other problems, I was proud of mine, yet I was anxious to have my own.

People have always told me how pretty I am, and girls always seem to envy me because of my looks, thinking that my life must be easy and that I was automatically lucky in love. I wasn't. All I ever wanted was someone to love me. Most of the men I dated in high school were only interested in having sex with me or having the "beauty queen" on their arm, but none of those relationships ever lasted.

Most of my past relationships didn't mean anything to me. I found myself always looking for love instead of letting it find me, and I have gotten my heart broken in the process. I felt that things would be different with James because for once I wasn't looking, and this is when it seemed that fate brought us together. At first he gave me a lot of attention and made me feel like a woman. I knew I loved him almost immediately. I fell in love with him because of how it made me feel to be with him. I would have done anything to be with him even though my parents disapproved. I felt that our relationship could stand just about anything and, the 1st year, it did.

After we were together for a while, he told me that his name wasn't really Angel and that he had a son from a previous relationship. He said that he had custody of his son because the child's mother didn't want him, but the mother was taking care of him while James was in the military. I understood why he waited to tell me—he wanted to make sure we would be together. I decided that I loved him and was therefore willing to be a mother to his son. I knew that they were a package deal.

After James and I got closer, he told me that he was married but that he was working to get an annulment. He said he didn't love her—his wife—and had only married her so that she could stay in the States. He told me about her when she was being transferred to Fort Bragg so I wouldn't be surprised. I was glad he told me about her when he did. I knew ahead of time that she would try to break us up with her lies, so I was prepared. I was glad when the annulment went through and knew that James had chosen me. I thought we would be together forever, but the more faithful I was to him, the less interested he became.

I didn't ask James a lot of questions about his life, because I figured if he wanted me to know things, he would tell me and I wouldn't have to ask. I was raised in the church and want to make my relationship with God better. I have asked James to go with me to church but he refused. He said that he was a Muslim and that I shouldn't try to change him.

I accepted him because I loved him. I trust James, but I know that sometimes he lies to me. We were together for almost a year before he broke up with me—saying that he didn't want to hurt me. I tried to go on with my life, but I couldn't get him out of my mind or out of my system. I knew if he ever wanted me back, I would go running. My mother introduced me to a lot of "church men," but I wasn't interested in them. I compare everyone to James. I liked some of the qualities the other men had, but they weren't James. It seemed I wanted a man with the morals of who my mother brought to me but who looked like James and smelled like James and talked like James. I prayed that God would bring him back to me, and eventually he did. We got back together on New Year's Eve, and I truly felt it was the beginning to a wonderful relationship, but I was wrong.

After we got back together, James told me he wanted me to have his baby. I was so happy because I felt that he wanted the same things I wanted in life, to get married and have a family. Our relationship became serious and we got busy trying to make our baby. I found out I was pregnant in April and I was so happy. I thought James would be happy as well, but I really couldn't tell. He wasn't very supportive during the pregnancy and made me feel like I didn't matter to him. I thought that having a baby might bring us closer, but it only seemed to make him less interested in me. I hoped that once the baby was born, he would change.

I gave birth to our daughter a week before Thanksgiving. She was beautiful. Everyone said how much she looked like me, but I was desperate to find traces of James in her. He seemed disappointed that she didn't look as much like him as his son did. For a long time, he acted like the baby wasn't his, but the more she grew, the more he would come around. But his interest was only in the baby. He began to ignore me. He told me that there was no "us" anymore because we had a baby.

I didn't give up on James because I love him. He hasn't really done a lot for the baby, but he explained that he can't afford to do much because he has to send money home for his son and pay his own bills. I don't complain as long as he does what he can. He buys her diapers every now and then. I hope things will be a lot better when we are married.

I'm getting tired of how James treats me. He talks to me like I am a child and demeans me every chance he gets. He makes me feel stupid. I am beginning to resent how much I changed to be with him. Sometimes I don't recognize myself. I used to want to be a model, but James is a Muslim and doesn't want me to wear makeup. I want to make him happy, but I don't feel that he does anything to make me happy. It just doesn't seem like he cares, even when she took her first steps. He goes weeks at a time without seeing her, and the only time we ever talk is when I call him. His phone is in my name and I find myself wondering if he is not talking to me, who is he talking to?

I've been praying a lot lately, and my pastor told me that I may end up settling for less than I deserve if I stay in the relationship. I love James, but I don't think he loves me as much, and I am afraid that when we get married, things will get worse instead of better. I want to have the same perfect family for my daughter that I had growing up. Every time I tell James I don't think it's going to work, he apologizes and promises that things will change. I don't know if I believe him any more.

I had a dream the other night that I was back together with my ex-boyfriend, the one whose heart I broke to go back with James. I don't want to have any regrets, but I don't really know what I want. I want to feel loved and appreciated, and James doesn't make me feel that way. Patrick, my ex-boyfriend, did. I wonder if I should call him and see how he is doing.

Initial Discussion Questions for Terry's Story

- What forms of idealized projection are important in her story? Look closely at her relationship history and role models and how these assumptions suggest that she is projecting her hopes and dreams and her angelic character onto James—her "Angel."

- How are her projections connected to how she feels about him, how are they connected to him representing her father's qualities, and how are they also part of why she falls in love with James?

- How are each of her projections challenged by the facts, and how does this tension between ideal and actual create relational tensions and conflict within their relationship?

- What forms of projection are also hinted at in the role of third parties in the story—female rivals, past boyfriends, his ex-wife, the baby, and so on?

- How do Terry's projections create a realistic or unrealistic picture of James, and how is this related to their subsequent relational conflict?

- What pressure do these assumptions put on James, and how do you think these idealized projections affect their communication and lead to conflicts in their everyday relationship?

- What, if any, are the negative forms of projection evident in her story?

- What forms of active and passive projections seem to be evident in her story and with what effect on their relationship?
- How might her projections affect the dynamics of their relationship in terms of using words as projectiles, the role of hooks and triggers, and their relationship as both lovers and possible enemies?
- What characteristics of James seem to form a hook for Terry's projections, and what issues or factors in her life trigger her projections?
- Try to imagine in detail how he might tell their relational conflict story from his perspective if he were being completely honest with you. How might her projections be sources of conflict for him?
- How might James's story contain elements of projection from his perspective in terms of what positive or negative projections Terry represents for him (note, for example, his reaction to her desire to model and how he talks to her like she is immature)?
- More broadly, how do Terry's projections limit her communication and her relationships in some important ways?
- How might you advise Terry to move toward more integration in her intimate relationship with James and in her relationships more generally?
- The story ends with her rethinking things with Patrick. How are her final thoughts, shared with us at the end of her story, also based on idealized projections?

Organizing Your Interpretations

Take your answers to the foregoing questions and summarize them around the following three interpretive research steps:

Step 1: Description

Describe the specific story examples of projection on both sides and how they affect Terry and James's communication. To do this, go through the story carefully and examine each type of projection and what it tells you about the people in the conflict and what it does within the various relationships in the story. Working with each example of projection in the story, from her school relationships with girls and boys and her family through to the present as she dreams about an ex-boyfriend, try to identify what rhetorical function it serves in constructing the qualities, characteristics, and particularly the apparent motives of James in the conflict. Indicate, also, what this might imply about Terry.

Step 2: Reduction to Themes

Thematize the examples so that you get a sense of the deeper meaning of their conflict. To do this, boil down the various examples of projection to how they cluster around core oppositions or themes (such as unrealistic or unmet expectations) between them that are central to why they are at this crossroads moment. Examine each of the oppositions and possible projections explicated in your description for the more fundamental or essential oppositions. Pay particular attention to how projections cluster around affirming desirable qualities for the narrator and negative qualities to the other.

Step 3: Interpretation

Interpret how these core oppositions generate the conflicts in their relationship and how these oppositions might provide opportunities for good topics and questions they might address in order to renegotiate their relationship. To do this, imagine how their habits of projection might actually provide useful ways of talking about their differences and their desires for a relationship. To interpret the meaning, you may have to decide which oppositions appear to be projections of the narrator's shadow (negative projections) and light (idealized projections) and which are just descriptors of the opponent that are obvious from the action and might be fair characterizations. You have to decide if something is being projected from the self in the depiction of the other and what those projections might be (for example, guilt, fears about being perceived a particular way, and so on) and why they occur. There are fairly direct projections, such as guilt, and there are more subtle projections that are connected to the hopes and fears of the narrator that may intensify or magnify a depiction of the other (for example, Terry's maturity and responsibility highlight James's immaturity and irresponsibility).

A Cautionary Note on Analyzing Stories for Symbolic Projection

There are a couple of cautionary notes that are important to consider at this point. First, guard against having an overly mechanistic or dualistic concept of projection, in which we see a self projecting interior experiences onto an exterior other—sort of like a movie image on a blank screen. Rather, we should consider projection as an ongoing co-construction in which the other participants are engaged with us in the unfolding of projections and their impact on the conflicted communication. Projections create the conditions for additional projections, and this dynamic interplay is important to understand in following the cycles and escalations of conflicts. This cautionary note is particularly important in terms of approaching conflict from a communication perspective in that we should not assume communication is merely the outward manifestation of people's psychology. Rather, as conflicts evolve, escalate, and polarize because of projection, particular projections will emerge as a result of the communication dynamics. These emergent projections will, in turn, fuel changes in the content and dynamics of the conflict. From the story we have and from imagining James's story, perhaps you can trace how projections might have emerged, solidified, and become reference points for each person's perceptions and communication as their relationship evolved and then devolved to where they are now.

Second, when analyzing conflicts that we are not directly involved with, we should also be cautious about how our subjective judgments impact how we portray the people and their projections. We should try to view the conflict from within the participants' frames of reference. This way, the projections we see in the conflict communication of others are not simply projections of our own desires and fears about ourselves as communicators. Projections are difficult to identify since they are, by definition, unconscious and unintended, so the key thing is cautious inquiry into what seem like important patterns of projection. We may not see all of the projections evident in communication. Similarly, we may see patterns that are not there as we bring our own experiences to the interpretive process. Not every quality or characteristic that one side uses to depict the other is a projection; sometimes that quality may actually be evident in their behavior. This caution is also particularly important in that we are engaging in interpretive research as we collect and interpret stories. As such, much of the time we are engaged in smart guesswork and working hypotheses as we interpret the meaning of other people's communication. If you could hear both sides of the story, there is probably one side that you would tend to agree with more than the other. Perhaps you see elements of yourself and your own relational history in the stories. Note how these might influence your reading of the story, and try to be conscious of those connections to you as you interpret the stories.

❖ PROJECTION AND THE SYMBOLIC RELATIONSHIP OF PEOPLE IN CONFLICT

As Von Franz (1982) shows us, projection involves the "unperceived and unintentional, transfer of subjective psychic elements onto an outer object" (p. 3). This outer object is usually another person, but it could be another group, gender, race, tribe, or nation (Karasawa, 2003). War rhetoric can be a good example of how we transfer negative qualities onto our enemies (Parry-Giles, 1994). This may go so far as to mean the enemy gets constructed as evil (Ricouer, 1967). In the case of more everyday conflict, it is usually the persons with whom we are in conflict that we construct in this way. Projections are usually of qualities, characteristics, or motives we see in the other that can be positive (idealized) or negative. In the case of positive projections, people project their own desires, wishes, qualities they see in themselves, and even their deepest passions onto another (Kearns, 1986; Thomsen, 1941). This is often based on feelings of empathy and complementarity with others whom we perceive as like ourselves or who we would like to be like in some way (Cary, 1987; Stein, 1986). In the case of negative projections, the unconscious or unperceived and unintentional nature of projection can be either active or passive. Each of these types and aspects of projection as they manifest in and structure communication have implications for conflict. As you explore projection, bear in mind the challenge that Hauk (2000) develops for us. Building on Kristeva's (1981) work, Hauk (2000) challenges us to acknowledge and own the differences and contradictions within ourselves and our identities rather than simply unloading them on to others through projections in order to build ourselves up.

Idealized and Negative Projections

Projection of idealized or positive qualities and characteristics often results in an overvaluation and admiration of the other. For example, if you desire to be seen as having particular qualities, such as wisdom, power, and good judgment, but you do not normally associate those qualities with yourself, then you may project them onto others in order to experience those qualities in action. The gods of ancient legends and mythologies often served this function for civilizations. In terms of human relationships, the other person then comes to symbolically personify those qualities as does the young man in the opening story. In relationships, if you have ever heard the phrase, "you remind me so much of my father (or mother)," and it's meant in a nice way, you are probably in an idealized projection scenario. It's useful to recognize that such a compliment comes with benefits and possible pitfalls as it is often based on a projection. In corporate settings, many of us tend to associate status and power with knowledge and wisdom because we desire status and power and the qualities we associate with them. Another typical projection in our culture is the association we make between beauty and wealth and happiness. Assuming that people are happy because they are rich reflects a desire many of us have for wealth and perhaps all of us have for happiness. Imagine in Terry and James's relationship how their projections helped construct a fragile and ultimately unsatisfying version of "happiness."

In intimate, family, and working relationships, we may also avoid opening up conflicts because we see them as more powerful, perceiving in them our desired qualities and not in ourselves. This way, conflicts are often avoided as the projector overestimates the power of the other. Last, a common source of relational conflict occurs when one or both parties create an idealized projected image of the other ("you're just like my father," or, "you're the perfect `girl next door' for me"), and then the other cannot or does not want to live up to that image. That person typically get pressurized to change and blamed for that failure by the projector if the change does not occur. I have heard this archetypal story many times in one form or another.

Negative projections are more common in the to-and-fro of conflicts as conflict tends to stir up emotions that are deeply and often unconsciously connected to our darker and more shadowy emotions, perceptions, and experiences. The idea is that we often make misjudgments about others based on some quality of ourselves that we project onto them. Normally we might correct such misjudgments based on insight—realizing that they are mainly symbolic manifestations of our shadowy selves or what Kristeva (1981) calls the stranger in ourselves. However, in the competitive environment of a conflict, we often cling to, and even accentuate, those judgments of others that are based on our own qualities or early experiences. We assume that the other is a tangible manifestation—a paradigm—of those qualities rather than a symbolic expression of them. Projection often has a profound impact on the dynamics of a conflict and the participants' ability to negotiate cooperation. Negative projection occurs when a current situation is reminiscent of an early experience of a negative quality associated with a particular category of people—fathers as tyrants, for example. The quality of "tyrant" is projected onto people who play a fatherlike or authoritative role. Working relationships with bosses might be an obvious application of such a projection. And the person may unconsciously behave just as tyrannically. The quality that people most dislike in others is, ironically, a projection of self. Think beneath Terry and James's relationship and imagine what conflict might have emerged if Terry had insisted on pursuing her modeling aspirations. Why might James have become something of a tyrant in that case? Are there elements of his own immaturity that he projects onto her that are important?

Passive and Active Projection

Passive projection or "unconscious empathy" (Von Franz, 1982, p. 16) occurs when the projector feels a sympathy that connects to the other. The projectors bring the other into relationship with them by detaching a feeling or quality from themselves and placing it onto the other. This is the basis of perspective taking and of the formation of social relationships, such as friendships. Hence, passive projection is the basis of developing *connection* or a feeling of combination with the other. For example, if a positive characteristic or quality, such as being caring or trustworthy, is projected from you onto another person, then you will see the quality that you value in yourself in the other person. This is one of the bases of feeling that you have things in common with someone and that you like that other person. As you might imagine, this passive form of projection is most commonly associated with positive projection and with the ability to work effectively with another with whom you may be conflicting.

Active projection occurs when you project a characteristic in order to create a distinction or *opposition* between yourself and the other person. This is most commonly associated with negative projection in that a quality or characteristic is projected from one person onto another, but the projectors are focused on showing how they are not like the persons with whom they are in conflict.

Given that we tend to associate negatives with others and not ourselves, active projection tends to be those things we most want to avoid seeing in ourselves. As you examine Terry and James's story, you might notice that most of the negative qualities they both point to in the other person are things that they do not want to be viewed as in themselves. Thinking beneath the story, you will start to see some key oppositions set up between the relational partners in which they point to a quality in the other that directly opposes a quality they see, or would like to see, in themselves. This is when you know that you are likely dealing with an interconnected and dynamic system of active and negative projections. Examining these interconnected oppositions is a very important starting point for possible dialogue and renegotiation of the relationship.

Discussion Questions

- What are the various positive projections that are evident in the relationship of Terry and James?
- What specific negative projections do you think are going on in their relationship?

- Where do these negative projections come from, and how do they fuel the conflict?
- Are there any passive projections evident in their relationship? If not, why not?
- How are the various forms of projection related to the quality of their relationship?
- How might you use these oppositions as a starting point for them discussing and learning from the conflict, if you could mediate between them?
- How do the aforementioned forms of projection figure into a significant recent, ongoing, or as yet unexpressed conflict in your life?

Discussion Questions for Further Exploring Terry and James's Projections

Now that you have explicated the possible projections in both sides of the story, use the following questions to discuss the effects that these oppositional projections have on Terry and James's conflict.

- How do the oppositional projections that you have uncovered form part of the underlying conflict patterns that are repeating between these people?
- How do the oppositional projections provide energy and direction for the conflict as it unfolds in communication?
- How might their communication in the face-to-face conflict and in their discussions with others about the conflict affirm and solidify their projections and related versions of each other in the conflict? How does communication help to constitute their perceptions that are the basis of their communication?
- If you were able to work with these people in helping them to understand and manage their conflict, what specific insights could your analysis of projections provide them in stimulating understanding and communication about the conflict? Create a list of these as possible topics for discussion and questions they might explore together.
- What do you need to be cautious about as you interpret their conflict for their projections?
- What habits of projection in *your* conflicts, if any, come to mind as you analyze the two sides of Terry and James's conflict?

❖ PROJECTION AND CONFLICT
    DISCOURSE PATTERNS AND DYNAMICS

Projections are part of the underlying meaning structure of conflicts. Projections seem to provide both the means by which people understand their mutual roles in conflicts and many opportunities to misunderstand each other. Projections provide part of the meaning of conflicts and are, at the same time, often constructed from the communication through which the conflict takes place. This interplay of projections can lead to repeating patterns of conflict, emotional distance, and loss across several generations of relationships such as in families (Taylor, 2003). This interplay can also be linked to the escalation of conflict in that projections tend to feed off each other and make the other seem farther and farther away (Holtz & Miller, 2001). Murderous images of others and violence toward them may even be connected to the projected externalization of one's own fears and desires (Kimbles, 2000; Loewenberg, 1999; Mizen, 2003). How might Terry and James's relationship devolve into one that is hateful in some ways?

From Projections to Projectiles

Von Franz (1997) describes the process by which unconscious negative projections can become directed into attacking the other. She says, "As soon as a person projects a bit of his [sic] shadow onto another human being he [sic] is incited to ... rancorous speech" (pp. 19–25). Projection in a conflict can lead to words becoming projectiles. This boundary between projection and projectile is crossed when words get thrown at the other person instead of engaging him or her and the issues of the conflict. Then conflicts start to be about attacking others and their positions in the conflicts and their "face" and may even be associated with feelings of wanting to harm or destroy them. The words that hit the other person—like projectiles—symbolize and carry the negative flow of energy directed against the other by the one who is projecting. As Von Franz explains, "When one becomes the target of another person's negative projection, one often experiences that hatred almost physically as a projectile" (p. 21). Words are coming at you and feel hard to take. In turn, you will often have a physical reaction that can be equal and oppositional. You may want to throw hard words at them in response. The conflict can escalate quickly into a mutual verbal attack.

Discussion Questions

- What specific words and phrases in the story provide clues for us that Terry and James might, under certain circumstances, use words as projectiles?
- How would projections help to create such a context, and what might be some of the projectiles that they might throw at each other?
- Think of a time in a conflicted conversation when you used words to attack another person. Did you feel like harming them? What effects did your attack have on the conflict?

Hooks and Triggers in Conflicted Communication

One way to examine hooks is to think about the characteristics of someone with whom you are in a close relationship that drive you nuts or that make you automatically see that person as the bad person. Another way is to examine your preconceived notions about certain types of people. Complete the following sentences as an example of how to tap into these hooks: "I automatically trust people who . . . "; "I automatically distrust people who . . . " You can change the sentence to "am attracted to," or "am not attracted to," and so on. You likely make assumptions about people based on those characteristics you have built associations with in your earlier life.

When you are able to hook a characteristic onto another, then something will likely trigger the projection. Previously, I have discussed the important role of so-called hot buttons in promoting volatility and stimulating conflicts to emerge or erupt (Kellett & Dalton, 2001, p. 7). A hot button is a form of trigger. Triggers get pulled when we see specific characteristics that are hooks for us in the behavior of the other. For example, think about how Terry builds up a picture of James based on a few characteristics, such as his angelic persona and, later, his immaturity and irresponsibility. What is it about him that provides both the hook for that assumption and everything else that goes with it and then triggers the projections that are suggested in her story? Usually, there is some reminder or characteristic that the projector is able to connect the projected image to. For example, if the person shows some element of tyrannical behavior, then the full image of the other as a tyrant can be projected. The scripted but unconscious way of dealing with tyrants is then triggered.

Discussion Questions

- What characteristics or qualities seem to be hooks for Terry and James to stereotype each other, and how do these hooks get triggered into projections for them?
- What are some of the hooks that are important to you in generating conflicts with certain types of people or with someone you are close to?
- How do these hooks get triggered into projections and then into conflicts?
- What do these hooks enable you to project onto them?
- How can understanding the hooks and triggers of someone you are close to, and your own in relation to that person, help account for the type of conflicts that the two of you have?

❖ THE CONNECTION BETWEEN PROJECTION
AND ENEMY MAKING AND BLAME

Negative projection is not always about constructing enemies of others, but it is closely connected. Sometimes we project what is culturally devalued, feared, or misunderstood onto others to build ourselves up. They become the shadow—the qualities about ourselves we wish to deny—and we become the light—the qualities about ourselves we wish to affirm. It may also be that in the to and fro of conflict, the shadow and light are reversed for them—we become their shadow as well. This synergy of shadow and light is often at the core of our conflicts as it allows us to distinguish ourselves from the others and place ourselves above them—and vice versa. Both of these are important aspects of creating the opposition of a competitive conflict. For example, Griffin (2001) provides an interesting account of chauvinism based on projection. A portrait of the other is drawn in which the parts of the self that the chauvinist most wants to deny are made dark to the self and projected onto the other—hence, for example, to a man, a woman is seen as irrational and overemotional. This also allows him the construction of a false self, one that stands for valorized qualities: rationality and emotional control. Competing over these definitions and what they mean is often what people fight about in conflicts. Fjerkenstad (2001) similarly traces the rhetoric of criminality to the construction of an image of the criminal as a representation of all that the rest of us do not want to be, and therefore we become reasonable and law abiding. Thus, projection is one way of creating the self as virtuous and other as the villainous bad guy.

It is not very far from this sort of negative projection to enemy making. In fact, Keen (1991) goes so far as to challenge us to think about ourselves as *Homo hostilus*—the enemy-making animal. It's not a very heroic image but one that does capture a great deal of how we humans spend our energy—making enemies of others so that we feel good about ourselves. This notion of *Homo hostilus* suggests that we rhetorically construct the image of the enemy through projections of our own undesirable qualities and characteristics that can demonize the other. This works most obviously in a political and rhetorical sense in terms of constructing the other during wartime, but it also captures how we often relate to others in personal conflicts as our temporary enemies. This enemy making serves the vital dual purpose of (1) allowing those qualities that we cannot tolerate in ourselves to be unconsciously and painlessly attributed to our enemies, thereby (2) absolving ourselves of the guilt of those qualities (Zweig & Abrams, 2001, p. xvi).

Projection thus helps us create enmity and this is central to generating the energy for conflicts. At the same time, the enmity is connected to our typical narrative goal in conflicts, that of being viewed as the hero or victim and not the villain. The evil is seen to be in the actions and heart of the other, and this can become a ready-made archetypal argument for our actions in the conflict. Projection is in this way tied to both redemption—the removal of evil, guilt, or blame from the self—and to virtue—the maintenance of valor and goodness. Reduced to the basics, projection enables us to blame the other; it also allows us to avoid blaming ourselves even as we escalate and polarize the conflict. Herein lies the greatest challenge as we look for ways of working with projections and their relationship to communication. As Dan Bar-on (2000) shows us in relation to the Palestinian-Israeli conflict, it is not always giving up the war or the conflict that is the hardest part of achieving peace. Rather, a visible enemy and the rhetorically energizing force that the enemy provides can be the most difficult thing to give up.

The key to becoming more intelligent as a communicator is to understand patterns, and one of the important patterns here is the relationship between self and other as light and dark. The challenge is to become more conscious of the representation of another as our own shadow. The unconscious imagery and archetypes by which we construct our enemies and by which they construct us are keys to understanding why they are, in fact, partly our enemies and at the same time partly ourselves. If we could act on this intelligence, the results in our conflicts might be quite meaningful.

Discussion Questions

- We cannot know for sure what Terry and James are projecting per se and what judgments are based on reasonable interpretations of their opponents' actions. Given this caution, what qualities do you think might be being projected onto the other and what qualities are therefore being affirmed in themselves?
- In what ways do they have the potential to be hostile to each other?
- In what ways do both narrators experience and construct the other as their potential enemy, and on what qualities or actions of the other is this enmity based?
- In what specific ways does redemption of the self and blame of the other get constructed in each side of the story, and how are projections important in this process?
- If their conflict escalated into a very difficult and emotional exchange, what would it take for each of them to give up the other as their enemy, if that is even possible? What might be some important first steps if this seems unrealistic?
- How would you advise Terry and James to become more conscious of their patterns of representing themselves and others? For example, how might they explore other conflict experiences with similar people for clues about their patterns of projection?

❖ THE LIMITING EFFECTS OF PROJECTION

Although projection seems to be a normal part of how people engage in conflicts—certainly in the escalation phase—it can be limiting in how we relate to people and the kinds of solutions and resolutions we achieve. As Taylor (2003) argues, it is often difficult to think beyond conflicts into a different future state when the story we have does not support change. It is work to change the patterns we have become locked into. Nagy (1991, p. 84) expands this point by challenging us to "emerge" from our projections where possible, because our reliance on projection can limit us in the following important ways:

- First, projections can keep you *unconscious* of important aspects of a conflict. In particular, it can limit your ability to see beyond the characteristic you see in the other. Therefore, you may remain blinded to your own qualities, characteristics, and possibly dark motives as a participant in the conflict. You can get caught up in the busy rhetorical work of constructing the other person and lose sight of who you are in the conflict. You may also remain blind to the meaning of the conflict as you focus your communicative energy on the other person and what he or she represents to you.

- Second, this blinding aspect of projection can make you overly *vulnerable.* If you are focused on either idealizing or simplifying the other down to some characteristics that enable you to view yourself as the good guy and the other person as the bad guy, you will become vulnerable to the complexity of a conflict. If you are focusing your energy on projecting motives and qualities onto the other, you will likely miss some of the possibilities in the conflict for change, learning, and resolution. You may also miss the other person's true motives and characteristics, and this can make you vulnerable to making tactical moves in the conflict that are not wise. Also, as you are focusing on the other person, the conflict process can evolve in a direction that you are not ready for. Another important vulnerability is to the negative emotions that are often connected to projection, such as jealousy, envy, anger, and so on.

- Last, habitual projection can *inhibit your maturation* as a communicator. To see the other simplistically as idealized or villainous reduces your ability to see your own involvement in the conflict and take responsibility for it. It also limits your ability to take the perspective of the other, which is a key component of a mature and tolerant communicator. You cannot grow as a communicator if the other is always the villain and you are always the victim or hero.

Discussion Questions

- In what ways do Terry and James remain unconscious of important dimensions of the conflict as well as important dimensions of themselves?
- In what ways do they make themselves *and* the process of conflict vulnerable to escalation and breakdown?
- How might maturing beyond the level of projection they display help them in other aspects of their relationship, as parents, and in their lives as communicators?
- What advice would you give to help them to approach the conflict with a more developed sense of how they are limiting their communication through projection? How might this advice help them develop perspective-taking skills?
- What could both of them learn about their conflicts from your analysis?

❖ FROM PROJECTION TO INTEGRATION: NEGOTIATING NEW MEANINGS

Projections are not as easily corrected as simple misjudgments about people might be. Rather, they can become deeply held, unconscious patterns that are repeated and staunchly defended—as in Terry's case, from her childhood family through her adolescent relationships to her adult relationships. These qualities become exaggerated so that they are dominant in the other, and vice versa. The psychic and communicative distance between people can be difficult to change. Imagine how quickly Terry and James would distance themselves from each other if they decided to part ways.

However, building on Gordon's (1995) metaphoric notion of the bridge, we can make an effort to explore our patterns and habits of projection as they provide paths for insight into the relationship between our inner and outer worlds and connectors between states of a relationship that enable us to become more intelligent communicators. The five following steps could be a useful set of dialogue topics to help Terry and James decide what to do with their relationship. Imagine that you are helping them to move beyond the crossroads at which they find themselves. The stages and the related discussion questions could form the basis of them negotiating a new meaning for their relationship. Use the following main negotiation questions as a framework for their discussion and imagine where they might go from here:

Negotiation Framework for Dialogue

How can each stage toward integration provide valuable insight from Terry and James into

- the ideal relationship they desire and the constraints that those ideals create?
- the minimally acceptable level of relational quality and needed change that they would be happy with?
- the concessions that each of them might make in order to get closer to the other person's ideal level?
- the demands that each of them would want to make of the other in order for the relationship to work and be redefined?
- what conditions would indicate that the relationship will not work and therefore should end?

Von Frantz (1982, p. 9) provides us with five overlapping and progressive stages in the withdrawal of projections and the movement toward integration. These stages involve both (1) the recognition that you are implicated in the images of the other that you see in the other's communication and (2) that you are able to distinguish the person from the characteristics and motives as the person might see in themselves. This is the basis of perspective taking in conflict (Kellett & Dalton, 2001, pp. 62–64). As you examine the three stages of projection, imagine using the related discussion questions as a basis for a productive dialogue between Terry and James. Follow the principles of negotiation and dialogue as you explore possibilities for managing this conflict through the meaning of the projections at its core.

1. *Recognizing the archaic identity:* This occurs when the projector recognizes the identification of the other with the projected quality. The projector realizes that the constructed identity of the other may be faulty or archaic. For Terry and James, assume for the sake of this exercise that they are open to learning from this concept of projection and want their relationship to work but recognize that it might end. Try to imagine how they might both answer the following questions:

- What specific qualities or characteristics am I seeing in the other through how I tell my side of the story?
- Is this really what the person is like, or is there a possibility that I am seeing these things or reading these things into his or her words and actions from my viewpoint in the conflict?
- What are some important ways that my identification of the other might be faulty, limited, and limiting for our communication?

How might the insight from these questions provide valuable possible concessions and demands for both sides that help meet the needs of both Terry and James as they negotiate?

2. *Differentiation:* Differentiation occurs when the projector is able to identify the difference between the other person and the projected images of him or her. The difference between the other and the constructed image tells what is being projected. Building on the insight gained from the first stage, the projector is able to recognize that there are some important differences between the opponent in the conflict and how that opponent is being seen. It is important to question the characteristic and assumed motives of the other that the projector holds as true. Try to imagine how Terry and James might answer the following questions:

- What are the specific ways that the other is probably different from the qualities and characteristics I have been projecting onto him or her?
- How might that other person likewise be projecting his or her qualities and characteristics onto me?
- How are we both different from how we are constructing each other?
- What happened to that important difference in the dynamics of our conflict—why did I not see it?

How might the insight from these questions provide valuable possible concessions and demands for both sides that help meet the needs of both Terry and James as they negotiate?

3. *Moral evaluation:* This critical evaluation of the projection is based on the recognition that the projected image is not necessarily a manifestation of the person and that this projection has a moral and ethical component and implications for communication. Try to imagine how Terry and James might answer the following questions:

- How do my projections onto the other person result in moral and even unfair judgments of that person?
- How are these judgments based on qualities or characteristics of myself?
- How can I become more critically evaluative of how and what I project onto others?

How might the insight from these questions provide valuable possible concessions and demands from both sides that could help meet the needs of Terry and James as they negotiate?

4. *Illusion:* This stage is based on the recognition that the projection can be illusory images of others: We could be, and probably are, as wrong about them as they are about us. This is often the most difficult stage because it is very difficult to accept that the way we see people is an illusion of our own making. Even if we know it is a projected image, and we have morally evaluated it as such, we tend to hold onto our images of the other. This is partly because we do not like to accept that we are working on a false construction, and partly it is because in our own storying of the conflict, we piece together the evidence that proves that our perceptions are true—even if they are based on an illusion. It is quite difficult to change our projected image of the other because even though we know it is a projection, we still believe that the

evidence suggests that how we see the situation may be true, even as a projection of something about ourselves. It is very hard for us to accept that our version of an event could be wrong; we all tend to believe that we are right most of the time. Try to imagine how Terry and James might answer the following questions:

- In what ways are my assumptions about the other in this conflict based on an illusion?
- What do I still believe to be true about the other person, even though I recognize the illusory nature of my account?
- What would it take for me to give up these illusions and perhaps replace them with more accurate or fairer and balanced images?

How might the insight from these questions provide valuable possible concessions and demands for both sides that help meet the needs of both Terry and James as they negotiate?

5. *Reflection:* This final stage is based on asking how the image could have become so powerful in judging the other and on recognizing the ways that it structures and fuels the conflict. Try to imagine how Terry and James might answer the following questions:

- How do these judgments affect my communication with the other and, in particular, the style and direction of the conflict we are in together?
- How could the projected image of the other have become so powerful and true for me?
- What can I learn from the insight gained by challenging the projected images in my own account?
- How does my evaluation of projection in a conflict create points of connection and opposition that can be used as discussion topics that are the basis of a more productive dialogue process?
- What are some other projected images that have become powerful in my intimate relationships?

How might the insight from these questions provide valuable possible concessions and demands for both sides that help meet the needs of both Terry and James as they negotiate?

Of course, it is important to recognize that projections are rarely only from one direction. Conflicts can spiral off into arguments based on mutually negative and equally inaccurate projections from both sides. I think we have seen this to some degree in Terry and James's conflict. Negotiations could easily devolve into name-calling and finger-pointing, matched by Terry imagining a new relationship with Patrick.

Once somebody projects an image onto you that you know to be false, the conflict naturally starts to focus on defending yourself from that projection and perhaps returning the tactic. It is also possible that you may find yourself the target of projections from the other person that you recognize as based on an inaccurate version of you. Learning how to help others recognize and work with their projections that they may be unconscious of is also a very considerable communicative challenge.

An important key to meeting this challenge is to approach the conflict as an opportunity to *find points of possible dialogue* that can take the participants to a deeper level of understanding. Terry and James are at the point where they are negotiating either an ending or a new beginning. Reexamine their story one last time for possible ways that they can question and move beyond their projections to a better understanding of each other. Assuming that you were working to mediate their conflict and got them to frame it as a reconciliation, try to reconstruct the conflict from that moment onward as they renegotiate the meaning of their relationship from one of disappointment to one of new beginnings. Recognize that it will not be easy and that a quick, happy ending is less likely than a lot of difficult argumentation as they strive for meaningful dialogue.

❖ LESSONS FROM THE FIELD OF PRACTICE:
  AN EXERCISE FOR EXPLORING PROJECTION IN CONFLICT

Working through the following exercise will challenge you to think about projection within your own field of practice—your everyday life.

Projection Exercise: Examining the Ideals and the Negatives You Bring to Relationships

Think of a time when you were in an intimate relationship with someone and found yourself or the other person using any of the following archetypal conversational scripts that suggest that projections are in action. Maybe they were used early on in a relationship and came back as issues when the relationship went through conflict. These are just a few examples; you may find other archetypal projections that are worth noting and discussing.

A Sample of Ideal and Negative Projection-Based Archetypes

- "You remind me so much of my [father, mother] in a good way." (An idealized quality is being projected which sets up false expectations.)
- "You are so different from my ex-[husband, wife, boyfriend, girlfriend], thank goodness." (The person is being compared in order to make up for the failures or incompatibility of the last partner.)
- "You seem to be perfect for me." (The person represents a cluster of idealized qualities. You may be perfect for them, or vice versa, but these need to be examined for their accuracy and reality with the actual person and for the underlying assumptions about what the inherently ambiguous term "perfect" means.)
- "Why can't I seem to do anything right for you?" (The other person is projecting personal feelings of inadequacy or imperfection onto you: "You should be perfect because I know I am not.")
- "Who were you with and what were you doing—are you cheating on me?" (If there is no realistic reason to be suspicious or jealous, then the person may be projecting personal guilt associated with actions or thoughts of a similar nature.)
- "I don't play games, but why do [men, women] always seem to be trying to play me?" (This is a projection of a negative quality onto a category of people, typically enabling denial of game playing on the part of the projector. This also sets up the justification for playing games as a defensive response to other people's games. "I am playing them before they can play me," is a typical pro-action.)

Discussion Questions

- Why do you think the particular archetype was used in your conflict?
- How did the archetype possibly relate to projection of an ideal or a negative quality by you and by the other person?
- What effect did the archetype and its related projection have on the relationship in setting up unrealistic expectations, relational pressures and tensions that resulted in conflicts, or creating negative depictions of you or the other person that resulted in competitive or conflicted communication, for example?
- How did the projections you have uncovered affect your relationship?

- What would you do differently to work with the projections if you could go back, and how would you do things differently in future relationships?
- What other archetypes have you come across in relational communication that seem to be connected to projections?

❖ CONCLUSION

Projection of both idealized and negative qualities seems to be a normal part of what people do in conflict. Projections are closely connected to our desire in competitive conflicts to portray the other as the villain and therefore ourselves as victim or hero. It is an issue of great concern when that normal habit crosses over into constructing the other as the enemy and makes it seem reasonable to use words as objects to throw as an attack.

Through this chapter, I hope you have seen how this phenomenon can close down dialogue, even create rancor, and yet at the same time also offer participants points of possible insight and even starting points for moving beyond negative projections toward more collaborative dialogue. It is possible to renegotiate the meaning of relationships based on exploring projections and how they impact those relationships.

If we have to engage in projection, perhaps we can all strive for ways to make divisive or violent conflict itself the villain of our stories that we are responsible for creating, so that the other can become a potential collaborator in managing the conflict. All of the divisive and collaborative processes discussed so far are based on our ability to use language in particular ways. Our interpretive and conflict management skills are also closely tied to our ability to see beneath and beyond the language of a conflict to problematize it and question and work from its meaning.

Part IV

Using Story Dynamics to Understand and Negotiate Conflict

8

Heroes and Sheroes, Villains, Victims, and Fools

Using Story Archetypes to Understand Conflicts

❖   ❖   ❖

> *[The purpose of dialogue is to remind us of] that which we have forgotten to remember.*
>
> —Maya Angelou
> (as quoted in Brown, 1995, p. 155)

> *Behind the story I tell is the one I don't. Behind the story you hear is the one I wish I could make you hear [or the one I don't want you or myself to hear].*
>
> —Allison (1996, p. 36)

A student met with me privately recently to discuss a very difficult conflict that she was encountering. She told me about being a single mom working her way through college and desiring very much to finish school before having more children. She had met and briefly dated a baseball player who was playing in the United States during his off season from Venezuela. They had sex one evening after he wined and dined her. She told me he did things to her that no one else had done, and she was enjoying the sex very much when the condom came off inside her. She jokingly suggested that he switch to a smaller-sized condom. She didn't want him to stop, he didn't want to stop, and they finished having sex unprotected. Several weeks later she was amazed to find herself pregnant with his child. At the point when she was telling me this story, she was 9 weeks into the pregnancy. She broke the news to him and he became furious—demanding that she get an abortion that he said he would not pay for. He had been text messaging her several times a day telling her to "get rid of it" and to "stop trying to ruin my life." He also told her that she must never contact his parents as it would bring terrible shame on him and that they may even demand that he marry her, which he had no intention of doing. He went back to Venezuela to play baseball. She went to the abortion clinic alone and could not bear the sights and sounds that she encountered. She is now left with a difficult conflict experience with the father and with her family and a difficult decision to make alone. She would like him to pay for the abortion. The longer she waits, the more difficult and expensive the decision will be. As you read this story, who strikes you as the villain of the story? Who is the victim, hero, or fool, if there are any of these characters in the story? How important are the details and form of the story told, and its relationship to the story possibly not told, in shaping the characters and the agency and blame? The ways that conflicts are shaped by story archetypes and the implications for representing and possibly renegotiating conflicts are at the heart of this chapter.

To connect this concept to you more personally, think of a time when you recounted a conflict in which you were a participant but the person with whom you were sharing the story was not. What role did you portray yourself as playing in the conflict? How did you portray the other person or people in the conflict? What main moral or idea were you trying to present to the listener? What subtle or perhaps even blatant changes to the story did you make so that the story fit the meaning that you were trying to communicate about yourself and the conflict? Are you still convinced that your account *is* what really happened and is *all* that happened? How might the other person's story differ from yours and, if it were different, why would it be different if you were both in the same event? Last, how might you both have used archetypes to more effectively negotiate the conflict by working to create a shared story, if that were possible? We come back to these questions later but, for now, realize that they are at the heart of this chapter. As the opening quotes suggest, telling the stories of our conflicts through particular archetypes guides how we actually remember those events. By the same token, perhaps we can also explore those memories for opportunities to question our stories, discover the limitations of our representations, and engage the possibilities for negotiating new, more collaborative stories through dialogue.

When people tell the initial story of their involvement in a conflict, they rarely portray themselves as the villains—unless as the villains, they find redemption. Rather, there is a distinct tendency to portray others as the villains—allowing oneself to be the victim or the hero or the fool who learns a hard lesson. These symbolic personae enable us as narrators to create the story of conflicts that make sense as archetypal stories. People come to strategically represent or symbolize key aspects, themes, or motives in a conflict in particular ways and therefore not in other ways. Our own villainy disappears from memory, and subsequent events often reinforce the archetypes we have chosen consciously or unconsciously. This narrative construction of the characters in a conflict has major implications for the process, progress, outcomes, and representations of conflicts.

Just as there are only so many characters in a typical account of a conflict, there are also only so many conflict stories that people live through and tell about. In examining several hundred stories, I found patterns of archetypes commonly repeated across many conflict experiences. Conflict stories are unique and real to their participants and at the same time, they tend to be variations on a few themes and stories. Besides containing archetypical characters, plot structures and devices, lessons and morals, and so on, conflicts have real personal and relational meanings. It is this relationship between the archetypal narrative structure and lived meaning that I want to tease out and work with.

This chapter explores how conflict participants construct their accounts of conflicts through archetypal characters and plots and other structural devices and the implications of those characterizations. Questioning the symbolic representation of the people, plots and motives, and portrayal of meaning is a key to opening up dialogic space for people to renegotiate their conflicts. This chapter shows how striving for exchanges of meaning, negotiating those constructions, and exploring the possibilities for using archetypes to renegotiate conflicts can create newer, more collaborative stories.

Main topics and learning goals in this chapter:

- Archetypes, meaning, and the construction of conflict stories
- Some cautionary notes on interpreting archetypes

- Questioning archetypes in a family conflict
- Impasses, double binds, and conflict archetypes
- Using three-cornered narratives to open up story possibilities
- Lessons from the field of practice

❖ ARCHETYPES, MEANING, AND THE
CONSTRUCTION OF CONFLICT STORIES

Archetypes and Narrative Traditions: Character, Motives, Plot, and Meaning

Archetypes are deeply habitual modes of practice that might be termed "patterns of behavior" (Shelburne, 1998). Jung characterizes these patterns or archetypes as being reflective of a disposition of the unconscious in that they manifest and are seen through the symbolic expression in human activities, such as dreams and myths and, for our purposes, how people experience and narrate their conflicts. Archetypes underlie and form the deep structure for much of the symbolic activity through which people express and share the meaning of their human experience. Archetypes are based on the need to structure and make familiar what is unfamiliar or shadowy. Hence, many of us share similar images, symbols, and story structures in our dreams and other activities. Archetypes are the product of a common universal heritage of people embodied in the collective unconscious (Davis, 2003). Other animals may also have their archetypes. Cats seemingly engage in dreams, which people interpret as them being chased as prey or chasing other animals as prey—deep, conflicted archetypes for cats. As humans, we draw on common archetypes to translate our personal experiences—of stress, for example, in being chased but not able to move, falling through space, teeth falling out, and so forth. Archetypes, like symbols, cannot be fully articulated or known—they are buried deep within the human psyche—but they are seen as they manifest in symbolic action such as communication (Moore & Gillette, 1992). The most obvious example is in fairy tales and myths in which the archetypal oppositions of good and evil and the struggle between heroes and villains are clearly and simply played out (Von Franz, 1997). Other very clear examples include such universal myths as the life-death-rebirth hero archetype that many cultures and religions embody in the narratives they hold dear and true (Davis, 2003). Other common archetypes at a very broad level of culture include the return of the true king, the search for the Holy Grail, the quest for an all-encompassing story of ourselves, and finding true love (Midgley, 2003). Within these archetypes, there are localized and specific details and story structures that bring them to life. Hence, in many conflict stories, you see the symbolic echo of heroes (lover; king; warrior with courage, kindness, and humor), heroines (perseverance and fidelity), villains (tyrants, weaklings, and evil forces), and so on. Similarly, you will see oppositions being played out through plot structures in which courage and cowardice, envy and innocent generosity, kindness and malice, self-sacrifice and lust or greed do battle in the twists and turns of the story and eventually establish the moral or message. Because conflict is a common human experience that is deeply tied to symbolic activity and narrative form, we are likely to find important and revealing archetypal images in conflict stories. They might not be as simple as the fairy story motifs, but if we dig deep enough, we find the archetypes that help us understand the meaning of our conflict stories and the possibility for discovering alternative or long-forgotten possibilities that we might use creatively to negotiate our conflicts effectively.

There has been some quite insightful research done on the presence of archetypal dramatic structure and characters in fictional literature and other narrative forms of storytelling in our culture (Bernardo, 1994; Black, 1994; Briller, 1999; Burke, 1990; Labre & Duke, 2004; Li-Vollmer & LaPointe, 2003; Meyer, 2003; Solomon, 1979; Zehnder & Calvert, 2004). This research provides valuable understanding of some of the most powerful archetypes used in our culture as they work their way into everyday personal narratives and, in particular, conflict practices. For example, Burke (1990) provides an account of the relationship between heroic and villainous protagonists in entertainment films as they reflect the audience and social needs at the time for such archetypes. He shows that hero-villain conflicts are at the basis of much popular media and are also used to structure the narrative relationships of people in many media events and genres, from political campaigns to situation comedies.

Of course, there are many other archetypes and their relationships within dramatic stories that have a bearing on our understanding of conflict stories. For example, characters and their motives, plot devices, and story morals or lessons are all pervasive as narrative devices in conflict stories. There is a vast literature on folklore and story traditions of how particular characters, plot, and morals are interconnected, that I refer you to as a resource (see Campbell, 1949, 1972, 1988; Hook, 1943; Klapp, 1962; Liszka, 1989; Rank, 1964; Willeford, 1969).

Here follows a brief summary of these concepts, with some examples that apply specifically to conflict stories. It is easiest to begin with *morals* as these often help the characters and plot to make sense, as they usually connect to establish this moral. (Sometimes a story has multiple morals or lessons.) Sometimes the title of a story reflects the moral; sometimes it is connected to the main lesson that one or more of the characters has to learn through the conflict. Some of the lessons I see people narrate over and over in friendships include the following: don't assume best friends last forever, the betrayal I never expected, and how we stayed close through a difficult time. Some of the lessons I have heard repeatedly in intimate relational conflicts include boy meets ideal girl, boy almost loses girl, boy wins girl back; getting to know the real person; negotiating sex, money, and power; facing our imperfections (or differences) together; learning to live together; overcoming an unforeseen event, threat, or enemy; and are we moving closer or falling apart? Some of the archetypical morals of family conflicts include the secret that explains so much, the secret revealed, working through a normal stage together, we worked out together the abuse that haunts me still, how can we be family and enemies at the same time, and new generation—same old conflict.

Supporting these lessons are the *characters* that function as protagonists, good and evil personae, victims (persons who appears to be dominated or subject to the actions of others in the conflict), villains (persons who embody the qualities oppositional to the heroes—often unethical, devious, or deviant), and fools (those who appear foolish but are wise or those who learn important lessons through their own folly). There are also supporting cast members who add to the story, move the plot forward, or introduce twists and turns and information that add to the plot, reveal an important secret, represent institutions and forces outside the story, and so on. In examining the characteristics and qualities, actions, and motives, you will discover the representational choices made (and not made) in how people are portrayed in order to tell the story a particular way. For example, heroes usually show nobility and integrity in some important way, triumph over adversity, or vanquish evil. When female, they are referred to as "sheroes." Either gender may be reluctant heroes, not driven by the love of the spotlight but powered by righteousness, such as in the case of freedom fighters and guardians of the weak and vulnerable. They may have superhuman qualities and yet be accessible as real, often flawed, people. They may almost lose to the forces of evil and have to struggle back to find redemption, to be the person in the story that they alone can be.

Characters achieve the moral of their stories through the twists and turns, ups and downs, and ins and outs of the plot and the various subplots that help make the main plot vivid and believable. Breaking a story down to the scenes and plot moments that make up the story reveals the choices by which the reality of the story is constituted. For example, you can explicate the phases of events that link the first premise of "boy meets girl" to the final event, where "boy and girl meet again"—this time with a deeper understanding of each other (we have to learn how to live together) or knowledge that this is the right and only person, previously unrecognized.

In the following explication of plot, you are documenting the twists and turns, moments of insight and necessary learning for the characters, turning points, false starts and wrong turns, moments when they hit rock bottom and all seems lost, events that pull them back together through the conflict, and so on. You also need to document any subplots that are used to reflect other aspects of the moral or its opposite—for example, when the evil force or villain is vanquished and gets his or her just deserts as the hero and heroine get theirs.

Look at Sam and Matt's story in light of these morals, character types, and plot structures, and you will begin to see the narrative basis of their conflicted reality. It is simply the way it happened for them, but it will start to come to life for you as *a story*—one among many possible ways that it could be told, crafted from bits and pieces of archetypes, and as such, open to your ability to ask good questions about a good story.

Pulling these threads together, archetypes provide the narrative vocabulary by which stories get constructed. These archetypes reflect cultural assumptions; storytelling traditions; and sometimes ancient myths, legends, and sagas to give meaning to everyday conflict practices in particular ways. However, we are not talking about a mechanistic or even fully conscious activity of making choices. People rarely think strategically about how they can tell their conflict stories so that they can be seen as the hero or the victim. Yet such practices are quite pervasive, especially in deeply divisive and acrimonious conflicts. Rather, archetypes reflect deeply and long-held cultural habits of storytelling practices. This is why we refer to these elements as archetypes: because they are beyond even what might be considered culturally typical; they are *archetypical* or foundational habits and practices. Some say such archetypes are expressive of structures and images deep within the human psyche and ingrained into such widely varied human endeavors as how we create historical accounts of human existence and how we dream about our own personal daily experiences at night. Think about the archetypal elements of a conflicted dream, such as running from an evil figure or force but not being able to move, for example. Exploring these archetypical practices is extremely valuable for understanding the narration of conflicts, the possibilities for questioning such practices, and how to collaboratively negotiate a conflict.

Familiarity with archtypical storytelling practices is crucial for us in examining the rhetorical and persuasive function of stories. More specifically, archetypes can be valuable rhetorical tools for examining three crucial communicative goals of conflict stories: First, how people construct the *agency* for conflicts—who and what forces did what to create the conflict. Second, when characters are represented within the plot structure of the story and as they connect to the moral, they take on *motives*—their actions have meaningful consequences within the story. Actions always imply particular ways that they should be valued and judged by the audience. Third, archetypes can be useful in examining implied and stated assumptions about *blame* in conflicts. Blame has to do with linking agency—who did what—through motive to the effects of that agency on the conflict—why those actions are responsible for the conflict, for its escalation, its negative and positive effects, and for its resolution or movement forward as a story. Linking the use of archetypes to the representational goals of the narrator and examining the limiting effects of those representations to the conflict that the stories represent is precisely what I want you to do as you examine the case study stories that follow. First, consider the following cautionary notes about archetypes and their analysis.

❖ SOME CAUTIONARY NOTES ON INTERPRETING ARCHETYPES

- *Conflicts are complex.* We need to recognize that real life is rarely as simplistic as an archetypal story of hero versus villain and the simple plot in which villainy is destroyed by righteous heroes. In real conflicts, there are multiple layers of experience, history, evolution of the conflict, and a variety of textures to the characters that make it difficult to invoke simple formulae. In fact, if a conflict story were presented to you in this fairy story simplicity, you probably ought to be suspicious that the narrator is not invoking the rich detail of the story as it might be told. This is often, actually, a good starting point for deconstruction of conflict stories when you problematize the archetypes and look for ways to open up alternative representations in the story-text.

- *Meanings differ.* We also need to recognize that the meaning of archetypes—what they represent—can change dramatically depending on who is telling and who is hearing the story. Very often, when two people tell their versions of a conflict, the characters and their motives are reversed and oppositional. The very use of oppositional archetypes—you are the villain in the other's story and the other is the villain in yours—tells you that the narratives reflect the conflict and are constructed to express that opposition. Similarly, it is important to recognize that sometimes the meaning of conflict stories, and how agency is constructed from the choice and combination of archetypes, is highly personal and quite deeply audience centered. The understanding of characters and their meaning for the story depends on what meaning the hearer (or viewer) wants to see. For example, Burke (1990) shows us that for some audience members, Glenn Close's character in *Fatal Attraction* is a homicidal psychopath, for some she is an avenging angel, and for some she simultaneously embodies aspects of both villain and hero archetypes as a richly textured analogue of both. We rarely tell and retell the same story the same way; being conscious of our audience, we may change characters, their motives, and even the moral of the story in subtle and sometimes gross ways to fit the communicative context. These various interpretive and representational issues can also be useful starting points for deconstructing the conflict itself.

❖ QUESTIONING ARCHETYPES IN A FAMILY CONFLICT

As you examine the following story, try to identify the specific characteristics, communication styles and behaviors, historical details of the person's life, and so on, that are connected together to create the villainy of the person with whom Matt is in conflict—Uncle Sam. Consider how the persona of Matt, his and Uncle Sam's relative motives, the plot, and the meaning of the conflict are interconnected. Also, try to identify how the portrayal of self and others and context are reliant on this construction of the uncle as the villain. Here are some questions to guide your initial analysis of the story as you read through it:

- How is Uncle Sam's villainy constructed so that their conflict gets portrayed in a particular way and so that the other parties exist as archetypes to him—as victims or heroes and so on?
- How do the specific details of the story help to construct Uncle Sam as a multifaceted person rather than as simply a cardboard cutout villain? Notice how he is believable as a real person as well as an archetype, because the story includes enough detail to construct him as a real person. He also has momentary efforts to get out of the villainy, false starts and efforts that show the possibility of his being someone other than the villain that he seems to continue to prove himself to be.

- How does the characterization of him seem to be self-fulfilling in that it proves that Matt is right? Isn't Matt also a little self-righteous about their differences on health and issues? Why does Matt make such a point of sounding so neutral and innocent as he portrays it to us?
- How might Matt be the villain to Sam in Sam's version of their relationship, and what does this tell you about how characterization helps them negotiate the continuing existence of their conflict?
- Are they in fact mirroring each other's behaviors and projecting similar characteristics onto each other—and could this be a possible point of dialogue and renegotiation between them?
- How does Matt construct himself as the hero of the story and partly as the victim?
- How does he construct the reluctant hero persona to give depth and texture to his own character?
- Are there ways, such as with saving money, that you see similarities between the characters?
- How do the two create a polarity with each other when in some ways they are similar?
- How do *your* portrayals of others draw on these archetypal devices and characterizations in similar ways to Matt?
- How does this affect your communication with that person and the form that the conflict takes?

"Slimeball Sam" (Matt)

My mother's three brothers have been part of my life since I was a child. My oldest uncle is 10 years older than me, the middle one—Sam—is 8 years older, and the youngest of the uncles is 3 years older than me. Sam is the uncle with whom I have the conflict. He is the wildest of the three but has become over the years quite a talented folk artist, creating a business selling pottery. His pen-and-ink drawings are also quite marvelous. He has also been known to abuse alcohol and has a history of criminal activity.

However, he has reformed from drinking out of fear of losing his wife of 5 years. He also has a great ability to save [money]. Not only does he make a healthy income but he saves like a miser. He is very tight and has a bit of money, I suppose. I have difficulty remembering a time when I was talking to Sam when something about the wisdom of saving money didn't come up. He often asks what I intend to do after college. When I make the normal undergraduate reply of, "I don't know" or "I'm not sure," he usually continues to give some condescending advice and tells me that I will probably not be able to find a decent job. Because of his success, he is puffed up in his mind, putting most of his interest and emphasis on his financial standing being above others.

The thing that makes dealing with his arrogance the most aggravating for me is that he has little integrity and is disrespectful of others. Basically, he is a slime-ball. Once he went to jail for taking liberties with a minor who happens to be my 10-year-old sister. I always tried to overlook the fact, but 10 years later, when the topic came up, he actually placed the blame for the incident on her. Once when his wife and children were on a trip to Florida, he explained, with hope in his voice as we shared some beers, that he would get several hundred thousand dollars if the plane were to crash. As the conversation progressed, he explained that he could kill his wife and burn her remains in the pottery kiln, leaving nothing but teeth. These are only a few of the examples of what type of personality I am dealing with in my conflict. It might be alright if someone was a little self-righteous or arrogant, but he goes way beyond that.

Even after all of the low-down things, I always tried to overlook the fact that he had little integrity, and remained friendly. We enjoyed playing blue-grass music together, and from time to time we were at least sociable. Our personalities would not be in such conflict if I didn't have to see him.

The thing that has relevance to this situation is that I live with my grandmother who is also his mother. My grandmother raised me since I was 12, and I moved out at the age of 21. Sam had already moved out by the time I moved in. Six years later, my grandfather died and left my 66-year-old grandmother alone. Around the days of the funeral, the question of grandmother's security and emotional health came up. Some of the family suggested that someone should stay with her and, because I had lived with her for 12 years of my life, she suggested that I would be the most likely candidate. This arrangement was suggested to me by all three of my uncles, but even loving my grandmother dearly, I explained that I really did not like the idea. However, because of the close proximity of my grandmother's house to my full-time job and my concern for her well-being, I accepted the responsibility to stay with her a few days a week. At the time, I had been staying in a house that belonged to my father and enjoyed living alone. But I felt it would be the least I could do for the lady who had helped me so much. Her house was close to my work, she is a great cook, and she has always been there for me. Another important point is that my grandfather and me never really got a long very well. He was really a jerk, very unfair to me and very disrespectful. I was the least favorite of all of his family, and his actions displayed that most of the time. He was regarded as a good person in the community but not to me most of the time. I, on the other hand, am a great person who might have some trouble with people sometimes, but I wish the best for everyone, *always*.

As time progressed, I was looking forward to starting back to college, and my grandmother suggested that I could stay at her house full time and commute to the University. This would be of benefit to both of us—I would not have to pay for food and rent and she would have some company. It has worked out very well, as I am almost finished with my major and have saved loads of money.

The one drawback has been in dealing with my Uncle Sam. He has become one of my greatest enemies over the last 2 years. Every time I hear his voice, I cringe because of the attitude and disrespect I feel he delivers to me. He is always condescending and talks to me like I am a small child who is unable to do anything for myself. I can truly say that I have come to hate him. So the conflict is between our personalities and our value systems. He loves the power that comes from money and has little use for integrity, while I respect truth and virtue—so we have differences.

The conflict started to emerge not long after I started attending college. As I came in early one morning from a jog, I greeted Sam and my Grandmother in the kitchen of her house. He often comes over for meals and to visit with his mother. We made small talk as I poured a glass of water. After some time, I innocently said something to my grandmother about the contributions that country ham makes to the general health of people. It was a perfectly sound statement, and my tone was joking. As the conversation continued over the course of breakfast, I asked my uncle Sam if he had quit smoking yet. He replied no, and I suggested that it was not very healthy. All the while, I was simply making conversation, as anyone does, around the breakfast table. Then as my grandmother left to get ready for church, my uncle said a few words about the disrespectful comments I had made about his smoking and about the morning dish of ham. I insisted that I had not at all been disrespectful to my grandmother, as I had only intended to make small talk. He gave me more about the smoking idea and then he said some of the most heart-cutting words I had ever heard from a person. He said,

"Well, it just seems funny to me that when my father was alive, you weren't allowed here, but now that he's dead, you suddenly appear."

I was flabbergasted at this statement that seemed so out of place. After saying something that I do not remember now for a rebuttal, he insisted that he was only telling me the truth. Then I informed him that he didn't know the truth, never had, and probably never would. In a heated discussion the next day, I informed him in a heated moment in the debate that from that point on, he was my enemy and that the ball was in his court if he wanted to change. Until this day, nothing has changed, and I do not have to look very far in his attitude to reinforce my picture of Sam as a slimeball.

These characterizations collectively function to maintain a competitive, distributive, and polarized sense of right and wrong. According to Matt, Uncle Sam is to blame and has all of the responsibility to change. According to Sam, I would guess Matt is to blame for his disrespect and his materially opportunistic relationship with his grandmother. They have managed to construct an almost perfect impasse. There seems to be no way out unless it involves the other person changing or not having to see each other. They are deeply double bound; being right requires the other to be blamed, to be wrong. We move on to explore the interrelationship of characters, plot structure and devices, and motives in Matt's story as a way to understand the meaning of his conflict story.

❖ IMPASSES, DOUBLE BINDS,
   AND CONFLICT ARCHETYPES

Sam and Matt have reached a point in their conflict where they provide each other with an enemy that then supports their own sense of
righteousness and the sense that each is the victim in the relationship.
They have also probably reached a point where both of them believe
they have done all that they could and that now it is up to the other
person to make things improve. Negotiation seems unrealistic at this
point. They also are likely to believe that most of the conflict is the
other person's fault. These are all characteristics of a conflict that has
reached an *impasse*. In an impasse, there seems to be no way forward,
the other person is in the way, and the only answer is to exit the relationship or try to dominate the other and force change that moves
them out of the way, symbolically or physically. The archetypes of
character and plot we referred to earlier are intimately tied to this
stalled and double-bound state of their conflict. Let's go back through
the story and try to deconstruct this relationship between the archetypes and the state of the conflict, and perhaps we can gain some
insights into how their impasse came about and what it might take to
work with their relationship. Of course, they may never want to have
a relationship beyond mutual enmity and hate; people can sometimes
come to rely on this to fuel their senses of self or believe trying
to change it is not worth the energy. However, it can be useful to
imagine what it might take to loosen or shift such a deeply conflicted
relationship.

Hawes (2004) provides valuable insights into the relationship
between impasse, double binds, and archetypes. In conflicts, there are
often many intersecting levels of opposition that create impasses—
points where dialogue has failed and the participants are locked in
opposition. It is at these narrative points or moments that discourse can
devolve into double binds such as oppressor–oppressed, victim–villain,
and so on. Each side will likely claim a need for justice and to be heard,
while the other appears to perpetuate the conflict or is portrayed as the
aggressor. They begin to sound alike as they draw on parallel archetypes to build their common opposition, and they will more than likely
locate the blame with the other. This leads to deeper entrenchment of
the conflict, as the archetypal portrayals of self and other become all the
more vivid and true. For Matt and Sam, the double bind occurs when
each of them needs the villainous portrayal of the other in order to portray himself as the victim-hero in the conflict. As Hawes explains,

In dialogue at impasse, in which participants are struggling with double binds, victims and victimizers ... sound increasingly alike in so far as each locates choices, agency and responsibility in the other, in effect blaming each other as the double bind becomes increasingly entrenched. (p. 178)

It is at this point also that defensiveness and its related tactics of anger, aggression, and intensity get produced and in turn deepen the impasse. They will each find the proof of their side of the story and will defend it against evidence that challenges that account or possibilities for change. Once this defensiveness sets in, the risks associated with listening beyond one's own account become greater and greater. Unless someone is willing and able to open up new possibilities for improving relations, violence is often also not far away at this point.

Yet as Hawes (2004) reminds us, listening beyond our own impulse for our story to be the truth and to deny the story of the other is a crucial risk to take if we are to negotiate movement beyond impasse and double binds. People may not want to listen, and they may not want to see the relativity of their own stories and the reality that their conflict is co-constructed as they hear the story of the other. The impulse might be to shift the relationship to memory, to history, to relational death; yet in listening is the possibility for speech, and as Hawes states, "speech is where the possibilities of dialogue incubate" (p. 179).

As you examine Matt's story, imagine what Sam's story might be like. Try to read between the lines of the people involved, and imagine how they might be both parallel and oppositional. This is where you will explicate the doubly bound reality of their relationship as they construct their conflict together. To help you uncover the archetypes by which they share in the co-construction of their relationship, answer the following questions:

- How is Matt constructing Sam as villain and himself as victim through the details of the story?
- How is Matt constructing Sam as the aggressor and himself as the reasonable person guided by justice?
- How is Sam made to appear as the one perpetuating, as well as initiating, the conflict?
- How do you imagine that they would sound alike or different as they might share their versions of the conflict?
- How does Matt specifically build his case that Sam is to blame for the conflict?

- What are the clues in the story that this has become a deeply entrenched conflict with seemingly no way out?
- What clues are there in Matt's story that both of them might be defensive about changing their account to explore the idea of reshaping their relationship?
- What are the clues that Matt is not ready to listen to Sam or that when he does listen to Sam, it is only to support his own version of reality?
- What do you think it would take to get these relatives to listen to each other and possibly talk about their divisions and connections, and what exchanges of concessions and demands it might take to move the conflict forward?

Hawes (2004) describes several key characteristics for a double bind to occur. Examining these characteristics in the action of Matt and Sam's conflict will help you to understand how they got to the point in the conflict that we now find them. Examine the story using the following related questions that will enable you to explicate their conflict as a double-bound relationship.

The Conditions for Double Binds to Occur

First, there are two or more persons, at least one of whom is designated a victim, whether by self or others.

- How does Matt designate and construct himself as the victim in the story?

Second, Matt and Sam have repeated experiences with each other so that the double bind becomes ingrained into their way of relating.

- In going back through the stages and sequence of the relationship that are revealed to us, how does the oppositional relationship of Matt and Sam devolve into more and more entrenched division and double bind?
- How do subsequent experiences get interpreted as further evidence of Matt's account—showing that their double bind relationship is ingrained?

Third, there is the primacy of a negative relationship, such as avoiding punishment, rather than the presence of nurturing.

- In what ways is their relationship based on specific negative thoughts, experiences, and communication rather than on nurturing?

- What do these forms of negativity do to build the divide between them?

Fourth, a second layer of negative injunction occurs but at a more abstract level (e.g., don't see this is punishment, but . . .).

- Do Matt's attempts to reconcile or make an effort to work on the relationship seem believable?
- How genuine does his claim to be making neutral small talk at breakfast seem to be?
- If Matt's claims are not genuine, then what is the negative motivation that gets portrayed as a positive intent beneath the breakfast talk?
- Are there other examples of deeper negative themes and issues going on in the family (for example, between Matt going to college and jogging and how Sam is portrayed)?

Fifth, a third layer of negative injunction occurs in which the victim cannot escape from the conflicted "field": They are interconnected as family, for example, or there is a promise of change that binds them together.

- What binds these people together? It is probably not love, but in many double binds, this is the third layer ("Can't live with him, can't live without him" in an archetypal third-layer double bind).
- What stops them from simply severing the relationship?
- How is Matt's grandmother an archetype of this third layer?

Sixth, the narrator starts to see the whole relationship and even their shared world in double-bind terms. It becomes difficult to see the other as anything but an enemy. At this point, one part of a double-bind sequence (one comment, for example) is enough to invoke the totality of the double-bind experience. Even attempts to talk about the conflict can be interpreted as double-bind tactics and add to the double bind and undermine dialogue. At this point, the worst conversations are about "where did this begin" and "who is to blame."

- What are some moments in Matt and Sam's relationship when there was the archetype of "almost a breakthrough," and what do you think triggered the relationship to fall back into the totality of a double bind?
- Why is having them sit down and try to trace the origins and responsibility for the conflict not necessarily a good conversational direction to take at this point?

The key to getting beyond this level of conflicted discourse and to know what is going on in a conflict, according to Hawes (2004), is to examine the conflict more at the level of *ontology*. Here, we move on to discuss the deeper ontological questions that we might ask of their conflict and that we might have them discuss if we had the ability to mediate their conflict. The question Hawes picks up at this point in his discussion is how do we dissolve doubly bound dialogues in which both claim the truth, and yet, neither truth works at all for the other? Part of the answer is to explore processes of *dominance* within the double-bound discourse as this is connected to truth claims. Making the other person the villain, presenting oneself as superior, and forcing the story to show that the other is the one who needs to change—all these are typical acts of dominance. Examine the following questions to explore dominance in their relationship:

- What are the narrative and relational tactics through which one or both are struggling for dominance in the conflict account in terms of portraying the other and asserting the superiority of the self and the other as the locus of the need for change?
- In what ways does this struggle create a character—a person—who is subordinate *and* who appears to deserve to be subordinate?
- What details of Sam does Matt build into his account that make his own dominance in the relationship seem reasonable, even necessary?

A second strategy is to explore the process of problematizing their truths as truths in relation to the other. Telling the truth and problematizing those truths as being intimately connected to power and the struggle for dominance and superiority in the relationship is a crucial dialogic process.

- What are we expected to take as true about Sam that might blend truth and fiction?
- What might Sam's story of their relationship be like?
- What might Sam try to have us take as truth about Matt and their relationship that shifts the meaning of their conflicted relationship and calls Matt's story into question?
- How might Sam's account differ in key aspects of representation and blame from Matt's? Perhaps Matt might consider how his own tactics push his uncle into his villainous role.
- What does he do to create his uncle as the villain, and why is this connected to truth claims? What ontological function does Matt similarly serve for his uncle?

- How can these people really listen, begin an exchange about their stories and their relationship, and possibly begin renegotiating their relationship?
- What would be a good starting point for allowing speech to incubate dialogue when they seem to hate each other so much?

Another aspect of this truth-based ontology question that connects to the quote at the beginning of this chapter has to do with exploring deeper levels of truth that these two have chosen not to consider in their accounts so far or for which their double bind has made them unconscious. Perhaps both Matt and his uncle might consider why they need each other as enemies in their particular family.

- What does the conflict they share do for them as uncle and nephew in this family?
- How might previous conflicts and ongoing patterns be a deeper part of their current relationship (we are given hints of problems with the grandfather when he was alive, for example)?

These types of questions are deep and often too close to home to manage for oneself. In such cases, a third party can sometimes work effectively through three-cornered narratives.

❖ USING THREE-CORNERED NARRATIVES
   TO OPEN UP STORY POSSIBILITIES

Intervention by a third party to help the people in the relationship to negotiate more dialogically—what Hawes (2004) calls a three-cornered narrative—is a complex and problematical practice, although it does offer the chance of moving a relationship forward. Even if Matt and Sam desired to work on their conflict out of their own volitions or for the sake of their grandmother-mother, it would not be a simple process of dissolving the conflict through communication. There are several dangers and guidelines as well as related strategies that should be followed to help ensure that the dialogue progresses productively. The dangers are, first, that the people in the double bind may see the intervener as vested in the outcome rather than just neutrally involved, as it is a competitive relationship to begin with.

In this example, Matt and Sam will likely at least initially see you, the intervener, as taking the other person's side. They may also not recognize that they are in a double bind or that they are part of creating it. Matt and Sam are likely to portray things as the other person's fault and that they could personally let it go if it were not for the actions of the other. When they are confronted with the double bind by you as an outsider to their conflict, you risk a certain amount of denial and even collaboration between the participants against you. Remember that they are family despite their enmity. Similarly, there may be deep levels of distrust both between the participants and with the mediator, as double-bind relationships often involve the overestimation of the power and choices that the other has and the underestimation of one's own power and access to choices (I've done all I can, but he keeps . . .).

A second danger is that the intervener may be positioned in the double bind–discourse as a rescuer—someone who makes things right and brings justice back. This sets up expectations that create failure in which the victim, here probably both relatives, holds onto the archetypal identity of the oppressed (I have . . . minimal power, limited resources, compromised choices, and lack of accountability) and leaves the mediator with the impossible task of rescuing the relationship for them. A relationship of blame by the oppressed and guilt by the villain can also emerge and become entrenched. The participants often turn at this point to righteous indignation. There are clues that Matt has perhaps reached this point.

Third, denial and defense can also cycle together. As Matt and Sam deny their double-bound relationship, they may become more defensive about having a problem at all. These cycles put the intervener in a strange position: the intervener has to be undaunted by resistance and negative portrayal and yet can easily end up doing the work of convincing the participants that they have a collective problem for which change is possible. This may feel somewhat like an imperialistic viewpoint on the lives of others. Here are some questions to guide you as if you were mediating the conflict between Matt and Sam:

- How might you make sure that Matt and Sam would see you as a neutral third party?
- How do you think they would react as you show them their double-bound relationship?
- How do you think they would react as you show them carefully how they helped to create and maintain this dysfunctional conflict?
- What would you do to manage these reactions and make sure the two don't undermine your attempt to help them?
- Do you think that they might deny the double-bound reality of the conflict or even collaborate against you?
- How would you work with their levels of distrust for you and for each other?

- How might you address your role and your boundaries and limits so that you do not get portrayed as the rescuer with all the answers?
- How do you think some of the destructive cycles, such as denial and blame, might emerge from working with Matt and Sam's conflict, and how would you manage those cycles as they emerge?

These are all very difficult questions and are often difficult to predict in terms of how and if they might manifest, but they are worth considering before you might step in and try to intervene. After all, you do want the discourse to focus on their relationship and not on questioning you or undermining the process.

Useful Guidelines and Strategies for Managing Three Cornered Narratives

The important strategies for maintaining open dialogue and a negotiation-based exchange include the following:

- First, try to get Matt and Sam to share multiple responsibilities for roles and feelings such as suffering, compassion, and guilt. To get them to recognize that they are part of the construction of the conflict and therefore partly responsible for it is a big step toward getting them to see the conflict as something that they have co-constructed. This will not likely happen immediately—it is too big a step—but as you work to question and destabilize their notions of truth and blame (see the steps that follow), you will create dialogic room for this to emerge.

- Second, destabilize the polarized narratives by asking recursive questions about will and desire, resistance and reality, and so on, that have unknown answers. These force participants outside of their fixed account into the realm of imagination. "What are you willing to do . . . ?" "What would happen if . . . ?" are good examples of this type of question that stimulate a negotiation mentality. These questions can turn double-bound discourses inside out if the participants approach them willingly and allow their imaginative talk to incubate dialogue and to think about what it would take from the other to concede certain things and to move the conflict forward.

- Third, focus on the content and dynamics of their communication as they talk. For example, getting them to speak in the first person from their lived experience of the conflict, rather than in terms of double-bound archetypes, is a useful strategy. Listening carefully to what is being said and what is not being said, and asking the participants to do the same, can also be valuable strategies. Focusing the talk wherever possible on getting the participants to develop more and more possibilities—sometimes called "expanding the pie"—is a constructive way of framing the dialogue as a positive process. Changing the metaphors rather than the topics is another way of framing the discourse so that dialogue can emerge. For example, a "feud" is a very different image from a "rebuilding process" and can, if accepted by the participants, reframe the conversation accordingly. Encouraging mistakes and reassessments rather than staying on the level of politeness allows the participants to admit mistakes and also go back to issues without fear that they are breaking a surface preoccupation with politeness and cordiality that can mystify and obscure the expression of true feelings and experiences. Last, it is important to assume a desire for growth that enables you to focus on positive aspects of the double-bound discourse. This relies on your ability to see the participants other than in terms of them having a problem and you being the rescuer or hero of the story—which would put you in a form of double bind yourself with both people in conflict—as potentially reasonable people who might change if they could develop the right three-cornered narrative pathway out of their impasse.

❖ LESSONS FROM THE FIELD OF PRACTICE: AN EXERCISE
    FOR FURTHER ANALYSIS OF NARRATIVE ARCHETYPES

**Exercise: Reflective Questions for
Uncovering Your Own Archetypes**

Use the following questions to reflect on your experiences of representing people and relational dynamics in conflict stories that you tell and stories told by other people in which you have found yourself to be part.

• Think of the last time you were portrayed in a conflict story in such a way that it surprised you. What was it about the other person's representational choices that surprised you? How did their portrayal of you make you feel? What reaction to their story did you have as a defense to or extension of their portrayal?

• Think of the last time you heard another person's account of a conflict that you were involved in or witnessed that was quite different from how you would have told the story. What were the key differences? How do these differences affect how the conflict is portrayed or represented? Why would your account be different?

• Think of a time when you were conscious of retelling the story of a conflict in which you actively changed the emphasis, selected aspects for exaggeration, and left details out. Why did you do this? How did your changes shift the meaning of the conflict that the listener was supposed to get from your account?

• Think of a series of conflicts in different contexts of your life—close relationships, friendships, family, workplace colleagues, and so on. What aspects of how you lived through and managed those conflicts were similar? What patterns of story structure and process, characterization of people, and moral tend to remain across those conflicts for you? In other words, what archetypes do you tend to rely on to represent your experience of conflict? What do these patterns tell you about yourself as a conflict communicator? Are there any of these patterns that you might question or that you would change if you could?

• What conflict archetypes would you like to add to or develop in your repertoire? For example, you might want your stories to establish a particular narrative moral that you believe is important in relationships. Or you might want them to end differently. What might you have to change about how you actually do conflict in order to make those archetypes real as new possibilities for you? How might you tell the conflict stories that you wish you could tell but perhaps are not doing so at this point?

• Which conflict story archetypes do you wish you could reduce your reliance on? Why do these undesirable archetypes seem to persist in your conflict experiences? What would it take to change your reliance on them? What would this mean for how you do conflict and how you might change your representations of people, forces, dynamics, and processes of conflict?

❖ CONCLUSION

Archetypes, we have seen in the main story of this chapter, are at the same time profound and questionable. They are profound in that they connect cultural values and even ideologies, deeply historical traditions and practices of storytelling, and the everyday communicative practices of people doing conflict and organizing their experiences into narrative form. In this sense, people's stories can provide windows into each of these interrelated dimensions of conflict stories. Similarly, exploring these dimensions of conflict—culture, storytelling traditions, and everyday practice—as they contribute to the symbolic vocabulary of the narrative in the form of archetypes can be an excellent source of understanding and a starting point for open dialogue and negotiated exchange about the conflict.

Story archetypes provide a sort of vocabulary that influences the ways that people engage in conflict and limits the possibilities that they are able to talk about and see, both during a conflict and as they look back on it through that lens. Archetypes limit the ways that people do conflict and provide a vocabulary for how we talk about conflict. As we have seen in the case of Matt and his uncle, archetypes can also provide the opportunity for reflexivity into the way that conflicts are managed.

A truth about dialogue is that it is the quality of communication that enables deeply held beliefs and assumptions to be brought to the surface, questioned reflexively, and potentially changed. Hence, archetypes are eminently useful in the sense of enabling the deconstruction of conflicts and the creative reconstruction and redirection of conflict stories and relational realities.

Some conflicts, you will discover, are more open to reconstruction than others. You would probably agree that April and John's conflict in the next chapter has a lot more hope of reconstruction and redirection than Matt and Sam's. But you never know until you try, and perhaps we need to explore our archetypes of "hopeful" and "hopeless" conflicts for ways that they structure the assumptions and expectations embedded in how we interpret and judge conflict stories. Perhaps "you never know until you try" is a better archetype to work from as a mediator than "hopeful" versus "hopeless" because it invites the dialogic energy to at least make an attempt. Assuming that negotiation is possible is important. Sometimes the most entrenched and double-bound relationships can surprise you, and sometimes the ones that seem simple can quickly get more complex and further from resolution. Recognizing and questioning the archetypes that we bring to the analysis and understanding of other people's archetypes is another crucial form of reflexivity that we should strive to develop as an important interpretive skill.

9

Learning to Tell
the Next Chapter

*Story Archetypes and the Negotiation and
Mediation of New Meanings in Conflicts*

❖   ❖   ❖

*Mediators are interested in employing strategies that will
take some of the intensity out of the conflict and destabilize
it to the point where alternative stories can be considered.*

—Winslade and Monk (2001, p. 6)

A student of mine, Eddie, shared his family conflict with me recently and asked me what he should do about it from where it now stands. As requested, he began to tell me the background. He had grown up in a very strict, very conservative "Christian" home in which the Republican Party was regarded as the only true Christian party. He felt that he had grown up going along with his parents' ideals but that during college had begun to think for himself more, challenge the tenets of his family beliefs, and develop his own perspectives. The current conflict came to a head when he went home to vote during the presidential election. He was driving to the local fire station with his dad to cast their votes when they began talking about their intentions to vote. It was at this point that his dad began to argue that Kerry wasn't a true Christian because he was Catholic, pro-choice, and for equal rights for gays and lesbians. Eddie told his dad that he thought he was a bigot and a hypocrite—and threw Bible verses at him about judging people. Things escalated to yelling, pointing, and screaming. His dad told him that his liberal professors had brainwashed him. Eddie felt chastised and ridiculed and could not understand his dad's refusal to accept his differences. The conflict made him not want to come home. He remains angry and the conflict with his dad is unresolved.

This brief sketch of their conflict suggests to me that there are several possible paths ahead for them. They can simply put the conflict on hold and avoid it. They can become estranged and allow the things that divide them to take deeper root in their respective stories of their family experience. They can agree to differ and not discuss this difficult subject but focus on the things they do have in common. They can hash it out and try to get to the bottom of their differences and see where that takes their relationships. They can try to explore what each of them most wants as a resolution to the conflict.

My guess is that Dad wants to be recognized for the good parenting he provided—something that Eddie might be willing to do. My guess is that Eddie also wants to be recognized for being a grown-up who is on his own journey into developing his identity and beliefs—something his dad might be willing to do. Would sharing these desires be a possible starting point for productive dialogue between them? Could they also ignore these common interests and focus their energies on building a story of estrangement that creates years of space between them? It happens this way quite often. Of course, both forks in the road are possible. There are many possibilities for the next chapter of their relationship, depending on what they want, what they are willing to give, and how well they communicate about and coordinate those interests. The communicative choices that each of them makes at this point will dictate the next chapter that they experience together.

This process of uncovering possibilities and developing the dialogic negotiations that make the most desirable version of the next chapter into reality is what we explore in this chapter.

Main topics and learning goals in this chapter:

- Archetypes as opportunities for dialogue, negotiation, and mediation

- Learning to tell the next chapter through narrative mediation
- Lessons from the field of practice

❖ ARCHETYPES AS OPPORTUNITIES FOR DIALOGUE, NEGOTIATION, AND MEDIATION

Managing conflict using a narrative approach is a lot like learning how to tell the next chapter of the story that you find yourself in. The main story in this chapter illustrates a moment of truth where the couple—John and April—seems to desire to move forward and create a happy relational story, but something is holding back the moment that will push their story forward.

Perhaps you've experienced a similar situation, where a relationship is stuck at a particular chapter and because of conflict, the story is stalled. Perhaps you do not know what you want the next chapter to be. Perhaps the story is poised at the point of transformation or ending—the archetypal crossroads—and you are too afraid to face the responsibility for directing the story along to the next point. Perhaps moving forward would cause you or the other person to question and perhaps change the archetypes that you have come to rely on and that have brought you this far in the story. Perhaps also the story is stalled through relational inertia, and you need a good energizing conflict to move it forward to a new understanding and mutual definition.

All of these are moments in relational conflicts when effective communication becomes crucial. One of the big challenges is in not knowing the ending of the story, which would make it easier to figure out how to get there from where you are now. Rather, most relational conflicts call for extrapolation skills: knowing how to move beyond the current configuration to create the next step in a largely unknown sequence of relational phases. To do this, insight into archetypes of character, plot, and narrative dynamics can help develop an understanding of how to move forward together to create a new chapter through the current conflict.

As you engage in your first reading of the following story, think about opportunities for creating dialogic negotiation between the conflicted couple so that they can emerge through the conflict into a new relational chapter. As you start to look into the relational world of John and April through her story, what would it take for him to become a more complete hero? Where could the story go next? How might they actively choose to get there by initiating changes to the archetypes and characters they are playing? What does each of them most desire from the other, and what would it take for them to exchange that concession for something they desire? As you will see, April has expectations for creating a fairy-tale relationship. As their-helpers in moving their story forward, think about how you would do this difficult narrative work— helping them to recognize the limitations that such an idealized arche- type might involve. Follow the guidelines and related questions that follow to discover how to use narrative mediation techniques and story archetypes as the bases for understanding and managing conflicts dia- logically (Winslade & Monk, 2001). I chose this story because it is emi- nently possible to discover a solution-based narrative to this conflict. It is full of hope and full of possibilities to be discovered by them and by you.

Having analyzed the construction of a conflict through narrative archetypes, we move on to focus on a relationship that is significantly more rescueable. The relational story you are about to examine ends well—the two are happily married, although at the time the story tells about, they faced a difficult conflict in their relationship. Between where they are in the story and the happy ending, your challenge is to interpolate—to think about—how you might help them to complete the intervening steps that connect the two states. Your challenge is, more specifically, to use narrative archetype principles and devices to imagine a communicative path between the story they want to tell at the end and the conflict they are in at the moment of conflict. As you read April's story, imagine what the two need to exchange or negotiate in order to connect the present to the future they want.

"Still a Little Hung Over" (April)
John and I (April) have been dating for almost 2 years. What began as a sum- mer flirtation, sparked by more than a few drinks, has turned into a serious long- term-commitment. At first I thought that our relationship would be just physical because, although John was handsome, I wrote him off as a brainless ex-high- school football star. We had fun together and I enjoyed kissing him, but I never expected to enjoy having a conversation with him. As we evolved into a couple, I began to be attracted to John on an emotional as well as physical level. He was kind, to people and animals, and had impeccable manners. He treated me like I wanted to be treated. Instead of always mumbling that I was pretty, John told me that I was intelligent, a good writer, and a good friend. He appreciated the subtle aspects of my personality that not many others had even noticed. We had more in common than I realized at first, and I had to admit to an error in judgment. John was not the jock I had at first thought he was. He was a unique person who I loved very much.

However, as in every fairy tale, there was an evil force working against the happiness we had created together. Although I did not notice his erratic behavior at first, after a few months of being with John, I started to see several upsetting patterns. He would bring a pint of Crown Royal with us to the movies and sip it. He would promise to meet me somewhere and then never show. I would later find him passed out in either his car or bed. He showed up at my room one morning at 8 o'clock demanding to be let in. He woke up half the girls on my hall yelling at me. When I finally let John in, he fell on my bed and passed out for 16 hours straight. One night, at a barbeque, John became enraged that I was showing his friends some pictures he found inappropriate. He yelled at me in front of a large group of our friends while denying that he had anything to drink. I found out later that he had chugged a half gallon of fire water that afternoon.

I should have broken up with John at that point, but I have always been attracted to wounded birds. I wanted to help him. I thought that if I loved him enough to make up for his Mom dying when he was 8, he would stop drinking. So I would hold him when he closed down the bar and then started to cry because he did not know where he was. I would talk to him at 4 in the morning, so drunk that his voice seemed to be struggling to be heard from underneath water. I took care of him and waited for him to realize that he was hurting both of us, only he didn't.

On Christmas Eve, John was arrested for driving while impaired. His blood alcohol was almost four times the legal limit in Virginia. This gentle guy assaulted a police officer and used his urine to paint the walls of the holding cell. He decided to enter a treatment facility and went dry a year and a half ago.

Although he is now sober, our relationship is still struggling to overcome the damage done to it while John was drinking. Although I attended counseling sessions with him, I never said what I really felt; I didn't want to make him feel guilt for hurting me. I didn't want him to know that I didn't trust him. I thought it was more important to help him get better than to heal myself.

Today, instead of the evil being the alcoholism, what has infected our relationship is more complicated. I cannot be angry with him for drinking anymore, and I can't protect him, but I don't know how to treat him. I am trying to trust him but if he is 20 minutes late, I start to worry. I envision him passed out at the wheel or salivating in front of a liquor store. This is irrational because John has an amazing will. Once he decides to do something, it gets done. I don't really think he will ever drink again, but in some sick way, a small part of me wishes he would. As miserable as our relationship was while he was drinking, I knew my role, and I had the confidence of knowing that I was a superior person.

I am fairly certain that John and I will get married. He has worked really hard to have his own self-respect. He has developed a sense of self-pride. He goes to class and makes good grades. He supported himself for a long time and has concrete goals for the future. I love the person that he is today, but I am still getting to know him. This John is not at all the person I started dating, and I am still adjusting to life with him.

Some Initial Questions for Understanding
Plot, Character, and Motive in the Story So Far

The following questions will help you to dig deeper into the story that we have so far for April and John. From this point, we will explore and apply the technique of narrative mediation as a way to move their story forward.

Character and Motive Questions

- What are the qualities that characterize John as a hero figure in April's story?
- The relationship evolves from a "flirtation" to a "long-term commitment." How do these archetypes carry assumptions and expectations that are important to the conflict?
- What archetypal role has April come to rely on playing in the relationship?
- How is her attraction to "wounded birds" suggestive of her archetypal role in the relationship?
- What is John's main flaw—his Achilles' heel—as the "hero" of the story, and how does his flaw connect to April's archetypal role as his lover-nurturer who does not know what to do next?
- How does this archetypal role and plot twists hold back the story from progressing?
- How does the seeming double-bound plot archetypes of loving him but not knowing how to treat or protect him offer a moment of insight into April's assumptions of her role in the relationship?
- Is there a victim in the story?

Plot Questions

- How is "filling the gap that his mother left" an important plot archetype?
- How is his "hitting rock bottom" an important plot device in terms of a turning point in the story?
- The "unspoken truth that haunts her" seems to be an important theme that April is wrestling with. How is this unspoken truth an important plot archetype in her conflict and in conflicts more generally?
- The driving force of the conflict seems to be a transition between the relationship archetypes of "magical beginning" and "the challenge of learning to live with each other." How is this learning

period positioned as an important plot device between the magical beginning and the hope to live happily ever after? How does this archetypal transition give you hope for the couple? How might it be the basis for helping them move forward in their story? What does this transition between archetypes tell you about the moral of this story? Are relationships, for April, a combination of magic and the work of learning to make it work?

- What positive attributes of John as the hero offer hope to the story?
- What details of his life and his behavior point to the possibility that they will get married and quite possibly live happily ever after?
- What controlling or even dark ("evil") forces have led the story to the tangled point where we find it?
- We find the story poised in a complicated moment, suffused with dramatic tension and all sorts of possibilities. How does the plot get to this complicated period, and what are the possibilities that leave the story poised and full of possibility? For clues to these possibilities, think about their hopes and fears and the dangers to the relationship at this threshold to the next chapter.
- How would you summarize the main moments in the plot so far, using an archetypal "boy meets girl" storyline as your guide? The story begins with "girl meets boy"; what are the main plot moves from there until the end of the story? How does this plot structure rely on specific qualities and forces inside and outside the characters to move the story through this storyline?

Questions for Moving the Plot Forward

- What would have to happen to those forces, whether to replace them or defeat them, so that both of the main characters and the plot can move forward?
- What is the moral of the story so far, and how might the protagonists question or change that moral or central theme that the story is organized around?
- What are some alternative ways that this couple might talk about and think about the characters and plot structure of their relational story?
- What redemptive turn can you imagine that might move them, and their story, forward? Look closely at April's description of what is and what was the source of "evil" in their story that brought them to this turning point.

- What would it take to reach this redemptive turn or even a much smaller plot development that might help them to achieve their next chapter?

Use the insights gained through the foregoing questions to imagine how you might help this couple move their relationship forward. To do this, follow Winslade and Monk's (2001) technique of narrative mediation. To guide you in your mediation work with this couple, remember that they did get married and are doing very well together, so they did discover a way forward with their story. You now have to imagine how they might have done that through strategic and ethical communication.

❖ LEARNING TO TELL THE NEXT CHAPTER THROUGH NARRATIVE MEDIATION

It is important to recognize some of the main assumptions about the narrative paradigm and specifically about narrative approaches to mediation as we begin to outline such an approach to moving April and John's story along. First, stories ought to be regarded as constitutive of the reality of a conflict (Winslade & Monk, 2001, p. 3). We have to believe that *the story shapes and is partly shaped by the conflict experience* rather than simply functioning to report a given reality or truth. This is a key assumption because we are about to develop a process by which April and John can reshape their story. We have to believe that the reshaping of the story will be reflected in the lived reality of their relationship. Looked at another way, there is little point in working at developing the story if the reality of the relationship does not parallel the narrative changes.

Second, and linked to the first, is the idea that *stories generated to mediate conflicts do not necessarily have to be completely true*. Rather, it is important to acknowledge that stories often blur the lines between fact and fiction, between literary texts and lived social and conversational discourse. As Langellier (1989) aptly puts it, stories are boundary phenomena—they blur the lines between fact and fiction. If we accept this, we are free to think creatively about stories. We can think of stories as powerful devices that we can use to evoke possibilities for people in conflicts and that might help generate better stories of the future because they energize and create direction and flow in a conflict.

Third, it is important to begin the process of mediating a conflict using a narrative approach with the understanding that you should *work from the stories that represent the lived experience of the people in the conflict.* In order for people to buy into a narrative process in which they are rebuilding or redirecting the story of their relationship, they would naturally want to start with their current story as a representation of their viewpoints and places in the conflict. Recognize also that as the mediator, you are helping create a third narrative—a three-cornered narrative, as was discussed earlier. Given the first two assumptions, there are responsibilities associated with helping to create a new story that then becomes reality for the participants in some senses. The quality of your advice and leadership in the process will have a direct impact on the formation of the next chapter of their story and, therefore, perhaps the next chapter of their relationship.

The main task for you as mediator of this conflict is to help the couple open up room in their story for alternatives and for a new direction for the story as a result. Within the story so far, and the characterization of the people in it, are judgments and accusations and depictions of people that create "totalizing descriptions" (Langellier, 1989, p. 5). *Totalizing descriptions* occur when the archetypes used to tell the story limit or close down opportunities to expand or change it. Totalizing descriptions are often seen in connection to the moral of the story when the conflict is portrayed as an overly simple or obvious case of something. They are also seen in connection to the way that characters are depicted, particularly in terms of double binds and enemy relationships, when people are seen as simplistic archetypes. Think back to Matt's story of his relationship with his uncle, and you will see very clear totalizing descriptions of his uncle and their relationship. The totalizing descriptions in John and April's story are perhaps more subtle and less obviously judgmental and accusatory. Their relationship is much more full of hope than Matt's, I think. However, if you dig into the plot, moral, and archetypes of character, you may find some opportunities to help John and April question the underlying judgments, assumptions, depictions of characters and forces, and even perhaps accusations. Use the following questions to help you to develop your own approach to opening up space in their relatively tightly woven story so far.

- How would you try to create narrative space in their conflict stories—particularly hers, as that is the one that we have? What questions and topics would you prepare for them, to achieve this opening of dialogic space?

- What assumptions, judgments, accusations, and depictions would you help them to question together, and how might this discussion help them exchange important demands and concessions as they negotiate?
- Would you characterize any of April's account as containing totalizing descriptions, and if so, how would you get them to see that these limit the story?
- How might questioning these narrative archetypes lead to an opening of the story to build on the "learning to live together" plot archetype?

Strategies for Opening Up Discursive Space

To help you open up discursive space within their story, Winslade and Monk (2001) offer several important mediation strategies. First, they illustrate the importance of *building trust* in the mediation process and in the mediator. Your job as mediators is partly to destabilize and question the story so far through helping April and John to see the limitations of their representational archetypes. This can be a threatening process unless you and the process you are managing are trusted. You will have to make sure the participants clearly see that you understand where they are in their relationship and in their conflict without appearing to take sides. Fairness and impartiality are important connectors to trust. As soon as you start to get people to question their stories at a deep thematic level, they will often become defensive and will, initially at least, prefer to find ways to reinforce their senses of injustice, betrayal, victimization, or mistreatment. Respectful listening is a key communication skill. You must convey to the participants that you take their story of the conflict seriously and that you are simply trying to help them discover additional or alternative story lines that will benefit them.

- It seems that the archetypes of "magical meeting" and "living happily ever after" have already broken down for this couple. How might you help them more fully destabilize the story—separately or together—in such a way that they trust you?
- Are there ways that either or both April and John might become defensive as you encourage them to question their archetypes in the story?
- I don't sense much in the way of betrayal or injustice in April's story, but do you think John might experience some of this when he finds out she does not fully trust him?

- How would you make sure you listen to each side respectfully and fairly as you move into these somewhat difficult conversations about secret fears and unspoken truths?

Second, Winslade and Monk (2001) show you how to *develop externalizing conversations*. This powerful technique involves getting the participants to talk about the conflict less as something that comes from within themselves and more from the context of their relational domain. Simply, you need to get the couple to talk about the conflict as a story that exists outside of them that can be told, talked about, and questioned as if they were not part of it, as something that is external to them. Have them imagine that their conflict is a movie that they are watching together or as something that they are observing as third parties to the story. This will tend to neutralize the intense energy of the conflict and will help them to step outside of their story and look back on the archetypes they have relied on to construct their conflict story so far. These archetypes are particularly useful to analyze, as differences in telling the story can help to focus the talk and ideas for change in that story. Changing characterization, plot, and so on is one way to do this. You might have the couple play with changing archetypes in the story and imagining how the story would change as a result of those choices. This gets them in the mode of focusing on the story and how it might be changed and away from any blame or other totalizing and personalizing or internalizing aspects of the story so far. Of course, you must also be sensitive to the fact that this *is* their story, and they will also need to talk about it as something deeply personal and true for them.

- How would you briefly paraphrase the story for them so that they can see it as an externalized account that they can step away from and look at as a story?
- In what key ways might you expect their stories to be similar and different if they were told as if about someone else or from a movie script?
- What central archetypes in April's story would you have them both play imaginatively to help them see more possibilities?
- Might there be any issues of blame that you would have to work with in this conflict? Think of self-blame as a possible issue for John. April is careful to blame an external evil force. Is he likely to do the same? Might he blame her for not communicating her fears to him more freely?

Third, Winslade and Monk (2001) show you how to help the couple *map the effects of the conflict*. This process involves getting the participants to enrich the archetypes of the story by expanding their description of the historical context and evolution of the conflict they are storying for you. This generates a richer description of the understandings that are the backdrop to the meaning of the conflict for each of them and also provides you all with insight into the archetypes they have drawn on to construct their story. An important aspect of filling in the meaningful backdrop has to do with exploring the patterns and rhythms of the conflict as they manifest in their current account. Going back into archetypes used and abused in previous relationships or in their parental marriage relationships might offer insight into the current crossroads moment they face, for example. Also, exploring patterns of escalation, avoidance, build up, displacement into other aspects of their relationship, and so on can be valuable for the mediator and can lead to deep *aha* moments for the couple.

It is crucial to get the couple to talk about the effects of the conflict, how it affects them and their emotions and sense of belonging in the relationship. It is also important to get them to discuss the effects of the conflict on others—family members, for example. Knowing where the conflict comes from and how the backdrop plays a role in shaping the current conflict can be an important step in externalizing the conflict and talking about it as part of an ongoing set of patterns or cycles that can be questioned and possibly changed.

- How would you get April and John to talk about this conflict in terms of more historically grounded experiences and conflicts in their families and prior relationships?
- How would you get them to talk about their own relationship as the context in which this particular backdrop makes fuller sense? Their relationship is portrayed through an "evolutionary" archetype by her. What aspects of their relationship would you question them about to see how this conflict relates to any relevant patterns or cycles in their relationship?
- How would you think they would describe the effects of this conflict on themselves and their relationship? How do you think that each other's stories would be a surprise for the other person?
- How might they describe the effects of the conflict on other people around them? Would their close friends be surprised that they have this conflict?

Fourth is the *deconstruction of the dominant story lines and archetypes* and their effects on the constitution and maintenance of the conflict. Winslade and Monk (2001) state that "cultural norms invoke particular patterns or styles of relating that are enacted in particular ways" (p. 14). It is important to help the conflict participants deconstruct the cultural norms and expectations of roles, identities, and choices that are implied by the archetypes they use to construct their stories. The patterns or styles of relating have ideological and cultural foundations that can be revealing for the participants to examine. These ideological dimensions of conflict stories are particularly salient in terms of understanding culturally based prescriptions of gender roles, family roles, relationship expectations, double-bound relationships, and so on that form the foundation for how the story is constructed. Dialogue can focus on explicating the constraints and limits that such expectations imply.

Dialogue can also be focused toward imagining directions that the story might take if certain expectations were lifted or suspended. In dialogue, there is the magical possibility of imagining options that are somehow never dreamed up in the conflict itself and yet might provide the direction and energy that the conflict needs to move to the next— hopefully coauthored—chapter. Linked to the practice of explicating the cultural context is the key dialogic skill of being able to name and problematize the dominant themes and discourses that underpin the story. For example, if the story is one of a "flawed hero and a nurturing princess who needs the flaw but wants the hero" as we might characterize John and April's story, then the naming provides a point at which they can explore those themes and how they structure the meaning of the conflict, especially if the themes are agreed upon by the participants. Perhaps they might discover a double-bound relationship between the two characters. Last, this deconstructive approach to archetypes ought to lead to *deconstructive conversations* (Winslade & Monk, 2001, p. 16). These can take place separately and then jointly, and the material generated in separate caucus meetings can be used as the basis for a joint deconstructive dialogue. The purpose of the deconstructive conversation is a deeper questioning of the implications and effects of the dominant themes and related archetypes of the conflict story. You might ask how the dominant themes make each of the participants feel, what obligations and entitlements the themes set in place, how the themes might burden and limit them and their relationship, and so on. You are likely to delve deep enough to stimulate reflective insight by the participants into themselves as well as the basis of their relational conflict with this type of dialogue. This can be the basis of real insight, understanding, and progress.

- Looking back on your answers to the initial questions about archetypes, how might you carefully challenge April, and perhaps John, to think about the cultural norms and expectations that are embodied in the archetypes of their story?
- What ideological issues of roles and expectations would you want them to explore through dialogue together?
- What limits and constraints do you think you might be able to get them to discuss if you approached this issue carefully?
- What possibilities for the future would you have them imagine, if you could?
- How do you think they would name the central archetypes of the story, and how might this help them to deconstruct the double-bound relationship of April wanting happiness together but desiring John to remain flawed?

Fifth, deconstruction ought to lead to reconstruction of the conflict, and most important in terms of moving the story forward, you should be able to help the couple to *develop shared meanings* about the conflict and its possible solutions and to generate possible future directions in their story-relationship. One way to start this momentum is to begin discussing what they would like for their relationship as an ideal. They may share a lot of this ideal, and this may form a good basis for negotiation between them. This shifts the dialogue toward questions of how to achieve that forward direction. The mediator can also explore moments in the relationship when the conflict was not dominant or aspects of the relationship that are not marked by conflict. This also shifts the frame to the positive aspects of the relationship and to areas that might stimulate "we-centered" talk.

Another way to develop shared meaning is to expand the number of voices in the dialogue. For John and April, this might not be particularly important, but in cases of more family-centered conflicts, other people may be able to enrich the dialogue and help deconstruct the archetypes in the story. It is important to start moving toward consensus, if this is a realistic outcome of the dialogue. This involves creating both a new direction in the story and a new set of corresponding agreements over the things that need to change in tangible behavior to make the lived reality match the story. Moments when the tone of the talk turns lighter often indicate this emerging consensus as well as when you can get the participants to tell each other what they appreciate and what they are willing to do to move the story forward. Shifts in the dominant themes of the story and mutual characterizations as archetypes also can indicate a move toward a new and preferred story. Once a preferred story emerges, it is important to thicken the plot and acknowledge that the archetypes have changed. Thickening the plot occurs when you get the participants to articulate changes they are willing to make to keep the conflict resolved and to imagine the future of the relationship with the conflict managed. You can also ask "unique account questions" (p. 26), which are designed to get the couple to reflect on how they were able to agree and create their new, more closely shared account of the possibilities for the future. Unique possibility questions also help to get the couple to reflect on good habits of communication and conflict that they are agreeing to put in place as well as the opportunities that such good habits might encourage in their life.

- Do you think April and John are both likely to work consistently toward the goal that they have for their relationship—to learn to live happily ever after?
- What questions would you get them to consider in terms of how they might start building the next chapter of their relationship story?
- They are likely to talk freely in terms of "we," but are there moments and times in their relationship outside of this conflict that you would get them to talk about so that they generate we-centered talk?
- As you tease apart the assumptions and effects of the archetypes that have to do with wanting to live happily ever after and also secretly fearing and needing his flaw, what additional or preferred story line would you expect to emerge from the dialogue?
- What new agreements in terms of communication and conflict would you like to see them develop?

There are a lot of questions posed for you to work with and a lot of variables to consider in any mediation process. If you carefully consider the possibilities, it is almost magical to imagine how narrative archetypes can be used to find new meanings.

❖ LESSONS FROM THE FIELD OF PRACTICE:
AN EXERCISE IN CREATIVE SCRIPTING

The family story that follows might be considerably more difficult to figure out in terms of what the next chapter should or even could be. In complex conflicts with long histories, multiple issues, and several participants, it sometimes helps to play with ideas about what the next chapter *could* be. The key to effective mediation and negotiation is to work from the viewpoint of *possibility*. Imagine you are helping them to write a movie script, and you are trying to work with several possible endings so that the story finishes on a note that you are trying to achieve. To brainstorm these possibilities, carefully read through the story as it has evolved so far for clues about what each person most wants from the conflict, what each seems not to want, what each might be willing to concede or give to make the conflict move forward, and how each person's emotional connection to the conflict and personality might impact his or her behavior in the next phase. Follow the creative scripting questions and directions that follow. Annie provides some useful background; then she captures the essence of the conflict in a poem. Your job is to play with possibilities so that you imagine a next chapter in which the story evolves into one where the best possible solution is achieved for the most number of people. Not necessarily a happy-ever-after ending, but as good an ending as might be possible given the complexity of the relationships of the people.

"A Happy Family Torn Apart" (Annie)

(Background to the story)

My parents got married in 1980. My dad played on a traveling softball team that competed in tournaments all over the South. My mom also loved to play softball, so this was a common interest that they could share. In the long run, it would be a huge issue that would ultimately play a part in my mom's "baggage" with my dad. My mom had a miscarriage in 1982, and I was born in 1983. I grew up thinking I was the luckiest kid on earth. My parents were still married (unlike the parents of most of my friends), we went to church, did stuff together, and were always going on family vacations. I thought that they had the perfect relationship. I never saw or heard them argue. It wasn't until I was a senior in high school that I learned that their relationship wasn't so picture perfect. By 2002, I had seen a significant change in my parents' relationship, and things slowly got worse.

No child wants to believe that their parents are having problems, especially after 22 years of marriage. By the end of 2003, my mom couldn't handle or hide her unhappiness anymore. From January 2004 to April 2004, I don't think my parents ever had a real conversation. They never showed affection to each other, and the words, "I love you" became automatic reactions rather than a true feeling.

Everything came to a head one weekend when my dad went away and didn't call. It was at this time that my mom made the decision to leave. She stayed for a couple more weeks—just long enough to find a place to stay and discuss what was going on with my brother and me. I was so mad at her. She was destroying my family and hurting my father. I was so ashamed of what people were going to think of my family. People were always complimenting me on how happy my parents looked, and it had to be a show that whole time. The anger I felt toward her slowly changed to understanding when I learned her reasoning. A lot of things had gone on in their relationship that I didn't know about. My parents never truly talked about what was happening to their relationship. My mom moved out, and it has been a year now. They still don't communicate effectively, and I can see those patterns in myself and my brother. The following poem is a journey through my parents' relationship and the conflict which led to their separation and to where we are now. Currently I live with my mom, and my brother lives with my dad. My ideas on what "family" means have definitely changed. My relationship with my mom is very strong, but I struggle daily to have a good relationship with my dad.

A Happy Family Torn Apart
A man and a woman with two separate lives
Come together in marriage, she made the perfect wife
After toil and strife their first miracle arrived
A bundle of joy at the perfect time—
was what they needed to make everything alright
Four years passed and they were blessed again
With a bouncing boy with blue eyes and a perfect grin
Everything was great, a happy family of four—
Surrounded by love, but was there more?
The kids grew up, the couple grew apart
And with the blink of an eye they had a change of heart
The girl went to college and moved away
The boy went to high school—
Did this add to their dismay?
Mom and dad started arguing over the smallest of things
Who was to blame? Who brought the shame?
Dad went away, the whole time he didn't call
She needed answers but there were no promises at all
What would happen to this family of four—
that was surrounded by love but needed more?
Mom and dad had problems that they could not resolve
But what about the children, they were very much involved?
What would happen next was anyone's guess
Mom moved out; she thought it was best
Dad begged her to stay—
She knew in her heart that she had to get away
She had so much hurt that had built up for years
It was buried inside of her bursting to appear
Who would live with mom and who would live with dad?
No matter what was done, someone would be mad
The girl was daddy's princess, the boy the apple of mom's eye

A decision had to be made—
But who would comply?
And here is where we are now a year has passed
Still a family torn apart—So many questions to be asked
Holidays and birthdays are filled with confusion
Will it get easier or is it just an illusion?
We went from everything being great—a happy family of four
That was surrounded by love—to searching for something much more

Exercise 1: Imagining the Possibilities for the Next Chapter

a. Best-case scenario:
   (i) Go through the poem and list all of the issues that seem to be part of making this conflict as divisive and complex as it is. These issues can become elements of the story that you can play with in creative ways, and they can become the very things that can be negotiated. For example, in the next-to-last stanza, the family is a year into their separation, and they still have so many questions to be asked. So the issue of "unasked and unanswered questions" is one that you can imagine progress on. What if they actually sat together and asked those questions; what direction might the conflict go in? Another example might be the issue of "built up hurt" that has accumulated over many years. Imagine that Annie's parents were able to work on this issue; where might that take them? Another issue might be that of "repeating patterns" in that Annie sees elements of her mother and father's approach to conflict in herself and her brother. How might her parents' negotiations have an impact on Annie's and her brother's side of the story in terms of their approach to conflict in their own intimate relationships? Of course, these ideas may not be real, but the point is to get in the habit of seeing conflicts as evolving stories that can be partly, at least, shaped by our choices and our negotiations.
   (ii) On each of the issues you explicate from the story, try to imagine positive progress on that issue. What would it take to achieve that progress, and how might it impact the plot of the story and the relationship of the characters?
   (iii) Develop a short outline of the next chapter of their family relationship—say, a year into the future—based on them achieving significant progress on the key issues that currently divide them.

b. Worst-case scenario:
   (i) For each of the issues you have explicated for the first part
        of the exercise, imagine what would make the conflict stay
        this divisive and even perhaps get worse.
   (ii) What impact on the next chapter would such a worsening
        create in terms of each family member's experience of the
        conflict?
   (iii) Develop a summary of the next chapter as it might look if
        you imagined the worst-case scenario for each issue play-
        ing out in their story.

Exercise 2: Negotiating to Make That Next Chapter a Reality

Realistically, if this family went to mediation, they might achieve
a set of agreements and resolutions to the different issues in the conflict
that would be partly based on concessions made on issues that are
important to one or more of the others. A solution would likely also be
based on desired demands—things that another has conceded. The
probability is that the final solution would be somewhere between the
best case and worst case for each of the people in the conflict as you
have just imagined them. Your final task is to think about ways that you
might help them negotiate a solution that maximizes the desired goals
and needs of everyone in the conflict. Annie says at the end of the poem
that they are searching for something more. Our interest is in helping
them look for something that actually helps make them happy. The following steps will help you work on this difficult but challenging task:

- Examine the conflict story for those demands and concessions
  that each party would value highly.
- Map out a series of dialogue questions around these possible
  concessions and demands that might move the conflict in the
  most productive direction possible.
- Carefully consider the principles and guidelines of narrative
  mediation and outline for yourself how these would guide you
  if you were actually mediating this conflict.

❖ CONCLUSION

Becoming conscious of the narrative form of our experiences can be a
very empowering moment. Of course, we cannot always simply decide
what the future will be. There are variables or forces out of our control,

some of which are not even conscious. However, taking the time to explore one's own story of a conflict, allowing it to be open to the existence of other perhaps competing stories, and working with others to negotiate new directions for the stories of their relationships is at the heart of our goals in this chapter. Hopefully you have become more aware of how to listen to your stories and those of others for ways that both limit and offer new possibilities. Hopefully, also, you will become more aware of the choices you make and those that you allow others to make as you share the co-construction of the next chapters in your relational stories. Even if the plot line for the next chapter might be difficult to develop, as it might be in Annie's family, approaching its construction with the spirit of dialogic negotiation will likely help you find the story that works for all involved.

10

Putting It All Together

From an Old Story—to a
New Meaning—to a New Story

❖　❖　❖

Meanings are forged . . . in conversation, in discourse.
—Winslade and Monk (2001, p. 249)

In working through the book, we have explored a system of concepts and principles that enables you to both analyze and manage conflicts from the perspective of their meanings for the people involved. In this short concluding chapter, you are asked to consider how everything you have explored in the book connects together into a framework that can be used to interpret and make recommendations on any conflict for which you have access to the participants and their experiences through their stories. As the opening quote suggests, you are pulling everything together to have conversations about conflicts that hopefully lead to better conversations between the people in the conflicts. If they could hear your recommendations, all of this would hopefully lead to new meanings of their relationships for them. If existing meanings are forged in conversation, then new meanings can be created by learning to have different kinds of conflict conversations and relational discourse.

You can also, of course, choose a conflict from your own life and follow the steps of collection, analysis, and recommendations. I encourage you to do so as the final exercise of the book. For now, I will simply give you a fresh conflict and ask you to play with it as a case study. Gain as much insight as you can into the conflict, imagine the possibilities for dialogic negotiation for the people involved, and do the very best you can to think about how you might help these people move their relationship forward through the conflict. You can then apply the model to your own conflicts.

The following story is relatively long, but it is rich with possibilities and cuts across relational and family contexts, and it illustrates many of the issues, concepts, and principles we have worked through in the book. This exercise asks you to put all of the pieces together as you analyze how the conflict has evolved so far and as you develop recommendations for how the people in the story might manage the conflict from here forward. Rather than restate all of the many questions developed throughout the book, I have given you a few key questions from each chapter to work with, assuming that you will go back to those chapters to pull out more of the questions and finer details to help you to examine this conflict case. To recap the process: First examine the story of their relationship so far—the "old story." Then consider how you might help them to discover new meanings as you work to get them to explore their conflict. Last, consider how they might move forward to create a new story that reflects changes in their approach to their conflict—hopefully, through dialogic negotiation.

"Like Mother Like Daughter?" (Holly)

When I was 14, I met a guy named PK. PK and I were in a school musical together so therefore we found ourselves spending a lot of time together. Eventually we both realized that our friendship was turning out to be a bit more that just a friendship. PK and I eventually became a couple a little while after the musical was over. Our relationship progressed very fast. We were together for only a month before we started having sex. I was 15 then, and it was the first time for both of us. Our relationship seemed perfect, and neither one of us was pressured by the other to take our relationship to this level. We used a condom when we had sex, but I still wanted to get on birth control before we made sex a staple in our relationship.

I talked to my sister about getting on birth control. I planned out the perfect time to talk with her. We were coming home for a weekend at the beach with our father, stepmother and family. We drove separately and stopped to eat at Burger

King. We got our food and settled down at a table by the window. Our conversation went something like this:

"Sis, I need to ask you something," I said very reluctantly.

"Yeah what's up?" she replied, not knowing the seriousness of what I was about to say.

"Well . . . I think I need to go on some sort of birth control," I managed to stutter.

"Oh my God, are you serious? My little sister is having sex," she said, in shock.

"Yeah well, what I wanted to ask was . . . will you take me to the doctor sometime soon?"

"Have you already had sex?"

This was her last question before she sputtered out a list of more personal questions and tips on what to do if PK and I have sex again before I get on birth control. She is only 2 years older than me, but my parents and I knew that she was sexually active with her then current boyfriend.

After our return from the beach, I made the call to get an appointment with my doctor about getting on birth control. I got the appointment for a day when I was at my Mother's house but when she was at work. I had my sister pick me up from my Mother's house and we went to the doctor. She told them that our father and stepmother made her tell them what she was doing. I wasn't too worried about them finding out because we had already had a similar conversation about this before. I told PK about the appointment and he knew how nervous I was. The only person that didn't know what was going on was my Mother. I was scared about how she would react. My mother and I had only one conversation a long time ago about sex before marriage, but it was only on a superficial level.

I had my appointment and everything went fine . . . this is until I got back out to the waiting room. In the waiting room I saw my sister, PK who showed up for emotional support. In addition to those two, I saw my Mom's wife Lynn who came with her son for one of his allergy appointments. By this point I knew my cover was blown.

On the way back to my Mother's house I was freaking out! What was going to happen? Should I wait for my Mother to call me or should I call her? I knew that she was going to be upset; and she didn't like PK very much as it was. PK dropped me off and I called my Mother. By the time I called her she had already spoken to Lynn and my stepmother. She sounded like someone who didn't have anything left to live for. She even talked about committing suicide.

"I think I might just go outside and step out in front of a bus." This was one of the comments that she said to me, which I did not know how to react to. She sounded serious. I tried to reason with her and stop her from doing anything stupid.

"No, no, no," I cried over the phone. "This isn't about you. You shouldn't feel this way. It has nothing to do with you." I'm not sure if she managed to hear anything I said over my wailing and sobbing.

"My baby daughter has turned into a tramp!" She sounded cold and evil with this statement. It was intended to cut me deeply, and it did. She ended the conversation with, "When I come home, you better not be there."

I was scared to death of my own Mother. She was acting like a lunatic. It sounded like she wanted me dead. Still shaking, I called my Dad, packed up my essentials, along with as many things of mine as I could. I left my mother's house thinking that I would never have a relationship with her again.

I started living with just my father and stepmother. This was in opposition to what I was doing, which was living one week with my mother and 1 week with my father—a lifestyle I had been living since I was in first grade. I was very saddened that I had a mother who was so cold and unforgiving, and angry at the same time. Living just at my dad's house wasn't so bad. At least I could spend more time with my sister. She had a string of acting out and doing miscellaneous rebellious things that led to her having to live with our father full-time as well.

A few weeks went by where I didn't speak to my mother. I don't think that either one of us wanted to talk to the other. I did hear of her calling PK's mother and blaming this all on her "no good" son. Hearing that my mother did this made me want to talk to her even less.

One day my mother called my father up and they talked. The conversation ended with me having to go eat ice cream with her. I was angry at him for making me do this. I wanted to erase her from my life and even my memories. How can I talk to this woman who sounded like she wanted to kill me? Do I even know this woman anymore? She came and picked me up and gave me a long hard hug. The hug took me by surprise. When she hugged me, all I wanted to do was let go and run and hide. I was so angry and sad, I began trying to hold back my tears. I did not want her to see me cry. On the ride over to Baskin-Robbins, we were both quiet. She kept trying to make superficial small talk to which I gave short snippet answers. By the time we got to Baskin-Robbins, she was bawling. She asked me, "How could you do this to me?"

"It was a personal decision that had nothing to do with you," I said, hoping that she could finally see my side.

"You won't understand until you're a mother." She seemed to repeat this over and over again, as if it would make everything alright. I was still so pissed off at her. I knew I had to confront her now about the things she said on the phone.

"Well, when I am a mother and this happens to me, I won't call my own daughter a tramp . . . you called me a tramp, Mom!" I was basically screaming at her. I could not control my anger.

"I didn't call you a tramp, I said you were acting like one," she said back to me in a very stern and angry voice.

"You said them to ME, I think I would remember!"

Needless to say, we didn't eat any ice cream. Somehow we ended up driving back to my father's house. When she dropped me off, she made me promise to keep in touch, which I had no intention of doing.

Time went on and my mother and I started talking again. Things had changed, though. I lied a lot more now. When it came to talking about what I had been up to, and if it had to be with PK, I always just left him out of the retelling. I hated the look that she gave me when I talked about him, and I wanted to avoid her saying anything bad about him. Things went on like this for years, because I was still with PK. I sometimes make it seem like PK and I don't spend much time together when I talk to her. I catch myself now, though. I am getting too grown up for those kinds of petty games. PK and I are currently living together. I made her accept our relationship in another big blowout we had last year. She is gradually seeing that we are not going to split up, and that PK and I are a sure thing. PK and I talk about getting married and, if we know one thing is for certain, mom is not making a speech at our reception!

Some Insight From Holly to Help You

I have listed some of the insights that Holly shared with me that might take a little of the guesswork out of the analysis and might help you move through the learning cycle described with a closer or keener sense of the meaning of the conflict, at least for her.

- The conflict put a big wedge between Holly and her mother, and she has kept her distance from her mother since the conflict.
- Holly believes that the conflict revealed her mother's "evil side"—a part of her mother that she says she hates.
- Holly believes that she effectively took her mother's perspective and tried to understand her behavior in the conflict but feels that her mother did not reciprocate.
- She acknowledges that neither she nor her mother engaged each other on the level of the meaning of the conflict for each other but rather ended up arguing somewhat competitively (notice the name-calling).
- She feels that her mother was more interested in having her feel guilt and to come running back to her.
- Holly points to some important family dynamics and patterns that are revealing. Specifically, she points to the fact that mother-daughter relationships in her family history have often been difficult and conflicted. When Holly's mother revealed that she was gay, her mother disowned her. Ironically, Holly sees part of her grandmother in her mother and perhaps a little in herself. In particular, she sees a habit of having strong and somewhat judgmental beliefs, and when those beliefs are challenged, a strong reaction follows. Also, mothers and daughters in the family rarely have space and time in their relationship for talking about intimate issues and experiences so that when an issue of an intimate nature comes up, there is an uncomfortable lack of precedent for that type of conversation. They find themselves fumbling around for a conversational script for this context, end up fighting, or they avoid this type of conversation all together.

- Holly's mother had endured a marriage that she had to be in because she got pregnant as a young woman. She was only able to break out of the marriage after many years of unhappiness.
- Holly's mother is afraid that, as a lesbian, she will be judged more harshly by society than would a parent who is straight if her daughter makes big mistakes. The pressure to have "perfect kids" adds to her anxiety over Holly's behavior and choices.
- Holly wants a relationship with her mother that is quite different from the one she has. I think this is a crucial clue to hopeful possibilities for the future of their relationship. She wants her mother to be much more involved with her life. She wants her to get to know her boyfriend. She wants to be able to tell her anything and not have to worry that she will be overly critical, put her down, or disown her. She would also love to be able to talk to her about this particular conflict without it starting all over again and without it spinning out of control. Last, Holly believes that such a close relationship ought to be possible, given that they are mother and daughter. She also believes it is possible and desirable for her mother to be close to PK, the man she loves.

Your job is to take these insights and your own insights from analyzing the story and figure out how to help these people move forward with their conflict. Perhaps we can even help them to achieve the relationship Holly talks about in the last bulleted item. It is unlikely that her mother has much of an idea about the details of Holly's desire to have a closer relationship, given the wedge between them. It is also unlikely that Holly knows much about her mother's desire for their relationship in the future. And neither of them understands the barriers that the other feels are in the way of progress in their relationship or what they could do to remove those barriers. They simply have not had this type of conversation, at least in recent memory. Yet, Holly believes that a more productive and peaceful relationship with her mother *is* possible. Perhaps this might make a good starting point for your approach to helping them.

❖ THE LEARNING CYCLE OF CONFLICT NARRATIVES

The narrative approach we have taken throughout this book suggests that we begin with a story—the story so far. Then our task is to figure out what needs to change in how the people in the story practice conflict so that hopefully they learn how to bring about conditions so that they are able to tell a new story, one that speaks of a more productive and peaceful relationship. This new story would be distinct from the old one by the changes in behavior and communication that the participants have implemented based on your recommendations. This cyclic approach to beginning and ending with narrative is called *the learning cycle of conflict narratives* (Kellett & Dalton, 2001, pp. 94–98). We would like you to follow the steps of this interpretive cycle as you examine and imagine making recommendations to Holly and her mother on their conflict.

Step 1: Collecting the Story: What Is the Story So Far?

We have Holly's story of their conflict. This circumvents some of the challenges discussed in Chapter 1 concerning the collection of stories as data. It still challenges your sensitivity to working within the confines of narrative interpretive research, however, in that you have to figure out what the conflict means from the evidence presented in the story. I chose this story because it is a good story, in that it has clear evidence of conflicted interaction, opposition between Holly and her mother, characterization of people, and their motives around that opposition, and it evokes patterns and deeper meaning in the relationship. However, stories are rarely complete and final. Are there any additional questions you would ask Holly, to help you to tease out or develop any additional dimensions or details of the story? To do this, consider whether you are left wondering about anything that you would like her to add to her story. Would you also like to have her mother's story? If so, what specific questions and directions on writing about conflict would you give her so that she could write out the important details of the story for you? Would you prefer to interview her and piece the story together from her answers? The idea is that you need as much as possible of the lived reality of the conflict from the people in it, to build into the next steps of the cycle.

This systematic approach to conducting systemic analysis of the conflict ensures that the process of change is based on the meaning for the people in the conflict and not your own projections and guesswork as a researcher. There will always be an element of this researcher relationship to the data with any type of interpretive research, but you can take steps to ensure that your account is as accurate and plausible as possible without being present when the conflict happened and without having perfect knowledge of the people involved. Recognize also that in everyday life, you will rarely have all of these details on which to base your decisions about your conflicts, even though you are in them, but you can learn to approach them more systematically by adapting as much of this cycle of learning as possible.

Step 2: Asking Good Questions: Explicating the Dynamics of Conflict in the Story

For this step, you will need to go back through each of the main parts of the book and use the concepts from each chapter to provide you with the insight into the conflict that will enable you to help Holly and her mother move the conflict forward. Each chapter, and corresponding main part of the book, will help you uncover another important dimension or layer of the conflict. Each moment of insight will form a snapshot of an important dynamic in the conflict and its relationship to the way the conflict has taken shape so far. Behind and between these snapshots are possibilities for how things might be done differently and what it might take to negotiate such change. Note any clues to new possibilities as you read between the lines of the story. Each of the following questions relates to a chapter of the book. Go back to each chapter and see how everything in it helps you to explain something about the conflict between this mother and daughter, within the family and cultural contexts in which it occurs.

- Why does this conflict appear to take on such an important meaning for Holly and for her mother, and what does Holly's story reveal about why this is a particularly meaningful conflict (see Chapter 1)?

This question gets you to think closely about the meaning of the conflict from within the lives and times of the characters in the story. In some families, this story would have played out in a very different way. For some reason, the history and family context of their relationship shapes the conflict into the form and direction that it takes. So as you reflect on this story using the concepts from Chapter 1, I want you to focus in particular on why their conflict happens as it does. The answer to this question lies in your ability to understand the meaning of the conflict for Holly and her mother. The contextual meaning of their conflict also contains clues to why they have been unable to live up to the ethos of the first quote in Chapter 1, which has to do with finding peace in their relationship. Applying the principles from Chapter 1, see if you can discover why Holly and her mother are so far from the peaceful relationship Holly desires and what opportunities are there for them as you carefully work to uncover the meaning of the conflict.

- How well would you say that they have managed their conflict so far, through engaging the common and oppositional meanings that unite them in their relationship and divide them in their conflict? How could they change their conflict to become more centered on the relative meaning of the conflict for them (see Chapter 2)?

Chapter 2 begins with the challenge of learning how to work together through dialogue and negotiation where possible. As you consider the foregoing question, you might begin by carefully evoking the steps of interpretive methodology to enable you to get at the meaning of the conflict. You might also carefully consider all of the possible demands and concessions that the people in the story might value, based on the meaning of the conflict. This will give you a good sense of what is possible for Holly and her mother. Also develop some guidelines for how you might get Holly and her mother in the mode of engaging their conflict through the principles of dialogic negotiation.

- What does the language of their conflict and of Holly's story reveal to you about the meaning and dynamics of the conflict so far and what possibilities for change it embodies (see Chapter 3)?

With this question, I want you to reflect on the intensity of their conflict and, in particular, the verbal exchanges and name-calling. There must be clues in the language of their conflict to the meaning of the division between them. Also, look carefully at the fabric of the language in which Holly describes their relationship and this particular conflict, and think about what her choice of imagery and representation tells you. You might also carefully consider what possibilities lie behind and beneath the language for them to be able to talk differently, with different results for their relationship.

- What does the story reveal about how effectively Holly and her mother have balanced their senses of belonging together in a special relationship with the reality of their seemingly divisive differences (see Chapter 4)?

Clearly, Holly and her mother are in a lifelong relationship as mother and daughter. There are clues in the story that suggest that Holly is thinking into the future of her life and that as she does so, her mother remains an important part of that future. At the same time, they are currently divided, oppositional, and conflicted. The lessons from Chapter 4 include not waiting until the graveside to have an important conflict conversation and not helping to create nightmare relationships. So consider how Holly and her mother might more effectively negotiate the meaning of their differences and move toward a better balance of collaboration, to complement their experience of being held together by a deep sense of togetherness.

- In what ways are Holly and her mother at a crossroads moment, and how could they negotiate through that moment to move in the same direction so that they might look back on the conflict with a different perspective at some point in the future (see Chapter 5)?

Holly and her mother have a not entirely atypical parent-child relationship at a point where it could easily go toward estrangement and distance or it could be revived, based on the passion that is evident. Think about how the depth of feeling they evoke in each other, which is currently divisive, might be redirected toward developing a common path forward. Think about the clues in the story that hint that you might see them looking back on this conflict as a close mother and daughter and not from the viewpoint of divided and estranged family members.

- What psychological and cultural issues are being displaced in this conflict, with what impact, and how could Holly and her mother more effectively work with those displaced issues (see Chapter 6)?

Displacement is often brought on when people bring something to a conflict from some other dimension or area of their relationship or their broader life, as we have seen in Chapter 6. These displacements can be unconscious or conscious or even the result of tangled webs of desire. As you examine the conflict of Holly and her mother, try to figure out what, if anything, is being displaced. When you have explored the layers of displaced issues and their interconnections in their conflicted relationship, try to imagine how this understanding might be the basis of improving their relational communication.

- Are there aspects of themselves that both Holly and her mother might be projecting onto each other, with what effects, and how might they more effectively work through those projections and their effects on the conflict (see Chapter 7)?
- How do the plot, character, and motive archetypes by which Holly tells the story and by which she portrays herself, and her mother in particular, help you understand the conflict so far? What might be some aspects of representation that would be productive to change (see Chapter 8)?

Projecting things from the protagonists' own lives, personalities, and motives is a common thing in any conflict. It is particularly poignant in a story in which the mother does not want her daughter to make her mistakes all over again. This is the case in the conflict between Holly and her mother. The difficult task that Holly has is to respect her mother's motives and advice while making her own decisions. This is the tough path toward peace that gets muddied by projections, responses to projections, and counterprojections. As you examine the projections in the conflict of Holly and her mother, try to understand why words have become projectiles and how they might move toward integration from understanding their projections. Consider also how they might more effectively negotiate their relationship without the negative impact of either negative or positive projections.

- How might you help them use story archetypes to imagine and tell the next chapter of their story so that it might have more peaceful and productive themes to it (see Chapter 9)?

Holly's story has archetypes of plot, moral, and characters that suggest that she and her mother are in a significant conflict in their lives. Things have become polarized between them, and yet there is so much potential for change. Behind the story that Holly shares with us are possibilities for learning to tell a different relationship story, one in which she and her mother are working together and sharing a much more fulfilling relationship. Carefully consider the archetypal characteristics of Holly's story and what they tell you about her relationship with her mother and the meaning of this conflict more specifically. If you were working with them to help them find a more productive and peaceful story line, how might you manage the third corner of the story in ways that would help them to work together more effectively from their own corners in the conversation?

Step 3: Creating the Big Picture: Understanding Their Conflict
For this step, you are essentially taking each snapshot of insight that you have brought into focus in Step 2 and piecing them together into a bigger picture that provides clarity to the conflict as a whole. Here you provide an understanding of why their conflict happened as it did, given all of the dynamics of their conflict communication and behavior. You are also providing a picture of the underlying central issues on which they might develop a more open and effective exchange of demands and concessions.

- How do all of the dynamics of the conflict you have brought to the surface seem to fit together into a pattern of interrelationships that you might summarize in a paragraph or that might be something like a map of their conflict that you could draw? For example, how does projection connect to issues of being judgmental? How do the patterns of judgmental relationships connect to the quality of their dialogue and negotiation? Linking these dynamics will produce a picture of the internal workings of the conflict—the world behind the picture that the story describes.
- From the big picture of the conflict you have developed, what are the specific issues of great significance (important desires and demands) to each of the main participants in the story?
- What issues are Holly and her mother interconnected on in terms of having similar desires and demands, and which issues divide them as the basis of the conflict?
- Which issues might they be willing to make concessions on, and which would they be less willing to make concessions on?
- What do they each want from the conflict (demands) and what might they be willing to trade (concessions) that are of value to the other person, to make that goal possible?
- What would they likely demand from each other for each of the concessions traded if they worked together to negotiate change in their relationship?

Step 4: Discovering New Meanings—Developing Good Questions and Topics for Dialogic Negotiation

Careful analysis of the details of the story will reveal possible topics and questions that participants in the conflict might explore together and try to negotiate around and with so that they make progress on the conflict and in their relationship. In the case of Holly and her mother, you are likely to have explicated several core issues that they might focus their conflict dialogue on. Some of the more obvious topics for them to explore might include (a) how to talk to each other during difficult conflicts, (b) how to create more closeness and trust in the relationship, (c) how to avoid bringing in value judgments and projecting personal experiences, and (d) how to keep conflict discussions constructive. They will need to figure out how to negotiate these topics. Specifically, they will need to have the questions necessary to begin thinking about how and why they feel the way they do about these topics and how to cooperate to build shared agreements on how to work with them. Their talk is likely to surprise them in that it will reveal to each of them some of the perceptions and experiences that they did not know the other person had.

It is at this point when we can start to question a personal story in terms of its completeness and accuracy, hopefully revealing the blind spots that are created because we have decided, through our story, how things really are. Often, participants will begin to see that their own stories are not the whole truth. Ideally, as they share experiences and desires for their relationship, they will begin to reframe their conflict as something that they both have, instead of something that the other person is doing to them. This is when new meanings will start to emerge that can form the basis of agreements to change behavior.

- As you go through the story again in detail, list all of the topics that they need to explore together.
- What clues in the story indicate how they feel about each of those topics, and what impact might those feelings have on how they negotiate that topic?
- What specific questions would you set for each of them to develop collaborative answers to?
- If they approached these issues and worked on the dialogue topics and questions you think they need to, what opportunities for changing behavior and communication are they likely to start to uncover?

Step 5: Changing Conflict Behavior

The key is to build the knowledge gained from the analysis of the conflict so far to develop new habits and patterns of communication that would result in a more productive and peaceful relationship. Working to eliminate or at least minimize the impact of dysfunctional habits, tactics, and patterns would be a useful thing for both mother and daughter to do.

- How might Holly and her mother improve the dialogue in their relationship to create more open, empathic, and honest talk about their relationship issues and the things that are important to them? Bear in mind that your recommendations are based on Holly's account of their conflict and what you might imagine about her mother.
- How might Holly and her mother more effectively engage in conflict communication in which they balance the relationship between demands that are important to them and concessions they know are important to the other person?
- What communication habits or tactics that you think of as dysfunctional would be most desirable for Holly and her mother to eliminate?

- What desirable communication habits or tactics would you encourage them to develop and implement in their relationship?
- What might you consider to be some realistic constraints and challenges to changing behavior, for both of them?

Step 6: Changing Behavior Changes Relational Reality

Changing habits of communication ought to have an impact on the experience of being in a relationship with someone. If both Holly and her mother were to work on some of the negotiation goals and topics we have set for them, and if they were to make the changes that were suggested, then the reality of their relationship should change. They should experience more productive and peaceful communication. The more effective conflict behavior and communication should also have an impact on other areas of their relationship. For example, their mutual relationship to PK might be transformed if their own relationship becomes more effective.

- If Holly and her mother were able to move effectively through Steps 4 and 5, how would their relationship change in terms of becoming more productive, cooperative, and perhaps even peaceful?
- What other effects might the changes have on aspects of their relationship that are less directly related to the conflict they are working through?

Step 7: Toward a New Story: Changing Reality Changes Future Conflict Stories

The idea of the cyclical approach to working on conflicts is that after adopting changes that are practical and realistic given the nature of the conflict, the participants would tell a different story next time. It might be that one day, Holly and her mother could look back on this story shared with us and recognize important ways that they now do things differently. If they were in a similar conflict situation again, or if they were moving their relationship forward in productive ways, then we would expect the story of how they manage conflict together to be different. It should represent more productive and peace-oriented approaches to communication. It should represent at least some of the habits of dialogic negotiation that were not evident in their earlier story.

- If Holly and her mother were able to adopt more dialogic negotiation habits in their relationship, how might the story of a new conflict they might face be different than the one Holly shared with us?

- How might the story that Holly shared with us be a source of surprise or even humor as they look back on it from the viewpoint of their more effective relationship?

❖ CONCLUSION

We have looked closely—microscopically, at times—into the conflicted relationships of others and ourselves through the powerful lens of theoretically grounded questions, many questions. I hope that this close analysis has also resulted in a deeper appreciation on your part for the bigger—more macroscopic—picture of conflicts in terms of how the dynamics fit together and connect to bigger patterns from the past and from our cultures. Holly's story is a good case in point. I hope that the parts and chapter concepts from this book fit together into a bigger picture for you as you examined her story and all of the internal and relational workings of the conflict. I hope that such a bigger picture will enable you to examine and make recommendations on new conflicts that you encounter in your life or see in the world around you. I hope that you have become more aware of your position and responsibility in your conflicts in terms of understanding what we all do to shape the conflicts that we are inevitably part of. Most important, perhaps, in Holly's case and in our own lives, I hope that you have come to the understanding that *engaging in dialogic negotiation, based on the meaning of a conflict and the desires of those in that conflict, is a practical and ethical way to achieve more peaceful and productive relationships.*

References

Abramsky, M. F. (1996). Displacement: A major causal contribution to prolonged post traumatic stress disorder. *Psychology: A Journal of Human Behavior, 33,* 1–9.

Agar, M. H. (1996). *The professional stranger: An informal introduction to ethnography.* New York: Academic Press.

Allison, D. (1996). *Two or three things I know for sure.* New York: Penguin.

Arnett, R. C., & Arneson, P. (1999). *Dialogic civility in a cynical age.* Albany: SUNY Press.

Atkinson, P. (1992). *Understanding ethnographic texts.* Newbury Park, CA: Sage.

Aziz, R. (1990). *C. G. Jung's psychology of religion and synchronicity.* Albany: SUNY Press.

Bar-on, D. (2000). Cultural identity and demonization of the relevant other: Lessons from the Palestinian-Israeli conflict. In A. Y. Shalev & R. Yehuda (Eds.), *International handbook of human response to trauma* (pp. 115–125). Dordrecht, Netherlands: Kluwer.

Baxter, L. A. (1988). A dialectical perspective on communication strategies in relationship development. In S. Duck (Ed.), *Handbook of personal relationships* (pp. 257–273). Chichester, UK: Wiley.

Baxter, L. A. (2004). Dialogues of relating. In R. Anderson, L. A. Baxter, & K. N. Cissna (Eds.), *Dialogue: Theorizing differences in communication studies* (pp. 107–124). Thousand Oaks, CA: Sage.

Baxter, L. A., & Bullis, C. (1986). Turning points in developing romantic relationships. *Human Communication Research, 12,* 469–493.

Baxter, L. A., & Montgomery, B. M. (1996). *Relating: Dialogues and dialectics.* New York: Guilford.

Baxter, L. A., & Pittman, G. (2001). Communicatively remembering turning points of relationship development. *Communication Reports, 14,* 1–17.

Beebe, S. A., Beebe, S. J., & Redmond, M. V. (2005). *Interpersonal communication: Relating to others.* Boston: Allyn & Bacon.

Bernardo, S. M. (1994). Recycling victims and villains in *Batman Returns. Literature & Film Quarterly, 22,* 16–21.

Bilsker, R. (2002). *On Jung.* Belmont, CA: Wadsworth.

Black, E. (1994). Gettysburg and silence. *Quarterly Journal of Speech, 80,* 21–37.

Black, M. (1979). More about metaphor. In A. Ortony (Ed.), *Metaphor and thought* (pp. 19–43). Cambridge, UK: Cambridge University Press.

Bochner, A. P., & Eisenberg, E. (1997). It's about time: Narrative and the divided self. *Qualitative Inquiry, 3,* 417–439.

Booth, A., Crouter, A. C., & Clements, M. (Eds.). (2001). *Couples in conflict.* Mahwah, NJ: Lawrence Erlbaum.

Brewi, J., & Brennan, A. (2001). The emergence of the shadow in midlife. In C. Zweig & J. Abrams (Eds.), *Meeting the shadow: The hidden power of the dark side of human nature* (pp. 260–261). Los Angeles: Tarcher.

Briller, B. R. (1999). *Television Quarterly, 30,* 31–42.

Brown, J. (1995). Dialogue: Capacities and stories. In S. Chawla & J. Renesch (Eds.), *Learning organizations: Developing cultures for tomorrow's workplace* (pp. 153–166). Portland, OR: Productivity Press.

Burke, K. (1990). Heroes and villains in American film. *International Journal of Instructional Media, 17,* 63–73.

Campbell, J. (1949). *The hero with a thousand faces.* Princeton, NJ: Princeton University Press.

Campbell, J. (1972). *Myths to live by.* New York: Viking.

Campbell, J. (1988). *The power of myth.* New York: Doubleday.

Carey, J. S. (1987). Empathy and the expert witness. *Journal of Medical Humanities and Bioethics, 8,* 19–25.

Chase, S. E. (1996). Personal vulnerability and interpretive authority in narrative research. In R. Josselson (Ed.), *Ethics and process in the narrative study of lives* (pp. 45–59). Thousand Oaks, CA: Sage.

Cheney, G. (1995). Democracy in the workplace: Theory and practice from the perspective of communication. *Journal of Applied Communication Research, 23,* 167–200.

Cissna, K. N., & Anderson, R. (1998). Theorizing about dialogic moments: The Buber-Rogers position and postmodern themes. *Communication Theory, 8,* 63–104.

Clarke, A. J. (1998). *Defense mechanisms in the counseling process.* Thousand Oaks, CA: Sage.

Constantino, C. A., & Merchant, C. S. (1996). *Designing conflict management systems: A guide to creating productive and healthy organizations.* San Francisco: Jossey-Bass.

Conville, R. (1988). Relational transitions: An inquiry into their structure and functions. *Journal of Social and Personal Relationships, 5,* 423–437.

Conville, R. (1991). *Relational transitions: The evolution of personal relationships.* New York: Praeger.

Conville, R. (1998). Telling stories: Dialectics of relational transitions. In B. M. Montgomery & L. A. Baxter (Eds.), *Dialectical approaches to studying personal relationships* (pp. 17–40). Mahwah, NJ: Lawrence Erlbaum.

Coser, L. (1956). *The functions of social conflict.* New York: Free Press.

Cupach, W. R., & Canary, D. J. (1997). *Competence in interpersonal conflict.* Prospect Heights, IL: Waveland.

Davidson, D. (1978). What metaphors mean. *Critical Inquiry, 5*, 1.

Davis, R. H. (2003). *Jung, Freud, and Hillman: Three depth psychologies in context.* Westport, CT: Praeger.

Deetz, S. (2001). *Transforming communication, transforming business.* Cresskill, NJ: Hampton.

Deetz, S., & Simpson, J. (2004). Critical organizational dialogue: Open formation and the demand of "otherness." In R. Anderson, L. A. Baxter, & K. N. Cissna (Eds.), *Dialogue: Theorizing differences in communication studies* (pp. 141–158). Thousand Oaks, CA: Sage.

Denzin, N. K. (1997). *Interpretive ethnography.* Thousand Oaks, CA: Sage.

Earnest, W. R. (1992). Ideology, criticism and life-history research. In G. C. Rosenwald & R. L. Ochberg (Eds.), *Storied lives: The cultural politics of self-understanding* (pp. 250–264). New Haven, CT: Yale University Press.

Ehrlich, A. S. (2001). Power, control, and the mother-in-law problem: Face off's in the American nuclear family. In L. Stone (Ed.), *New directions in anthropological kinship* (pp. 175–184). Lanham, MD: Rowman & Littlefield.

Ellis, C. (1997, November). *Narrative ethnology seminar notes.* Seminar presented at the National Communication Association Annual Convention, Chicago.

Ellis, D. G. (2001). Language and civility: The semantics of anger. In W. F. Eadie & P. E. Nelson (Eds.), *The language of conflict and resolution* (pp. 105–120). Thousand Oaks, CA: Sage.

Feeney, D. J. (2003). Creating cultural motifs against terrorism: Empowering acceptance of our uniqueness. Westport, CT: Praeger.

Fisher, R., & Ertel, D. (1995). *Getting ready to negotiate: A step-by-step guide to preparing for any negotiation.* New York: Penguin.

Fisher, R., & Ury, W. (1981). *Getting to yes.* New York: Penguin.

Fisher, W. R. (1987). *Human communication as narration: Toward a philosophy of reason, value and action.* Columbia: University of South Carolina Press.

Fjerkenstad, J. (2001). Who are the criminals? In C. Zweig & J. Abrams (Eds.), *Meeting the shadow: The hidden power of the dark side of human nature* (pp. 226–232). Los Angeles: Tarcher.

Folger, J. P., Poole, M. S., & Stutman, R. K. (2005). *Working through conflict: Strategies for relationships, groups, and organizations.* New York: Longman.

Frijda, N. H., Ortony, A., Sonnemans, J., & Clore, G. L. (1992). The complexity of intensity: Issues concerning the structure of emotional intensity. In M. S. Clark (Ed.), *Emotion* (pp. 60–89). Newbury Park, CA: Sage.

Gallin, R. S. (1998). The intersection of class and age: Mother-in-law/daughter-in-law relations in rural Taiwan. In J. Dickerson-Putman & J. Brown (Eds.), *Women among women: An anthropological perspective on female age hierarchy* (pp. 1–14). Urbana: University of Illinois Press.

Galvin, K. M., Byland, C. L., & Brommel, B. J. (1992). *Family communication: Cohesion and change.* Boston: Allyn & Bacon.

Gaylin, W., & Person, E. (Eds.). (1998). *Passionate attachments: Thinking out love.* New York: Free Press.

Gemmill, G. (1990). The dynamics of scape-goating in small groups. *Small Group Behavior, 20,* 406–418.

Goldhill, S. (2004). *Love, sex and tragedy: How the ancient world shapes our lives.* Chicago: University of Chicago Press.

Goodall, H. L., Jr. (1989). *Casing a promised land.* Carbondale: Southern Illinois University Press.

Goodall, H. L., Jr. (1996). *Divine signs: Connecting spirit to community.* Carbondale: Southern Illinois University Press.

Goodall, H. L., Jr., & Kellett, P. M. (2004). Dialectical tensions and dialogic moments as pathways to peak experiences. In R. Anderson, L. A. Baxter, & K. N. Cissna (Eds.), *Dialogue: Theorizing differences in communication studies* (pp. 159–174). Thousand Oaks, CA: Sage.

Gordon, R. (1995). *Bridges: Psychic structures, function and processes.* New Brunswick, NJ: Transaction.

Griffin, S. (2001). The chauvinist mind. In C. Zweig & J. Abrams (Eds.), *Meeting the shadow: The hidden power of the dark side of human nature* (pp. 207–210). Los Angeles: Tarcher.

Guerrero, L. K., & Anderson, P. A. (1998). The dark side of jealousy and envy: Desire, delusional, desperation and destructive communication. In B. Spitzberg & W. R. Cupach (Eds.), *The dark side of close relationships* (pp. 33–70). Mahwah, NJ: Lawrence Erlbaum.

Hammersley, M. (1990). *Reading ethnographic research: A critical guide.* London: Longman.

Harris, S. K. (1996). *The courtship of Olivia Langdon and Mark Twain.* New York: Cambridge University Press.

Hauk, C. (2000). *Jung and the postmodern: The interpretation of realities.* London: Routledge.

Hawes, L. C. (2004). Double binds as structures in dominance and of feelings: Problematics of dialogue. In R. Anderson, L. A. Baxter, & K. N. Cissna (Eds.), *Dialogue: Theorizing differences in communication studies* (pp. 175–190). Thousand Oaks, CA: Sage.

Holtz, R., & Miller, N. (2001). Intergroup competition, attitudinal projection and opinion certainty: Capitalizing on conflict. *Group Processes and Inter-group Relations, 4,* 61–73.

Hook, S. (1943). *The hero in history.* New York: Humanities Press.

Isenhart, M. W., & Spangle, M. (2000). *Collaborative approaches to resolving conflict.* Thousand Oaks, CA: Sage.

Johnson, R. A. (1993). *Negotiation basics: Concepts, skills, and exercises.* Newbury Park, CA: Sage.

Jones, T. S. (2001). Emotional communication in conflict: Essence and impact. In W. F. Eadie & P. E. Nelson (Eds.), *The language of conflict and resolution* (pp. 81–104). Thousand Oaks, CA: Sage.

Jones, T. S., & Remland, M. S. (1993). Non-verbal communication and conflict escalation: An attribution based model. *International Journal of Conflict Management, 4,* 119–138.

Josselson, E. (1995). Imagining the real: Empathy, narrative, and the dialogic self. In R. Josselson & A. Lieblich (Eds.), *The narrative study of lives* (Vol. 3, pp. 27–44). Thousand Oaks, CA: Sage.

Karasawa, M. (2003). Projecting group liking and ethnocentrism on in group members: False consensus affect of attitude strength. *Asian Journal of Social Psychology, 6,* 103–116.

Kearns, E. A. (1986). Projection and mirror: The psychology of *The Scarlet Letter. Journal of Evolutionary Psychology, 7,* 57–68.

Keen, S. (1991). The enemy maker. In C. Zweig & J. Abrams (Eds.), *Meeting the shadow: The hidden power of the dark side of human nature* (pp. 260–261). Los Angeles: Tarcher.

Kellett, P. M. (1987). The functions of metaphors in discourse dynamics: A case study of metaphors in the dynamics and resolution of conflict interaction. *Belfast Working Papers in Language and Linguistics, 9,* 118–139.

Kellett, P. M. (1995). Acts of power, control, and resistance: Narrative accounts of convicted rapists. In R. K. Whillock & D. Slayden (Eds.), *Hate speech* (pp. 142–162). Thousand Oaks, CA: Sage.

Kellett, P. M. (1996). The process of organizational sense making: A semiotic phenomenological model. In L. Thayer (Ed.), *Organization—Communication: Emerging perspectives* (Vol. 3, pp. 103–116). New York: Ablex.

Kellett, P. M. (1999). Dialogue and dialectics in organizational change: The case of a mission-based transformation. *Southern Communication Journal, 64,* 211–231.

Kellett, P. M., & Dalton, D. G. (2001). *Managing conflict in a negotiated world: A narrative approach to achieving dialogue and change.* Thousand Oaks, CA: Sage.

Kellett, P. M., & Goodall, H. L., Jr. (1987). The function of metaphors in discourse dynamics: A case study of metaphor in the dynamics and resolution of conflict interaction. *Belfast Working Papers in Language and Linguistics, 9,* 118–139.

Kellett, P. M., & Goodall, H. L., Jr. (1999). The death of discourse in our own (chat) room: "Sextext" skillful discussion and virtual communities. In D. Slayden & R. K. Whillock (Eds.), *Soundbite culture: The death of discourse in a wired world* (pp. 155–190). Thousand Oaks, CA: Sage.

Kimbles, S. (2000). The cultural complex and the myth of invisibility. In T. Singer (Ed.), *The vision thing: Myths, politics and the psyche in the world* (pp. 157–169). Florence, KY: Taylor & Francis/Routledge.

Klapp, O. E. (1962). *Heroes, villains and fools.* Englewood Cliffs, NJ: Prentice-Hall.

Knapp, M. L., & Vangelisti, A. L. (2005). *Interpersonal communication and human relationships.* Boston: Allyn & Bacon.

Koch, S., & Deetz, S. (1981). Metaphor analysis of social reality in organizations. *Journal of Applied Communication Research, 9*(1), 143–160.

Kohler-Riessman, C. (1992). Making sense of marital violence: One woman's narrative. In G. C. Rosenwald & R. L. Ochberg (Eds.), *Storied lives: The cultural politics of self-understanding* (pp. 231–249). New Haven, CT: Yale University Press.

Kristeva, J. (1981). Women's time (A. Jardine & H. Blake, Trans.). *Signs, 7,* 13–15.

Labre, M. P., & Duke, L. (2004). Nothing like a brisk walk and a spot of demon slaughter to make a girl's night: The construction of the female hero in the *Buffy* video game. *Journal of Communication Inquiry, 28,* 138–157.

Langellier, K. M. (1989). Personal narratives: Perspectives on theory and research. *Text and Performance Quarterly, 9,* 243–276.

Lanigan, R. L. (1988). Phenomenology of communication: Merleau-Ponty's thematics on communicology and semiology. Pittsburgh, PA: Duquesne University Press.

Leets, L., & Giles, H. (1997). Words as weapons—When do they wound? Investigations of harmful speech. *Human Communication Research, 24,* 260–301.

LePoire, B. A., Hallett, J. S., & Giles, H. (1998). Codependence: The paradoxical nature of functional–afflicted relationships. In B. H. Spitzberg & W. R. Cupach (Eds.), *The dark side of close relationships* (pp. 153–176). Mahwah, NJ: Lawrence Erlbaum.

Levi, I. (1986). *Hard choices: Decision making under unresolved conflict.* Cambridge, MA: Cambridge University Press.

Li-Vollmer, M., & LaPointe, M. E. (2003). Gender transgression and villainy in animated film. *Popular Communication, 1,* 89–110.

Liszka, J. J. (1989). *The semiotics of myth: A critical study of the symbol.* Bloomington: Indiana University Press.

Littlejohn, S. W., & Domenici, K. (2001). *Engaging communication in conflict: Systemic practice.* Thousand Oaks, CA: Sage.

Loewenberg, P. (1999). The construction of national identity. In N. Ginsberg & R. Ginsburg (Eds.), *Psychoanalysis and culture at the millennium* (pp. 37–63). New Haven, CT: Yale University Press.

Main, R. (1997). *Jung on synchronicity and the paranormal.* Princeton, NJ: Princeton University Press.

Mansfield, V. (1995). *Synchronicity, science and soul making: Understanding Jungian synchronicity through physics, Buddhism and philosophy.* Chicago: Open Court.

Mauthner, M. H. (2002). *Sistering: Power and change in female friendships.* New York: Palgram.

Merleau-Ponty, M. (1979). *The phenomenology of perception* (C. Smith, Trans.). London: Routledge & Kegan Paul. (Original work published in France 1962)

Messman, S. J., & Canary, D. J. (1998). Patterns of conflict in personal relationships. In B. H. Spitzberg & W. R. Cupach (Eds.), *The dark side of close relationships* (pp. 121–152). Mahwah, NJ: Lawrence Erlbaum.

Meyer, L. H. (Ed.). (1998). *Making friends: The influence of culture and development.* Baltimore: Brookes.

Meyer, M. D. E. (2003). Utilizing mythic criticism in contemporary narrative culture: Examining the "present-absence" of shadow archetypes in *Spider-Man. Communication Quarterly, 51,* 518–530.

Midgley, M. (2003). *The myths we live by.* London: Routledge.

Mizen, R. (2003). A contribution toward an analytic theory of violence. *Journal of Analytic Psychology, 48,* 285–305.

Moore, R., & Gillette, D. (1992). *The king within: Accessing the king in the male psyche.* New York: William Morrow.

Mumby, D. K. (1993). *Narrative and social control.* Newbury Park, CA: Sage.

Nagy, M. (1991). *Philosophical issues in the psychology of C. G. Jung*. Albany: SUNY Press.

Nicotera, A. M. (1995). *Conflict and organizations: Communicative processes*. Albany: SUNY Press.

Noesner, G. W., & Webster, M. (1997, August). Crisis intervention. *FBI Law Enforcement Bulletin, 13*–19.

Ochberg, R. L. (1992). Social insight and psychological liberation. In G. C. Rosenwald & R. L. Ochberg (Eds.), *Storied lives: The cultural politics of self-understanding* (pp. 214–230). New Haven, CT: Yale University Press.

Parry-Giles, S. J. (1994). Rhetorical experimentation and the cold war 1947–1953: The development of an internationalist approach to propaganda. *Quarterly Journal of Speech, 80,* 448–462.

Pearce, W. B., & Pearce, K. W. (1999). Combining passions and abilities: Toward dialogic virtuosity. *Southern Communication Journal, 65,* 161–175.

Pearce, W. B., & Pearce, K. W. (2004). Taking a communication perspective on dialogue. In R. Anderson, L. A. Baxter, & K. N. Cissna (Eds.), *Dialogue: Theorizing differences in communication studies* (pp. 39–56). Thousand Oaks, CA: Sage

Pelias, R. J., & VanOosting, J. E. (1987). A paradigm for performance studies. *Quarterly Journal of Speech, 73,* 219–231.

Rank, O. (1964). *The myth of the birth of the hero and other writings*. New York: Vintage.

Richardson, L. (1995). Narrative and sociology. In J. Van Maanen (Ed.), *Representations in ethnography* (pp. 198–221). Thousand Oaks, CA: Sage.

Ricouer, P. (1967). *The symbolism of evil* (C. Kelbley, Trans.). Boston: Beacon.

Rubin, J. B. (2004). *Good life: Psychoanalytic reflections on move, ethics, creativity and spirituality*. Albany: SUNY Press.

Scanzoni, J. H. (1979). *Love and negotiate: Creative conflicts in marriage*. Waco, TX: World Books.

Schmukler, A. G., & Garcia, E. E. (1990). Special symbolism in early oedipal development: fantasies of folds and spaces, protuberances and concavities. *International Journal of Psychoanalysis, 71,* 297–300.

Schreiber, A. K. (2002). A transgenerational psychobiography of the British royal family: From Victoria to Charles and Diana. *Dissertation Abstracts International, 63B,* 2994.

Shelburne, W. A. (1998). *Mythos and logos in the thoughts of Carol Jung: The theory of the collective unconscious in scientific perspectives*. Albany: SUNY Press.

Smith, K. (1989). The movement of conflict in organizations: The joint dynamics of splitting and triangulation. *Administrative Science Quarterly, 34,* 1–20.

Smith, K., & Berg, D. (1987). *Paradoxes of group life: Understanding conflict, paralysis, and movement in group dynamics*. San Francisco: Jossey-Bass.

Smith, R., & Eisenberg, E. M. (1987). Conflict at Disneyland: A root metaphor analysis. *Communication Monographs, 54,* 367–380.

Solomon, M. (1979). The "positive woman's" journey: A mythic analysis of the rhetoric of STOP ERA. *Quarterly Journal of Speech, 65,* 262–275.

Spangle, M. L., & Isenhart, M. W. (2003). *Negotiation: Communication for diverse settings.* Thousand Oaks, CA: Sage.

Spitzberg, B. H., & Cupach, W. R. (Eds.). (1998). *The dark side of relationships.* Mahwah, NJ: Lawrence Erlbaum.

Stein, H. (1986). Social roles and unconscious complementarity. *Journal of Psychoanalytic Anthropology, 9,* 235–268.

Stein, M. (1998). *Jung's map of the soul: An introduction.* Chicago: University of Chicago Press.

Sternberg, R. J., & Barnes, M. L. (1988). *The psychology of love.* New Haven: Yale University Press.

Stueve, C. A., & Gerson, K. (1977). Personal relations across the life cycle. In C. S. Fischer (Ed.), *Networks and places: Social relations in the urban setting* (pp. 79–98). New York: Free Press.

Taylor, S. (2003). A place for the future? Residence and continuity in women's narratives of their lives. *Narrative Inquiry, 13,* 193–215.

Thomsen, A. (1941). Psychological projection and the election: A simple class experiment. *Journal of Psychology, 11,* 115–117.

Vaughan, D. (1986). *Uncoupling: Turning points in intimate relationships.* Oxford, UK: Oxford University Press.

Von Franz, M. (1982). *An introduction to the interpretation of fairy tales.* Dallas, TX: Spring.

Von Franz, M. (1997). *Archetypal dimensions of the psyche.* Boston: Shambhala.

Watt, J., & VanLear, C. A. (Eds.). (1996). *Dynamic patterns in communication processes.* Thousand Oaks, CA: Sage.

Welker, L. S., & Goodall, H. L., Jr. (1997). Representations, interpretations, and performance opening the text of *Casing a Promised Land. Text and Performance Quarterly, 17,* 109–122.

Whillock, R. K. (1995). The use of hate as a stratagem for achieving political and social goals. In R. K. Whillock & D. Slayden (Eds.), *Hate speech* (pp. 25–54). Thousand Oaks, CA: Sage.

Willeford, W. (1969). *The fool and his scepter.* Evanston, IL: Northwestern University Press.

Winslade, J., & Monk, G. (2001). *Narrative mediation: A new approach to conflict resolution.* San Francisco: Jossey-Bass.

Zehnder, S. M., & Calvert, S. L. (2004). Between the hero and the shadow: Developmental differences in adolescents' perceptions and understanding of mythic themes in film. *Journal of Communication Inquiry, 28,* 122–138.

Zweig, C., & Abrams, J. (Eds.). (2001). *Meeting the shadow: The hidden power of the dark side of human nature.* Los Angeles: Tarcher.

Index

About the Author

Peter M. Kellett is Associate Professor and Head of the Department of Communication Studies at the University of North Carolina at Greensboro. His research, teaching, and service focus on narrative analysis and dialogic management of conflict as this helps people build healthier and more productive and peaceful relationships. His most recent publication is "Dialectical Tensions and Dialogic Moments as Pathways to Peak Experiences" (with H. L. Goodall, Jr.) in Anderson, Baxter, and Cissna's *Dialogue: Theorizing Differences in Communication Studies*.